Ladies of the Court

Ladies of the Court

Grace and Disgrace on the
Women's Tennis Tour

Michael Mewshaw

LITTLE, BROWN AND COMPANY

I'd like to dedicate this book to Philip, Linda, Marc, Paul, Gene, Jim,
Desmond, Don, Peter, Josef, Walter, Mark, Peter, Lorenzo, Lucinda,
Tom, Rich, Kerry, Mike, Kevin, Steve, Matthew, and all the others
who have had to put up with my tennis over the years.

A *Little, Brown* Book

First published in the USA in 1993 by Crown Publishers, Inc.
First published in Great Britain in 1993
by Little, Brown and Company

A CIP catalogue record for this book
is available from the British Library.

ISBN 0 316 90583 6

Printed and bound in Great Britain by
BPCC Hazell Books Ltd
Member of BPCC Ltd

Little, Brown and Company (UK) Limited
165 Great Dover Street
London SE1 4YA

Contents

Preface   vii
La Bella Figura of Gabriela Sabatini   1
Italian Open   17
French Open   56
Wimbledon   109
The Austrian Ladies Open   164
The Forbidden Zone   187
U.S. Open   197
Virginia Slims of Philadelphia   260
Virginia Slims Championships   286
Epilogue   312
Afterword   324

Preface

As I observe late in this book, professional tennis has no real season, no linear progression from start to finish. Instead, the tour is cyclical and it leads to a condition rather than a destination. As tournament melts into tournament, a single match can come to sum up an entire career, and a gesture, a smile, or a spectacular point seems to encapsulate a player's character. Although I discuss at length events that transpired in 1991 on the women's circuit, my intention was not to present an isolated series of snapshots, and it certainly wasn't to report match results. Rather, it was to provide background information and texture, to use incidents and players from one year as elements in a comprehensive portrait, a broad, variegated mosaic, of women's tennis. It was an attempt to show how the tour has been shaped by its history, and how the rise of female athletes generally reflected, and in some cases foreshadowed, the progress of women in other arenas.

While I chronicle the triumphs and tribulations of individuals at specific tournaments, I believe that their experiences are representative. Jennifer Capriati's very public adolescent growing pains can't be understood without reference to those endured by Tracy Austin or Andrea Jaeger. And Steffi Graf's attempt to rebound from injuries and emotional turmoil cannot be appreciated unless one knows how players in similar situations coped or failed to. Gabriela Sabatini's struggle to become a complete player and a happier person, Mary Joe Fernandez's desire to remain "feminine" yet become a champion, Pam Shriver's ambition to be more than just a tennis player, Laura Gildemeister's effort to balance motherhood and a career—all these preoccupations are deeply personal and, at the same time, emblematic of the difficulties that generations of women players have experienced.

Even someone as seemingly unique as Martina Navratilova isn't without precursors, and what happened to her in 1991 cannot be fully comprehended unless one knows what happened to Billie Jean King a decade earlier and unless one recognizes how the issue of female sexuality has always been a source of uneasiness in tennis. While male players and their sexual preferences rarely prompt speculation, women are invariably put on the spot and in the spotlight. The greatest irony is that parents and tennis officials are so irrationally anxious about lesbians in the locker room, they have ignored far more pressing problems caused by fathers and male coaches.

Yet much as the past is prologue to the present, there have been radical changes in women's tennis, some on the scale of quantum leaps that can only be understood in their own terms. The advent of wide-body racquets and improved training techniques, along with an exponential increase in prize money, have put added pressure on girls to turn pro soon after they reach puberty. The ascendancy of Monica Seles, who at the age of seventeen became the game's youngest number-one player, signaled that 1991 was both a point from which to reflect on the tour's origins and a place to start speculating about the future. In effect, this one year serves as a sort of Janus face whose double gaze falls in opposite directions and whose contrasting expressions suggest that comedy and tragedy are as inseparable in women's tennis as they were in classical drama.

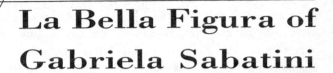

La Bella Figura of
Gabriela Sabatini

World-class tennis players are tribal creatures who, regardless of national origin, share the same mores, totems, and taboos. Whatever language they learned in childhood during those fleeting days before they left home for the accelerated training of a private academy or government-sponsored camp, they eventually wind up speaking a subdialect of English that has no codified grammar, no written literature, and, frequently, no distinction between past and present tense. Much depends on the repetition of key phrases that convey meaning through altered intonation. "Go for it" and "Just do it" appear like punctuation marks in almost every sentence.

Forced by circumstance to travel and live together, the tennis tribe places a premium on patience, discretion, and tolerance—tolerance of bizarre behavior, irrational outbursts, and varying sexual appetites. Players stay at the same hotels, eat the same food, and wear much the same clothes on court. Yet all this sameness serves to reiterate an obvious difference: At each tournament there are dozens of losers and only one winner.

In this tiny nomadic society, the migratory patterns are as inflexible as the scoring system. Thus it was that in early May 1991, Gabriela Sabatini departed from her home in Buenos Aires, Argentina, and flew to Rome for the Italian Open. She had won the title there twice and was determined to do it again and build on her record, which was the best in women's tennis this year.

Yet one couldn't blame her for looking beyond the Italian Open to the three upcoming Grand Slam events. Now was the time, experts agreed, for her to take over the top spot in tennis. Ever since she was fourteen, people had predicted she would become number one. With her heavy-topspin ground strokes, she had the baseline game to win the French Open. With her improved serve and volley, she looked capable of dominating players on Wimbledon's grass. As for the hard courts at Flushing Meadow, she had won there once and could do it again.

Although the U.S. Open was four months off, Sabatini sensed the arc of the season, the arc of her entire career, inclining toward the tournament, where, in 1990, she had finally triumphed over a host of real and imagined demons to win her first major title. Now at every press conference, journalists asked how she intended to repeat the victory, how she intended to cope with Monica Seles, Martina Navratilova, and Steffi Graf.

Upon her answers depended more than the odd tennis article or TV sound bite. If Gabriela hoped to command the kind of coverage that would carry her out of the sports ghetto and onto the style page, into the fashion section, and onto the late-night and early-morning talk shows, she had to do something besides wallop forehand winners and say, "I hit the ball hard. I feel a lot of confidence today."

With most players, victory ensured favorable exposure. But with Gabriela there had always been the danger of a boomerang effect. Her halting, monosyllabic encounters with the media often led to an un-flattering picture that risked putting off sponsors and undermining her morale. So as Dick Dell, her agent at ProServ, screened the requests and contracts that blizzarded his desk during the months leading up to the U.S. Open, he had to weigh the downside against the possible advantages to his client.

Dell had done what he could to tidy up Sabatini's image. Along with PR people from the Kraft General Foods World Tour, title sponsor of women's tennis, he had studied tapes of her press conferences and passed on tips about how she could punch up her performance. As her game began to show greater fluency and grace, he spread word that she was playing better because of a sea change in her personality; she was more confident, mature, outgoing, and articulate, Dell claimed.

One offer that intrigued Dell and excited Gaby was a proposed feature on Sabatini in the September issue of *Vogue,* which would hit the stands at the start of the U.S. Open. Because of the magazine's long lead time, *Vogue* had set up a photo session in Florida, dressed Gaby in evening gowns and cocktail dresses, and shot roll after roll of film.

Unfortunately, *Vogue*'s editor, Anna Wintour, didn't care for the photographs. She felt that Sabatini looked too meaty and muscular, too awkward in high-fashion wear. Wintour favored killing the project, but Peggy Northrup, the Health and Fitness editor, argued that Gabriela represented a new type of female beauty, a challenge to the hackneyed notion that an attractive woman had to be willowy thin and weak.

Peggy Northrup convinced Anna Wintour to postpone any decision until she had read the article that would accompany the photographs. Then Ms. Northrup asked me to write the piece. I was to meet Sabatini in Rome and spend forty-eight hours learning about her likes and dislikes, aspirations and fears, and, most important, the changes in her personal life that had allowed her to achieve her full potential in tennis.

Because I was about to do a book on the women's tour and knew it was harder to gain access to a top player than to line up an audience with the president or the pope, I viewed the assignment as a godsend— one that could save me weeks of wasted motion. Then, too, I was fascinated by the internal debate at *Vogue*. It seemed to reflect larger debates echoing throughout society. Was women's tennis part of a feminist breakthrough? Had female athletes truly come a long way, baby? And if so, what price had they had to pay? Did they, like legions of female doctors, lawyers, and business executives, have to fill dual roles—money-making professionals outside the home and traditional mothers-wives-lovers and nurturers in the home? Did they even have homes?

A flurry of phone calls interrupted my packing. Peggy Northrup said she had dropped my name to Dick Dell and he seemed to have misgivings. Then Dell himself called and mentioned that he had read *Short Circuit*, a book I had written about ethical and financial improprieties in men's tennis. He pressed me to tell him what I intended to ask Gaby.

Once satisfied that neither *Vogue* nor I had a hidden agenda, Dell explained that top-flight players were reluctant to talk to reporters and risk breaking their concentration during a tournament. But he had per-

suaded Gaby to make herself available for two days preceding the Italian
Open. That proved, he said, how much the feature in *Vogue* mattered
to her. What's more, it demonstrated her new expansiveness, her willingness to experiment on court and off. With the encouragement of her
new coach, Carlos Kirmayr, she had become a new woman.

And speaking of new women, he passed along a tip about a new
product. Gabriela's signature line of perfumes, already a success in
Europe, would be released in the States at the time of the U.S. Open.
As he proceeded to suggest questions I should ask Sabatini, I interrupted
to remind him of the reality of the situation. *Vogue* didn't like the
photographs and was lukewarm about the project. If we hoped to turn
things around, Gaby, Carlos, and I had to hit the ground running in
Rome. Since she refused to be interviewed during the tournament, I
couldn't waste time that weekend chasing her.

Dell assured me everything had been arranged.

O O O

The overnight flight to Rome provided an opportunity to review press
clips about Gabriela Sabatini. As described by sportswriters, she had
started off as another in an endless line of precocious teenage sensations,
the heirs apparent to Chris Evert. Like so many before her, she came
from a family of modest athletic accomplishment—her father had been
a first-division basketball player in Argentina, her older brother a prom-
ising junior tennis player—and they had introduced her to the game as
a child and encouraged her to excel.

She was said to be especially close to her father, Osvaldo, who had
resigned as a General Motors executive and assumed a role early on as
her manager and constant companion on the circuit. Her mother, Beatriz,
and brother, Osvaldo junior, often came along, too.

Gaby did well in the beginning. At fourteen, she was the youngest
player ever to win a match at the U.S. Open. By the time she was
fifteen, she was the youngest semifinalist at the French Open. Fame and
money flowed as smoothly as her passing shots. Long-legged and lovely,
she had a face framed by tresses as iridescent as a raven's wing; she
possessed a movie star's glamour, a ballerina's grace, and an Olympic
athlete's grandeur. (In 1988 she was a silver medalist in Seoul.) Young

boys adored her, older men sent mash notes, advertisers offered millions. She endorsed Sergio Tacchini tennis wear, Prince racquets, Longine watches, Fuji film, Seat automobiles, and Avis rental cars. Gleaming with perspiration, she inspired poet Clive James to pen an adulatory verse entitled ''Bring Me the Sweat of Gabriela Sabatini.''

Her rocket-burst arrival at the pinnacle of the sport seemed tantalizingly close, but when she failed to grasp the last rung of the ladder and win a Grand Slam event, flaws and fissures began to appear in her enameled image. She lost to Steffi Graf eleven times in a row. Monica Seles leaped ahead of her. Then thirteen-year-old Jennifer Capriati stole the hearts of spectators and sponsors. Wedded to a fatiguing baseline style, yet too weak to last three sets against the top women, Sabatini shucked one coach, a man whom her father resented, and hired another, a former Spanish Davis Cup competitor, Angel Gimenez, who put her through a punishing physical fitness program that featured lots of weight lifting. Soon she was much stronger—and much heavier and slower. Broad-shouldered and muscle-bound, she swaggered around the court looking, in the words of Teddy Tinling, like John Wayne—but a John Wayne who couldn't shoot straight and couldn't kill off the enemy.

Overworked by her coach and overprotected by her parents, Sabatini started to lose matches she should have won and to look moody and forlorn in the process. Always inclined to be laconic, she became more and more withdrawn. She had so few friends on the tour, she considered quitting and living on the millions she had won. But with almost no interests outside tennis, she had little alternative except to thud along in the same groove, playing a self-defeating style which Dick Dell described as ''robotized.''

In some quarters there was suspicion that Gabriela's one-dimensional game mirrored her mind. Having dropped out of junior high at thirteen, she had never had a tutor or taken lessons in anything more complicated than hitting backhands. When she was slow to learn English, her isolation increased, and so did the gossip about her brainlessness. Dell himself remarked that if a new coach could make her smarter, she'd improve by 15 or 20 percent. A childhood friend told *Sports Illustrated,* ''Gaby has tennis elbow in the personality.''

By the summer of 1990, Sabatini seemed fated to join that constellation of tennis dwarf stars who are no sooner visible than they burn out, leaving behind a fading remnant of their brilliance. The sad story sank to its nadir at Wimbledon, when an ex-boyfriend sold a scurrilous article to a London tabloid, recounting his affair with Gaby and describing her as waddling like "a fat duck."

Some cynics claimed the story was wildly inaccurate. Drawing on no greater evidence than their own imaginations, they claimed Gabriela must be gay. Others maintained that the right man could put a smile on her face.

Whether they believed she needed a man or a woman, people assumed that the answer to Sabatini's problems lay outside herself. Yet in the end it was her own decision to change coaches. Dropping Angel Gimenez—"It was like going from living every day with him, to nothing. Like a divorce," she told *Tennis* magazine—she hooked up with Carlos Kirmayr, a forty-year-old Brazilian so mellow and laid-back, he made a beach full of Californians look uptight.

Once a competitor on the men's tour, Kirmayr had won more with his wits than with his limited physical gifts. He knew the game well, had trained a couple of world-class players, and ran seven tennis schools. Though this might make him sound like a workaholic, Carlos was a carefree spirit in a sport remarkable for its murderous tunnel vision. He never took himself too seriously. In his spare time he had performed with a rock group called the Fleabags.

To shore up Gaby's shattered confidence, Carlos told her to stop planting herself at the baseline, stop turning every point into a battle of attrition. He urged her to attack, take risks and rush the net. She was tall, had great range and soft hands—the perfect combination for a serve and volleyer.

Halting her heavy metal workouts in the gym, Kirmayr preached speed and quickness. As he ran her through a regimen of jumps, lateral lunges, and sprints, Sabatini lost weight and gained agility. Her movement on court became more explosive, and so did her shots.

At the same time, she was conferring with Dr. James Loehr, a sports psychologist who encouraged her to show her emotions during matches and express them in writing afterward. As Loehr saw it, her problem wasn't simply to raise her level of play, but rather to recapture the childlike capacity to enjoy playing, to approach tennis as fun instead of as tedious labor, to view the tour as an opportunity, not a prison. He compiled an inspirational videotape of Gabriela belting winning shots to the background accompaniment of her favorite pop tune, the theme from *Top Gun*.

Along with Dick Dell, Carlos pushed Gaby to pursue outside interests. As Dell put it, "Tennis may be totally satisfying when you're winning, but when you lose, you have to have something else to fall back on." Finally Carlos advised her to stop playing doubles with Steffi Graf, who dominated Sabatini by sheer force of personality.

When Gabriela went on to win the U.S. Open, beating Graf for the title, the topic of every article switched from anxious tut-tutting about her arrested development to raves about her comeback. The girl who had been considered washed up, a sad, inhibited, uneducated, and easily manipulated adolescent, was suddenly presented as a woman in touch with her feelings, in charge of her life, and on the way to bigger and better things.

○ ○ ○

As we circled for our descent into Rome, bumping down through a canopy of clouds, rain rattled against the plane's fuselage and splashed over the runway. The pilot said it was fifty degrees.

The taxi ride into town ran past familiar landmarks, but none looked quite right. On this cold, dreary May morning, Rome had the haunted appearance of a house abandoned. Famous piazzas were deserted, and tables and chairs were stacked haphazardly at outdoor cafés like jetsam tossed up by high tide.

The Cavalieri Hilton, official hotel of the Italian Open, stood atop Monte Mario swathed in mist. In the lobby, fidgety players checked the practice court schedule and the availability of courtesy cars. At the reception desk, the concierge was keeping bouquets of flowers for Monica Seles and Martina Navratilova. Sabatini had already checked in.

From my room I dialed Carlos Kirmayr, as I had been instructed to do by Dick Dell. There was no answer. When I phoned the main desk to leave a message, the operator put me on hold, and I got my first inkling that much as the hotel might resemble a standard Stateside

Hilton, it had its share of local eccentricities. Instead of Muzak, I heard Joe Cocker wailing "You Can Leave Your Hat On."

For the rest of the day I phoned Carlos, listened to more choruses from Joe Cocker, and kept my hat on as the realization dawned that I was wasting my precious forty-eight hours. I dialed Gabriela's room, but there was no answer there either.

That evening I went down to the lobby, and while double-checking whether my messages had been delivered, I spotted Sabatini emerging from an elevator. The Women's Tennis Association media guide lists her as five feet eight and a hundred thirty pounds, but she looked much larger in a pair of tight jeans and a dark leather jacket with wide shoulders that called to mind Joan Crawford in football pads. Her face was fine-boned and chisel-featured, with glossy lips and teeth that shone unnaturally bright against her tan.

When I introduced myself, she smiled and inclined her head as if she couldn't decide whether I was someone she knew or just another giddy fan.

"*Vogue* magazine. The profile," I repeated. "We need to spend some time together."

She nodded dreamily, said, "Oh, yes," but drifted away, still smiling. Carlos Kirmayr took her place. He was smiling, too. A short, compact fellow with a freckled complexion and sun-streaked hair, he wore a blue denim jacket from the Hard Rock Cafe in Tokyo. The lobe of his left ear was pierced, but there was no earring. He said he and Gaby had practiced today at an indoor facility. The trip from Buenos Aires had taken eighteen hours, door to door, and a good workout was, in his opinion, the best way to recover from jet lag. This was as close as he came to explaining why he hadn't responded to my messages.

We strolled over to where Gaby waited with her parents. Mr. Sabatini was a seigniorial gent with white hair, a white mustache, and a firm policy of saying nothing to the press. Mrs. Sabatini was more extroverted, but there was little opportunity to speak to her before Carlos announced that they were off for a family dinner. Gaby and he would see me tomorrow at the practice courts. Panicky at the thought of losing them, I suggested we have breakfast together. He said no, they'd meet me at noon.

Next morning when I came downstairs at ten-thirty, Kirmayr and Sabatini were headed toward the door carrying equipment bags. I hurried over to ask whether there had been a change of plans.

"Yeah," Carlos said. "The courts won't be dry by noon. We're practicing indoors again."

Both Gaby and he were their polite smiling selves, but they had no intention of talking to me on the ride to the training center in Riano. "Gaby's parents are going with us," Carlos said. "You'll have to catch the next courtesy car."

There was no point in asking what would have happened if our paths hadn't crossed. This was the kind of foul-up that anybody who writes about tennis learns to expect. But given Dick Dell's assurances that everything had been arranged, given Gabriela's supposed eagerness to appear as a fashion plate in *Vogue,* I was surprised. My forty-eight hours were down to twenty-four and fast shrinking.

○ ○ ○

Two stocky German women with short hair—one had a buzz cut—shared the car with me. The Italian driver kept casting glances at them in the rearview mirror, but they weren't the self-conscious type. They introduced themselves as Gerda and Gisela, friends of Martina Navratilova's. Which, I assumed, was why tournament officials allowed them to ride in a car reserved for players and press. But it turned out that they were, in their own words, just "crazy Martina fans," not personal friends. They followed her from country to country all around the world. "Some friends think we're insane, but it's a lot of fun. You meet so many people."

They didn't just watch Martina's matches. They watched her work out even on days like today when it required cadging a lift and riding across Rome, up Via Salaria to the autostrada. Altogether it was a fifty-mile round-trip, and they intended to make it again this afternoon.

We passed a guardhouse and entered a fenced-in compound full of athletic fields and Quonset huts. Gerda and Gisela spotted a diminutive figure jogging through the drizzle. "Oh God, it's Cindy Nelson!" they exclaimed.

Cindy Nelson had come into Martina's life after the exit of her former lover, Judy Nelson. She was invariably referred to by reporters as Half-Nelson.

A canvas bubble covered two red-clay courts. On one, Navratilova was hitting with Mary Joe Fernandez. Craig Kardon, Martina's coach, and Ernesto Ruiz Bry, Mary Joe's coach, watched from the sidelines. The match was more than a contrast of Navratilova's net rushing against Fernandez's baseline defense. It was an opposition of fire and ice. Yet ironically, the pretty Hispanic girl was the icy self-possessed one, while the blond Czech generated all the sparks, laughing at her mistakes and cursing a blue streak. "Goddammit, bend your knees. Fucking balls won't bounce."

On the other court, Gabriela was stretching with Carlos while Mr. and Mrs. Sabatini sat nearby, bundled up like Eskimos. It wasn't much warmer in here than outside.

Except for Gerda, Gisela, and Mrs. Sabatini, all the onlookers, including the coaches, were men. As I would notice in the coming months, the women's tour was largely populated by male agents, umpires, linesmen, coaches, sparring partners, gofers, and journalists, not to mention the fathers, brothers, boyfriends, and husbands of the players.

Unlike the other girls, who appeared to have put on whatever lay close at hand—boxer shorts, bicycle pants, baggy T-shirts, rumpled sweat suits—Sabatini wore an elegant warm-up designed by Sergio Tacchini. As she started off stroking the ball at half speed and with none of her trademark topspin, Mama and Papa studied her racquet preparation with the sort of intensity that stockbrokers bring to the Dow Jones averages. Gradually Carlos and Gaby began hitting harder, their strokes as rhythmic as the rain beating against the canvas bubble. The session proceeded almost entirely without words and was as beautifully choreographed as a dance routine. From time to time Kirmayr applauded his pupil by slapping a hand against his thigh. Otherwise there was silence except for the X-rated chatter from Navratilova.

Perspiration purled down Gabriela's cheeks, falling from her nose and chin. She shed her warm-up suit, skinning down to a fuchsia shirt and a pair of shorts in a fuchsia and purple pattern. For a few minutes they did a drill in which Gaby produced delicate drop shots that nestled into the moist clay. Then Carlos moved to the net and Gaby tried to pass him. Whenever she missed, she shot him a malignant stare, but didn't utter a word.

When they stopped after an hour and a half, Sabatini stretched as carefully as she had before practice. She leaned back against the net post, and Carlos genuflected in front of her, letting her extend a leg and cradle her heel on his shoulder. By slow degrees he stood up to his full height, pulling her hamstring taut as piano wire. Crouching, he released one leg and raised the other in the same fashion while Gaby gazed straight ahead, her face as imperturbable as the sculpted figure on the prow of a ship.

I crossed the court thinking at last this was my chance to speak with her. But Carlos moved between us. Gaby, he said, had to hurry back to the hotel for a shower. The interview would have to wait. He told me to call him at 3 P.M.; he'd be happy to set up an appointment then.

"I thought I already had an appointment. I thought this was all arranged. That's what Dick Dell said."

Yes, yes, he nodded. "Call me. I'll take care of everything."

O O O

For the rest of that day and part of the next, I tried to keep my hat on as smoke streamed from my ears. There was never an answer at Carlos's room nor at Gaby's. I searched the lobby, the bar, and the restaurant at the Hilton, then had the Sabatinis paged—to no avail. Tournament officials said they must be at Riano; people at Riano felt sure they had to be at the Foro Italico. But it was raining at the Foro Italico, and no one had seen them there.

On Sunday I stayed at it—telephoning Carlos and Gaby, the Italian Tennis Federation, the tournament director, and the on-site Women's Tennis Association office. Shortly after noon there was word that Gaby had been spotted at the Foro Italico, where the courts were now dry. Although the WTA rep couldn't guarantee a reply, she agreed to pass along a message.

My message was as blunt as I could make it without burning all bridges. If Gaby wanted to appear in *Vogue,* she had to talk to me, painful as that prospect obviously was.

The WTA rep called back. Gaby wondered how long the interview would take.

Having been promised two days, I was down to haggling over minutes. "I'll need at least an hour."

"A whole hour?" The WTA rep sounded doubtful, but returned with the news that Sabatini had agreed to meet me in the players' dining room.

The road from the Hilton to the Foro Italico was a spillway of hairpin turns and wrecked cars, and as we sped down off Monte Mario, the cabbie kept repeating, *"Ecco Italia."* He pointed to gypsies begging at streetlights, to drivers double and triple parked, to a woman sitting insolently in her car holding up traffic while she applied lipstick. "You can't do anything in this city," he complained. "Even driving is a compromise, a deal you have to cut with every other asshole on the road. Look at that!" he screamed as a motorcycle zipped the wrong way down a one-way street. "Where are the *carabinieri?* I'll tell you where. They're all in a bar reading *Gazzetto dello Sport* and combing their hair."

Compared to his problems, mine seemed insignificant. It certainly wasn't worth wasting any of my hard-won hour badgering Gaby to explain her disappearing act.

The players' dining room reverberated with dropped plates and cutlery and the shouted greetings of old friends. Sabatini sat with her face fixed in a beatific smile, saying nothing, volunteering nothing, simply waiting for me to set up the tape recorder.

I began by lobbing at her the softball questions Dick Dell had planted. I figured she'd smash them away for easy winners, then once she found her range and rhythm, we'd move on to more substantive matters.

Her agent had told me she memorized song lyrics to improve her English. Was that true?

No. She used to, but not anymore. Now she was writing her own lyrics.

"In English?" I asked.

"No, Spanish."

Well, what about the guitar? Dell claimed Carlos was teaching her
to play.

"We didn't start yet," Gaby said. "But we will."

Was it true she had taken up photography?

Her smile brightened. "Yes, taking lots of pictures."

I waited for her to go on. When she didn't, I asked her to discuss
her other interests.

"Trying to learn some French," she said.

"How's it coming?"

She shrugged her broad shoulders.

Did she have a tutor? Was she taking lessons?

"I have a book and some tapes."

I observed that French grammar was difficult. She agreed, and that
finished that.

Among tennis commentators, there was general agreement that she
had changed in the last year. Was she happy because she was winning?
Or winning because she was happy?

"I think I'm winning because I'm happier. I think I'm going through
a good time. I feel more mature. So many things are changing inside
me. I think that's the reason I feel so happy."

When I coaxed her to discuss what had changed inside her, she
said, "I feel more confidence in myself, more secure."

In the United States women spoke of taking control of their lives.
Was that what she meant?

"Yes, I'm taking control of all the things—of my feelings. I'm
thinking more. Taking my time." Yes, she was doing that. A long pause
ensued.

I broke the silence and urged her to tell me about her change of
coaches.

"That's the reason I'm playing so well. First, I needed to change
coaches. That was a great motivation for me. I think Carlos is a great
person. We do a lot of things outside of tennis."

What did they do?

She pondered this. "We have fun." Pause. "We go walk on the
beach." Pause. "We talk very much."

I didn't dare glance at my watch. I had demanded an hour and was now groping to fill it. Since she had such difficulty discussing the new, thoughtful, feeling, and fulfilled Gaby, I retreated to strokes and strategy. Technically, how had Carlos helped her game?

"We're working more on coming to the net, to get more confidence."

Ah, back to the slippery subject of confidence. Okay, how had Carlos increased her confidence?

"Speaking."

I waited for her to go on. She stayed silent and studied my face, which I attempted to make a mirror of her sweet smiling countenance. "That's all," she said. "Just telling me, 'Go! Just do it.' "

I brought up sports psychologist Dr. James Loehr, hoping a reminder of their sessions might persuade her to dig deeper. But she cut off that line of inquiry. "I don't like to talk about it very much."

Since she was such a hero in her country, did that put her under greater pressure?

"I don't feel any pressure. I just keep doing what I have to do. I enjoy everything that's happening to me."

At that moment I couldn't make the same claim, for what was happening—and Sabatini appeared to be sublimely oblivious to the fact—was that she was killing any chance that *Vogue* would run a feature on her. I floundered for some way to get Gaby to convey in words a small portion of the fluency I had seen her display with a racquet in hand. Perhaps she was content to let her body do all the talking, to let her lovely face have the first and last say. Still, I asked, weren't there times when her beauty caused her difficulties?

"No," she said, but then added, "It's better to be a good person than to be good-looking or a good tennis player. Being a good person is for always."

Had she thought about life after tennis?

She laughed. "Yeah, sure. I have to think of it."

What had she thought?

"I don't know. It's hard. I always say I want to get married and have children. Maybe try to teach children. Maybe teach tennis. I like also to sing. Who knows, maybe in the future I will do something."

When I attempted to get an idea of what she did in Rome when she wasn't practicing or playing, she said she had seen all the sights. Although she had trouble recalling what they were, she didn't care to see them again. What she liked best about Rome was eating out with her family and friends.

"What's your favorite restaurant?"

Her face clouded. "There are a few." She frowned with concentration. "There's one with my name." She meant Sabatini's in Trastevere. "And I . . . " She struggled to name another. She had played here since she was fourteen. It was one of her favorite cities in the world. She ate out every night but couldn't say where. She was embarrassed, and so was I. "I mean I just love the food, the Italian food," she blurted.

This offered a polite excuse to change the subject and discuss her diet. "I think I eat very good food," she said. "When I'm playing tournaments, I eat pasta. When I'm just practicing, I eat fish and chicken and salad. But I don't have any problems. I eat very good."

What did she like best about life on the tour?

"Hmmm . . . " She mulled it over. "Just to go play tennis. Just playing, and it's good that I have a chance to see places."

What did she like least about the tour? Was it being interviewed?

She seemed torn. Perhaps she hesitated for fear of hurting me, but she couldn't hold back. "Sometimes the press is very bad. One day they say you are the best. Next day they say you are the worst. I don't like this very much."

I murmured my sympathy and asked whether fame caused other problems.

"You lose your privacy. Sometimes I want to do something and I don't feel free enough to do it. I mean people love me almost everywhere. But I don't feel free." Once again she ended on what would in the film world be called a slow dissolve.

"You started so young," I said. "Is there any way in which you feel you missed your childhood?"

"No, not now. Probably a few years ago I did. I wanted to go out more. When I'm at home in Argentina I like to go out with my friends. Go out dancing and go to bed late." She liked pop music; Chicago and

Phil Collins were among her favorites. "Nothing heavy. I like more the slow songs."

Was there any South American music that moved her?

"No."

Did she see any contradiction, any unfairness, in the fact that world-class women athletes had to bear the burden of being judged by their beauty and femininity, as well as their performance?

"No," said Gabriela. "I think every woman wants to be feminine and to look good. That's what I try to do—look feminine and look good."

O O O

Although I came away from the interview convinced that it was futile, I wrote a profile that emphasized Sabatini's on-court accomplishments, her discipline and diligence, and the beautiful expressiveness of her game. Weeks later when *Vogue* informed me that the project had been killed, I wasn't surprised. Yet while I didn't appreciate it at that moment, I would discover in the next six months that my search for Gabriela Sabatini hadn't been a waste. Her complicated relationships with family and coaches, her alternating persona as headstrong diva and heartsick ditzy adolescent, her determination to be fit yet feminine, her eagerness to court the public yet avoid the press, her wistful yearning for the prosaic pleasures of youth and for a freedom her millions couldn't buy her—all of these added up to a composite portrait of the best and worst of women's tennis.

Italian Open

Bella Roma, Bella Signorina

Throughout its history, the Italian Open's *torneo femminile* has been less a feast than a movable famine. Always second fiddle to the men's event, often shunted from site to site, it was first played in Milan, then moved to Rome in 1936, then canceled for fourteen years. Reinaugurated in 1950, the women's tournament took place at the Foro Italico every spring for the next three decades—except for 1961, when it was switched to Torino. Yet even when the women had a fixed address, the men's matches were showcased on Campo Centrale while the women were exiled to distant field courts.

In 1980, like rejected stepsisters, the women threw themselves upon the unreliable mercy of the road. For a while they played in the provincial town of Perugia. Then they wandered south to the port city of Taranto. In 1985 the tournament wasn't held at all.

In 1986, the women migrated back to Rome, where the Italian Open became a two-week event. But unlike Grand Slam tournaments, where the men and women play simultaneously, the women compete in Rome during the first week, then the men arrive. The women's prize money totals $465,000; the men get $1,280,000.

For spectators and corporate sponsors, the return of the women's tournament offered a great bargain. By paying a 20 percent supplement, fans could buy a box seat for an extra week, and sponsors got seven more days to flog their products. But while players and agents and the Italian Tennis Federation profited from this arrangement, the Roman public responded in a fashion best characterized as fickle. Unlike the men's event, which drew huge crowds, the women's tournament had to hope for increased attendance during the quarterfinals, semifinals, and final to compensate for acres of empty seats in the early rounds.

In 1987, fans flocked to the Foro Italico when Steffi Graf beat Gabriela Sabatini for the title. But Steffi hadn't been back since several ungallant Italian reporters printed cruel remarks about her looks. While she stayed away after being called a potato-faced German, Navratilova, Evert, and Seles had their own reasons for dropping out in 1989; Evert was injured, and Seles and Navratilova chose to prepare for the French Open and Wimbledon.

To guard against a repetition of this catastrophe, the Italian Open, like other tournaments, took steps to insure the presence of star players. It paid the men hefty guarantees, or appearance fees, that amounted to far more than a fellow might win in prize money. It wasn't uncommon for Connors, Lendl, Becker, Agassi, or McEnroe to demand in excess of $100,000 just to show up. These guarantees violated the rules and sometimes resulted in a player's pocketing the money, giving less than his best effort, and losing in the first round. Still, tournament officials felt they had no choice but to bribe top players to compete.

The Women's Tennis Association had long boasted that its members obeyed the rule against guarantees. According to its own Jesuitical reasoning, this might be true. Although most insiders assumed that Japanese tournaments do pay guarantees, it was possible that at other tournaments the women stars don't demand—or can't command—the enormous flat fees that men receive. But they get different kinds of inducements. They sign contracts with companies that pay them bonuses linked to specific events. They show up briefly at corporate receptions, drop by clothing and sporting goods stores, and collect handsome stipends for what Bud Collins describes as "tying their shoelaces in public." Seles, Sabatini, and Jennifer Capriati, all of whom had lucrative contracts with Italian clothing companies, returned to Rome in 1991, as did Martina Navratilova, who was represented by International Management Group (IMG), the American agency that owned the Italian Open.

Much had been made of this link between IMG and the Italian Open.

Some went so far as to claim that the agency saved the event from extinction. To be sure, the tournament had sunk close to insolvency, and while the women were wandering homelessly, the men held scant attraction for the public. In the early 1980s, when there was no break between the Italian and the French opens, and there was little more than loose change to pay guarantees, the top players decided they could do without Rome, and when the stars defected, so did the fans. In 1982 a total of nineteen thousand spectators, many of them with complimentary tickets, passed through the turnstiles, and the Foro Italico resembled a classical ruin. The slabs of porous tufa that served as bleachers were so empty they sprouted wildflowers and tufts of moss.

According to conventional wisdom, it was then that Cino Marchese, IMG's local rep, came to the rescue. He convinced his agency to buy the tournament and persuaded the Italian Olympic Committee to refurbish the Foro. As Marchese saw it, once the facilities improved, the players and the public would return. "First, the successful image," he told me, flourishing his index finger, "then the successful players will follow. We are building a new tradition."

Cino began that tradition building by constructing a hospitality village for sponsors and a VIP Village where celebrities of stage, screen, sports, and politics mingled in an exclusive enclave and discussed in a desultory manner whether it was worth crossing the road to watch tennis. Marchese's greatest coup came the year he managed to bring Alberto Tomba together with Alberto Moravia. Unfortunately, history has not recorded what, if anything, the Olympic skier and Italy's most famous novelist said to each other.

A genial rogue generally described by the press as a savior of tennis, Cino Marchese was essentially a salesman. For five generations, his family had been in the jewelry business and he admitted, "Tennis is often difficult and frustrating, but it's better than every year buying gold and going always to Tel Aviv to buy diamonds. There is no college for what I do. You prepare yourself by plunging in and doing. You go around and meet the peoples and get to be known. Then you either have the daring to do something or you don't."

Marchese had the daring—or call it the gall—to get involved in every aspect of tennis. Tall and white-haired, referred to as the Silver

Fox, he had served as an agent, a clothing dealer, a tournament director (he now ran the women's event in Milan), an arranger of exhibitions, a promoter of clinics, and a journalist who churned out articles and TV commentary on tournaments in which he had a financial interest.

Although he was a garrulous fellow of great charm and aplomb, he could, when crossed, show a truculent side. In 1983, I wrote up a few of his comments about guarantees, and his response was to have me physically removed from the press box, after which he banged my head against a concrete wall and regaled me with his flavorful command of English obscenities. Then along with another Italian Open official, he had me dragged into a storage room under Campo Centrale, where he threatened to hold me until I retracted what I had written. Since what I had written was transparently true—I had quoted Cino's assertions that the best players refused to play in Rome because the Italian Open could not meet their demands for guarantees—I suggested that an honest airing of this problem might help tennis.

"You think I give a shit about tennis?" Marchese shouted, shaking me by the shirt collar. "We're talking about money, not tennis."

To paraphrase the ancient aphorism, *in violence veritas*. Whatever else Cino Marchese might seem to be saying, in the end it came down to cash, and that was what so many reporters failed to consider when they marveled about the renaissance of the Italian Open. Nobody focused on the fact that the problems that IMG and Marchese supposedly solved were, in large measure, caused by them.

As representatives of most of the top players, IMG had had the power to starve the Italian Open of talent. Then when tournament revenues shrank and the facilities deteriorated, IMG was perfectly positioned to benefit from the disaster it had helped create. It bought the tournament on the cheap and as a bonus it came off looking civic-minded. When analyzed objectively, IMG's purchase of the event was less a rescue mission than a hostile takeover.

Now IMG was so flush, it could afford to make a marriage of convenience with its arch rival, ProServ, and let that agency market the TV rights and produce the telecasts of the Italian Open.

"It's simple," Marchese said as he explained this shotgun wedding to reporter John Feinstein. "We give ProServ something so we can get some of their players for the tournament. Tennis works this way. Everything is incest if you look at it closely.''

Understandably, tennis fans didn't care to look quite that closely. They preferred to watch Seles, Sabatini, Capriati, Navratilova, and Mary Joe Fernandez. Or to be precise, they would have watched if the weather hadn't been so wretched. Daily downpours turned the clay courts into blood-colored mud. The Umbrian pines surrounding the field courts served as giant umbrellas for the few souls who braved the rain. The thirty-eight green-and-white-striped hospitality tents, for which sponsors had paid seventy thousand dollars each, shuddered in the wind, their canvas walls bellying like sails in a hurricane.

Yet despite the *mal tempo,* the VIP Village continued to be crowded and Cino Marchese moved smoothly among the seven restaurants, the countless cocktail parties, and press conferences called to hype everything from new tennis products to another comeback by Bjorn Borg, the thirty-five-year-old Greta Garbo of the game. The latter event, a choice scene from Theater of the Absurd, transpired at La Galerie Peugeot, a swank bistro with busty papier-mâché caryatids, plush drapery, and a blue industrial carpet as squishy as a sponge. Seated on a stage lit by chandeliers shaped like sphinxes, the inscrutable Borg announced that after his first-round defeat last month in Monte Carlo, he had decided to forgo the French Open and Wimbledon and remain in Italy to train under Adriano Panatta, a former Italian ace who at the height of his career was well known for a conditioning program that consisted of liberal doses of wine, women, cigarettes, pasta, and bed rest. Now a rotund Davis Cup coach, Panatta sat onstage beside Borg, smoking and sweating profusely, looking like Jabba the Hutt.

Meanwhile, Borg's wife, a rock singer and exotic dancer named Loredana Berté, was off to one side, conducting her own Q&A session with reporters. Loredana wore stone-washed blue denims and a straw hat that resembled something you'd see on a horse pulling a carriage through the Borghese Gardens. Still recovering from a recent suicide attempt—like Borg a few years back, she had swallowed a fistful of sleeping pills—Ms. Berté sat snuggling a stuffed animal, a blindfolded chimpanzee.

After much discussion about the robust state of Bjorn Borg's internal

organs, one reporter, trying to connect this space cadet jamboree with
Planet Earth, asked what the Swede thought about women's tennis.

"Many of the girls have asked to train with me," Borg said, smiling.
"It's nice."

O O O

On those rare occasions when the rain stopped, the players rushed back
on court. Reporters rushed out, too, carrying something to mop up water
from the seats in the press section. Bud Collins came equipped with a
roll of toilet paper. Other journalists made do with brochures that Rado
Watches, a tournament sponsor, unwittingly provided.

Unlike grass courts or hard courts, which a light sprinkle can render
unplayable, European red clay soaks up moisture, and play can resume
not long after a downpour. But the nature of the game changes, especially
in Rome, where the pressureless Pirelli balls, slow and heavy under
normal circumstances, go dead as lumps of mozzarella.

The Italian Open also has a night program, and even in fair weather
the conditions are far from ideal. Regardless of the temperature during
the day, it plummets after dark, and spectators huddle under blankets
like fans at a football game. Every year the tournament's biggest upsets
and most bizarre incidents take place at night. Maybe it has something
to do with the setting of the Campo Centrale, which is sunk in an
amphitheater and surrounded by monumental marble statues of athletes.
Built during Mussolini's regime and originally intended as examples of
high fascist style, these statues have the appearance of inverted Peeping
Toms. Nude themselves, they seem to be staring through the iron un-
derpinnings of the bleachers at the crowds of fully clothed fans. A naked
skier adds a last touch of surrealism next to the scoreboard.

In 1987, during a night match that John McEnroe was losing to a
lowly qualifier, the stadium lights went out. When the electrical fritz
was fixed and Mac came back to win, reporters laughingly accused Cino
Marchese of pulling the switch to save a top seed. But the same thing
occurred in 1990 when the Sabatini–Capriati quarterfinal was interrupted
by a thirty-minute blackout. This year, the women's tournament would
again be plunged into darkness by an electrical malfunction.

OOO

During those days of monsoon rains when few matches were played, journalists had to scramble for stories. One subject always a sure bet to provoke debate was whether women deserved the same prize money as men. The girls got it at the Australian Open and the U.S. Open. Now they wanted it at the French Open and Wimbledon, and they refused to participate in a year-end event sponsored by the International Tennis Federation unless they received equal prize money there as well. At every press conference in Rome (post-match press conferences are obligatory for players; the alternative is a fine) the controversy came up, and since gender sensitivity wasn't the strong suit of most sportswriters and political correctness carried little weight in Europe, these interviews generated plenty of heat.

Much like fiery subterranean magma that periodically erupts with volcanic force to change the face of the map, repeated debate about prize money has not only shaped women's tennis. It literally gave birth to the tour.

Before the advent of the Open Era, all tennis players, with the exception of a handful of barnstorming mercenaries, were amateurs. In theory, both men and women played for the pure pleasure of participating at elegant, clubby events. Unlike other sports, where the sexes were segregated, tennis was seen as a social event for ladies and gentlemen, and its image was one of old money, white flannel, and blue blood. Anybody grubby enough to insist on being paid was supposed to be expelled from paradise, but, in reality, the Amateur Era had always been a bit of a sham. The only difference between amateurs and professionals was that professionals openly pocketed prize money, whereas amateurs accepted under-the-table payoffs. In some cases, ''shamateurs'' were making such a good living they couldn't afford to turn pro.

The hypocrisy ended in 1968 when a tournament in Bournemouth, England, publicly offered prize money and welcomed amateur and professional competitors. Other tournaments followed suit, and the phrase ''tennis pro'' ceased being synonymous with ''card shark'' or ''lounge lizard.'' Yet from the very start, women were paid less than men. At Bournemouth the men's singles champion received $2,400. The women's champ got $720. At subsequent events, the disparity grew progressively worse. By 1970, when Billie Jean King took the Italian Open, she won $600; the men's title holder got $3,500.

By September of 1970, the women, led by King and Rosie Casals, began agitating not for equality, but for a fair share of the prize money. They would have accepted 50 percent of what the men received, but their appeals were brusquely dismissed. The Pacific Southwest Open in Los Angeles offered the women a total of $7,500, to be divvied up among the final eight players. Early-round losers would get nothing. Meanwhile, the men's champion alone would take home $12,500.

The women boycotted the tournament in Los Angeles, and with the help of Gladys Heldman, editor of *World Tennis* magazine, and with funding from Philip Morris, they organized an event in Houston, which was named after a new cigarette—the Virginia Slims Invitational. By January 1971, Virginia Slims and *World Tennis* had inaugurated an eight-tournament women's professional tennis circuit. From it grew the Kraft General Foods World Tour, which still includes twelve events for which Virginia Slims serves as title sponsor.

Given the history of the women's tour, many players regarded the prize money debate as a feminist issue—equal pay for equal work—to which reporters wisecracked that most women's matches were finished in forty minutes while men fought on for hours. Yes, the girls snapped, and those hours were bloody boring. Tennis was show business, they argued. Entertainers should be paid on the basis of quality, not quantity.

Paid by whom? reporters demanded. The public, came the reply. Then where's the public this week? Even on a dry day, who'd pay to see Rachel McQuillan of Australia chloroform Federica Fortuni of Italy 6–2, 6–0? Oh yeah, well, who'd want to watch Carl Uwe Steeb against Slobodan Zivojinovic?

Lively as these arguments were, they couldn't compare to what occurred during dry intervals on court. Although critics complained that there were rarely any upsets at women's tournaments, ten first-round matches in Rome were won by the lower-ranked player, and in four cases a qualifier came through.

Bettina Fulco, a twenty-two-year-old Argentinean, once a semifinalist at the Italian Open and a quarterfinalist at the French, had suffered a series of injuries and slipped to 139 on the Virginia Slims computer. No longer accepted straight into the draw at most tournaments, she had to compete in the qualifying rounds the weekend before the main event. A harrowing rite of passage, the "qualies" have ended the careers of many players, but Fulco, small and frisky as a Pekinese, had squeaked through, then met Mercedes Paz, the fourteenth seed, in the first round. She beat the bigger, more powerful girl 6–1, 6–4, and also took her second-round opponent in straight sets.

In the third round, she ran into Manuela Maleeva-Fragniere, who had won the Italian Open in 1984 at the age of seventeen, dealing Chris Evert one of her rare losses on clay. Now the Bulgarian girl was ranked number ten in the world, and when she ripped through the opening set 6–2, it looked as if Fulco's long struggle—this was her sixth match in five days—was finished. But Bettina kept the second set close by clobbering high rolling shots to Maleeva's forehand, then crossing her up with low skidding balls to her two-handed backhand. When Fulco squeezed through 6–4, Maleeva seemed to snap, and ended up losing 6–1 in the deciding set of a two-hour-and-thirty-two-minute match.

In the quarterfinals, Bettina was eliminated by Mary Joe Fernandez, but it had been her best tournament in two years. The trouble was she had no chance to celebrate. She had to qualify in Berlin and Paris.

In the courtesy car on the way to the Hilton, she brushed back her spiky blond hair and said she was exhausted. She wouldn't have minded spending a few extra days in Rome, practicing at a relaxed pace. But even if she hadn't had to rush off to Germany, she couldn't have stayed here. Men in the main draw received free hotel accommodations for the entire tournament. Women had to leave as soon as they lost or else start paying two hundred dollars a day.

O O O

Cristina Tessi, another Argentinean, had begun playing tennis spontaneously at the age of three by belting balls against the garage wall back home in Buenos Aires. By the age of sixteen, she was the world's topranked junior. But then she set off on the pro circuit, coached by her older brother, Richardo, and was soon going nowhere. Tennis insiders blamed her brother, who sat at courtside screaming instructions and insults.

Although there were rules against coaching during matches, they were seldom enforced unless the violation was flagrant. Peter Graf had been cautioned for sending signals to Steffi, waving his arms like somebody bringing a fighter plane down on the deck of an aircraft carrier. Still, he was the soul of discretion compared to Richardo Tessi, whose shouts were audible to the entire stadium. People tried to reason with Richardo, arguing that neither his tactical tips nor his ugly rebukes helped Cristina. In fact, they seemed to paralyze her, filling her with dread over what lay ahead. When she lost, Richardo turned splenetic with rage.

There were horror tales on the tour about girls being berated or beaten by fathers, brothers, or coaches. Some said this had been true as far back as the Twenties with Suzanne Lenglen and her father. Others described times they had seen Patti Hogan, a player in the early Seventies, being whipped on the bare legs by her racquet-wielding father. They named juniors now being slapped around and destined to become the next generation of battered women. They speculated that certain girls who claimed injury and dropped out of tournaments—there was one suspicious case here in Rome—actually didn't care to appear in public with black eyes.

After Cristina Tessi upset Claudia Kohde-Kilsch in the first round, she was fortunate in the second round to play Jennifer Capriati at night, out from under the baleful eyes of her brother. With Richardo absent, Cristina's performance improved. She pushed the fifteen-year-old Floridian to the wall before losing 7–5, 7–6.

Capriati had her own explanation for this close call. She said she had been worried about her homework. It was the end of the academic year and she had a final assignment to complete. Her scholarly concerns impressed Italian reporters, all the more so when she described her typical day, which sounded like it would have daunted a Harvard grad student. "This year I'm studying more," she said. "I get up at seven, practice tennis, go to school, have lunch, practice again, go back to school, eat dinner, and go to bed at nine." She estimated that her schedule was comprised of 30 percent tennis and 70 percent school.

The next day Capriati brushed off Julie Halard of France 6–2, 6–4. Then accompanied by a pair of *carabinieri* wearing dress uniforms and swords in silver scabbards, she strolled past the courtside seats, shaking hands, signing autographs, and catching bouquets of flowers. Suddenly a railing collapsed and several fans tumbled onto the court at her feet. That sent her scurrying off to meet the press.

When the old interview room at the Italian Open was turned into a players' lounge, a new one had been improvised in a corridor under Campo Centrale. Windowless, furnished with folding chairs and a table covered with a green baize cloth, it was cold as a meat locker and seemed unsuited to the stature of someone like Capriati, whose grinning face had launched a thousand product lines.

Daughter of Denise, an airline flight attendant, and Stefano, an Italian immigrant and ex-soccer player, ex-movie stuntman, and self-taught tennis coach, Jennifer had been groomed since infancy to be a champion. Her father had had her doing sit-ups in her crib. By the time she was four, she was so adept at trading strokes with a ball machine that Jimmy Evert, Chris's father, took her under his tutelage. Before she turned professional just prior to her fourteenth birthday, she had been featured in *Time, Newsweek,* the *New York Times,* the *Washington Post,* the *Los Angeles Times, Sports Illustrated,* and a host of tennis publications. An IMG client, she had endorsement contracts with Diadora, an Italian clothing and shoe company, Prince Racquets, Oil of Olay, Gatorade, and Texaco, and was a multimillionaire before she played her first professional match.

Still, Jennifer insisted that she was just a normal kid—a kid who jetted around the world with her father and mother, her eleven-year-old brother, Stephen, her hovering minders from IMG, and often a United States Tennis Association coach. In one of those stunning paradoxes with which pro tennis abounds, this teenager with the Midas touch, this bubbly money-making machine who could have paid the tab out of petty cash, was receiving free coaching from the USTA.

Beset by hiccoughs and giggles that jostled her gold hoop earrings, Jenny Capriati said, Yes, it had been, you know, a tough match last night. It was cold and night matches are, you know, always tough. Today was like a totally different experience. Now she was looking

...terfinals, because, you know, she had never beaten
... now was the time.

...t your schooling? a reporter asked, referring to that trou-
...ar-end assignment.

...school was like finished, she said. "I'm really happy about
that. It's a big stress lifted. The only thing I have to do now, you know,
is keep a journal about the cities where I go in Europe."

Depending on one's point of view, Jennifer Capriati was either a
lovable, endearing adolescent or a walking advertisement for remedial
education. Many journalists expressed one view in print and another in
private. But Lea Pericoli, for many years Italy's top-ranked woman
player and now a TV commentator and tennis correspondent, was consistent in her attitude toward the American wunderkind; she felt sorry
for her. Although Lea had been a five-time doubles finalist at the Italian
Open and a three-time winner of the tournament in Monte Carlo, she
had no illusions that she or most of her contemporaries could have
competed against today's players. In her era, the girls had been much
less athletic and muscular, and more dependent on finesse. But she
wondered whether progress hadn't come at too high a price.

So many of the players seemed sad and lonely to Lea. Although
surrounded by sycophants, they had few real friends, and to maintain
a relationship with a man, they had to pay. "It's crazy," she said. "In
my day rich old women paid men to keep them company. Now young
girls do it."

She showed me an article in *Corriere della Sera* that described male
hitting partners and coaches as "tennis gigolos." "To coach, or just to
hit with, the top men on the tour, you have to be good," Lea said.
"But there are a lot of mediocre guys making a living off the girls."

In some respects it made sense for a woman to have a male coach
or hitting partner. If she could handle his pace, she could cope with the
most powerful female competitors. But there was more to training than
simply trading strokes with a coach. There was, Lea pointed out, the
matter of strategy and psychology—and who could do a better job in
that area than a woman? Look at Jimmy Connors. He had been coached
by his mother, and he was as cagy as anybody in the game. Technically
and tactically, how many men were superior to Billie Jean King, Virginia

Wade, Margaret Court, and other stars of Lea Pericoli's era? Very few, in her opinion. The increasing number of men on the women's tour was, she thought, another indication of how so many young girls were being exploited.

"To have no education," Lea said, "to have no femininity, what kind of life is that? Look at *la povera* Capriati, ruled by her father. How can she, how can any girl her age, make real decisions? You try to get an interview with her, you try to ask one question, and the father won't allow it. Last year I made six appointments to talk to her on TV. Stefano and she never showed up."

While any father worth the name would protect his fifteen-year-old daughter, Lea felt that things became complicated when the girl was the primary source of her family's income. Then the father had to be careful to put his child ahead of his ego and self-interest.

Since Lea Pericoli was a slim, attractive lady who frequently reported on fashion, I asked about one of her earlier remarks. Was she suggesting that current women's players had chosen to get ahead in the game by giving up their femininity?

"No, they didn't choose anything. I don't think they have a choice. Their fathers are pushing them. It doesn't matter what the girl wants."

○ ○ ○

As Rome endured its coldest, wettest May in more than a hundred years, talk at the Foro Italico revolved increasingly around the condition of the courts. Monica Seles said they were as soft as a sponge. Italians complained that they were as lumpy as a pot of unstirred polenta. While the rain offered the grounds crew a ready-made excuse, the real problem, claimed journalist Gianni Clerici, was that the courts weren't covered during inclement weather by the kinds of waterproof sheets that had become commonplace at other tournaments. Christening the Italian Open the World Cup of Mud, Clerici wrote that to win here a woman had to hit off-speed junk.

But Martina Navratilova would have none of that. In tennis, as in life, she had one style—straightforward and emphatic. Unlike so many women who were inclined to play defensively on all surfaces, Martina hit for the lines and rushed the net. Now nearly thirty-five, she had neither the patience nor the legs for long rallies. Against Elna Reinach, a tall, awkward South African who skidded over the clay as if on roller skates, Navratilova kept her game compact and simple. She would run into Reinach again that summer, but in Rome Martina had little trouble.

That is, she had little trouble once she got the service-line judge removed. She felt the guy was guilty of two blatantly bad calls. "What are you thinking?" she demanded.

Whatever the poor man had in mind, he continued his cogitations elsewhere. After his banishment, Martina beat Reinach 6–3, 6–0.

Intelligent, articulate, opinionated, histrionic, ferociously honest, and dizzyingly complicated, Martina Navratilova is the kind of character seldom seen anywhere except in novels. She might have been invented by Italy's modern fabulist, Italo Calvino. As a player, she had reshaped herself, metamorphosing from a butterball into a formidable mass of what lifters call "ripped" muscle. Then she went on to reshape women's tennis and proved how much more speed, power, and sheer athleticism could be brought to the sport.

Winner of eighteen Grand Slam singles titles, holder of the record in both singles and doubles for the longest winning streak, Martina would have been world-renowned even if she had accomplished nothing else. But it was what she had done outside of tennis that had cast her shadow far beyond the defined limits of sport. Attractive in her androgynous, gender-bending fashion, admittedly bisexual, survivor of a series of affairs and melodramatic, not to mention expensive, break-ups, she had, for many people, come to stand as an emblematic figure in an era of blurring sexual identity. While Margaret Court, the retired Australian champion whose records rivaled Navratilova's, criticized her as a bad role model, others praised her candor and courage.

Whatever one thought of Martina, it was difficult to imagine any athlete, male or female, who could have surmounted the disorienting experiences she seemed to thrive on. What if John McEnroe, for example, had grown up in a Communist country, then had had to defect to the West, learn a new language, and acclimate himself to a different culture? Would he have become a champion? More tellingly, how long would he have lasted at the top if it had been revealed that he was bisexual and had lived with a pro golfer, then a pro basketball star, then a popular gay novelist, then the divorced father of two sons? How could he have coped with the tumult of emotions, the public obloquy, the incessant distractions, the endless litigation? Would he, as Martina had once done, hire a transsexual to help stabilize his life and iron out his strokes?

No, it was inconceivable to think of living as Martina did. More artist than athlete, she seemed to require chaos as a means of stimulating a stronger flow of adrenaline. It was as though each great triumph in her career had come not despite, but *because* of some emotional trauma.

Later that week, after a hard-fought three-set win over a German teenage prodigy named Anke Huber, Navratilova said her goal was to win a tenth Wimbledon title. She would skip the French Open and start practicing on grass. As for whether her split-up with Judy Nelson affected her game, she insisted, "I find tennis a refuge from personal difficulty."

"At this point in your career, what is the place of tennis in your life?"

"It's a job," she said. "It's a job I like, but it's not the only thing in my life."

○ ○ ○

Monica Seles, seventeen, less than half Martina's age, was herself feeling the need of refuge. The new number one, the youngest in history, a growing girl from Novi Sad, Yugoslavia, she had migrated to the States at twelve and was now so Americanized she spoke a brand of English which, while less than perfect in grammar and syntax, seldom faltered in its grasp of slang. Unlike so many tongue-tied teenagers on the circuit, she showed no reluctance to speak her mind—and to continue speaking it long after her brainpan was empty. To the delight of journalists, she was eminently quotable, but they had problems keeping up with her nonstop rap. In Hungarian—Monica's native language—seles means "windy," and that she was.

The burdens of being number one—that was Monica's hobby horse this week, and she rode it hard. Before flying to Rome, she had had to finish a rain-delayed match on Monday in Hamburg, where Steffi Graf beat her in the final of the German Open. If that wasn't disappointing enough, she couldn't collect her runner-up prize of $31,500. The money had been frozen by a court order obtained by a Cologne-based management firm that claimed it represented Seles. The company, AIG, alleged that Monica's father, Karolj, had signed a contract in 1986, when his daughter was twelve. It charged that Seles had breached the contract by hiring IMG and it demanded 380,000 deutsche marks (about $226,000) in damages.

This wasn't the first time, and wouldn't be the last, that Seles found herself the center of controversy. "It always seems," she said, "that when people talk about me, they invent mean things. In the beginning I thought it would be a miracle to become the best, but today I cry about it."

She spoke in a breathless, bouncy voice even when complaining. "To be number one is a terrible cross. My life has become a prison. I can't go out of the house without having fans and photographers all over me. Sometimes it's scary. My new haircut helped. It gave me breathing space for about a week. Nobody recognized me. But then the first pictures came out and that blew it."

The new hairstyle wasn't entirely a bid for anonymity. It was a promotional deal with Matrix cosmetics. For cropping her formerly frizzy locks short, she had earned a fee of $600,000. There were, after all, a few attractive perks at the top.

Her hair wasn't the only part of her appearance that had changed. In the past year she had sprouted six inches to five feet ten. "It's very strange," Seles said. "I have the feeling I have grown even since Hamburg. I'm not kidding! When I look at other players, I realize there were some who were the same height three weeks ago and now I look down at them. I'd like to get to five eleven and a hundred thirty pounds. That would be perfect."

It was more probable that Monica would reach her desired height than that she would ever weigh 130 pounds again. Seles suffered from what Curry Kirkpatrick of *Sports Illustrated* called "a widening caboose." She ate butter on everything—meat, French fries, even pizza. "Ugh. Gross, totally grody," she admitted. "But I can't help it. I must be addicted to butter. I just can't eat any food without it. I know it all goes right to fat down there." She gestured to her hips, thighs, and behind. "I know I've got to switch my diet habits. But I'm waiting until after Wimbledon. If I quit cold on butter now, I'm afraid it would be too much of a shock to my system."

A more immediate shock to her system was how badly players yearned to beat her. As the reigning French Open title holder, the youngest ever, she had gone on to win the Virginia Slims Championship in a five-set marathon against Gabriela Sabatini. Then she had taken the Australian Open, where she was again the youngest winner in history. This year she had fought her way to the final of every tournament she played, but had been beaten twice—by Martina Navratilova and Steffi Graf—leaving her with a shaky purchase on the top spot.

In Rome, fatigued after playing five matches in five days in Hamburg, she ran into resistance in the opening round from Nicole Provis. A tall, suntanned blond from Melbourne, Provis had some luck swinging the ball wide and finishing points without long rallies. But Monica soon bounced back. Slugging each shot with two fists, unleashing a high-pitched, two-syllable grunt, she evened the score at 3–3, broke to 4–3, and was never in danger again.

Seles took every ball on the rise, forcing other girls to play faster than they wanted. As their shots lost punch, she advanced inside the baseline, and when she got a short ball, she pounced on it, pounding clean winners. Her serve wasn't particularly powerful, but it had good placement and deceptive spin, and her service return was among the most punishing on the tour. Although her long legs gave her the spindly look of an ill-coordinated egret, she covered plenty of ground and seemed stabilized by her broad beam.

Her game had only two weaknesses. At the net she was lost. And her two-fisted style off both wings reduced her range. Because she had to do more running than a one-handed player, Monica was vulnerable to ankle and leg injuries. While marveling at her power and tenacity, people questioned how long her body would last.

Still, she had more than enough muscle to spank Nicole Provis off the court, 6–3, 6–1, and she had plenty of energy to spare when she showed up at her press conference fizzing like the bottle of *acqua minerale gassata* on the table in front of her. Dressed in a striped pullover, a pair of tight slacks, and diamond earrings, she started off talking about her hair. "I was tired of having it long. I had to put so many hair pins into it every time I played, I thought I needed a break. Now after a match I don't have to blow-dry it for hours."

She was considerably less effusive about the political situation in Yugoslavia. "Last time I was there, in December, things were fine. Now they're not. Let's put it that way."

"How can you be so different off court and on?" asked an Italian. "You're so aggressive and hard-faced during matches and so sweet now."

"That's just my style. I don't want to grunt, I don't want to have an aggressive face, but that's how I started as a kid at seven and it's tough to change now. In fact," she said in her perkiest, champagne-sweet voice, "I'd like to make my game even more aggressive."

O O O

Later, in the lobby of the Hilton, I spotted Karolj Seles, Monica's father and coach. Although he wore a warm-up jacket and was ruddy and robust, he didn't look much like a coach or, for that matter, like anybody else in tennis. As author Peter Bodo has observed, a common denominator on the circuit is the ability of people to avoid eye contact. Bodo described Bjorn Borg's preternatural talent for crossing a crowded room without once letting his eyes meet another person's.

But Karolj Seles hadn't retreated behind a stone-faced stare. By profession he was a cartoonist and a documentary filmmaker, and his eyes were easily engaged. I stopped to talk to him about Monica. Or rather to attempt to talk to him. His English was rudimentary and among the few quotable sentences Karolj ever uttered are those he gave *Sports Illustrated,* comparing his contribution to Monica's game to the artistry of Michelangelo. "He [Michelangelo] didn't just carve a nice figure in stone. He brought out the spirit of the figure."

It was not entirely clear how he had molded his daughter's spirit or her strokes. Never a player himself, he managed to teach both his children with what he had picked up from instructional manuals. As Cindy Hahn of *Tennis* magazine wrote in an early article on Monica, Seles and her father had practiced on a parking lot near their apartment in Novi Sad. "For a net, they'd tie a string to the bumpers of two cars,"

Hahn reported, and Karolj urged Monica to hit with two hands because he believed that was biomechanically a better stroke. To keep her amused, he drew cartoon faces on her practice balls. Then presumably she grunted and smacked their fuzzy smiling faces off.

By the time Monica arrived at Nick Bolletieri's Tennis Academy in Bradenton, Florida, she possessed an arsenal of lethal, if unorthodox, shots. What happened in the next four years is a subject of dispute. Bolletieri maintained that he fed and housed the Seles family and coached Monica without compensation. Monica claimed Bolletieri gave her no more than advice. When she left the academy in 1990, she said she owed him nothing. If she had benefited from her sojourn in Bradenton, so had he by reaping a windfall of publicity.

Since Karolj seldom hit with his daughter these days, I was curious about their coaching relationship.

"I no good for English," he told me, smiling and patting my shoulder. "Talk to Monica."

When the pat turned into a gentle push, I assumed he was giving me the brush-off. But actually he was steering me toward Monica, who was at the reception desk asking for directions to a restaurant. Dressed in a black beaded and fringed miniskirt and black stockings, she looked like a rich Roman youth raring to hit the streets. She had her father's inquisitive green eyes and the same bump on the bridge of her nose. Over her forehead, above her right eyebrow, ran a long scar.

When I complimented her on the dress, she said that lately she had been doing a lot of photo shoots, like, you know, for fashion magazines. She had a contract to wear Fila on court; Gianni Versace was her current favorite off-court.

It was difficult to make out the color of her hair. It was some radiant hue that Monica, not Mother Nature, had decreed. But compared to her twenty-five-year-old brother, Zoltan, she looked understated. He had bleached his locks platinum blond and combed them forward like a Roman emperor.

"Who's coaching you these days?" I asked.

"My father's always my coach."

"I saw you hitting with somebody else."

She said that an Italian club-level player, Enrico Cocchi, was her sparring partner in Rome. When she moved on to Paris, she'd practice with the Iranian veteran Mansour Bahrami.

Just then there was a commotion in the lobby. Surrounded by squealing kids and autograph seekers, Jennifer Capriati scrambled out the front entrance and into a courtesy car. Hard on her heels, but ignored by the crowd, came Bjorn Borg and Loredana Berté.

"I'd love to meet him," Monica said, sounding more like a starstruck teenager than a fashion-plated sophisticate. "I'd love to hit with Borg."

I asked how difficult it had been for her to become a tennis player. At a press conference she had said, "In my town there wasn't even an indoor court, and you can't be a top-ten player if you can't play for five or six months in winter. Only football and basketball seem to count in Yugoslavia. It was hard to fight to get a court, to fight for everything."

She told me the battle hadn't just been about access to limited equipment and resources. "There's the whole attitude toward girls. Everybody thought I was crazy and my parents were crazy when I wanted to be an athlete, and there were all these discussions about whether it was good for me to play tennis. I think it's not good for a child to have to listen to all this. That's why I had to leave," she said. "Plus in Yugoslavia if you want to play sports, you still have to go to school."

O O O

On Thursday the sun reappeared, and it was so hot there was a rush on hats and suntan lotion. But the crowd couldn't have numbered much more than a thousand, most of them watching matches on Campo Centrale. On Court Four Leila Meskhi of Russia played Akiko Kijimuta of Japan in front of thirty spectators, the most vocal of whom was Meskhi's husband. Lizards slithered leisurely through the empty bleachers.

It was hard to know whether the sparse crowds reflected indifference to women's tennis or, as some contended, the vagaries of ticket distribution. Most seats had been sold in advance to corporate sponsors, local companies, and at least one reputed Mafia don. Other blocks of tickets were reserved for politicos and VIPs who called at the last second and expected to be accommodated. When huge numbers of people who had bought boxes failed to show up, the Foro Italico looked deserted, even though each day was theoretically a sellout.

To throw a baroque Italian twist into the situation, great numbers of tickets had fallen into the hands of scalpers. According to news reports, the scalpers had, in many instances, purchased tickets from VIPs who received them free from tournament officials. To round off the circle, the scalpers often sold them to companies that passed them on to their customers, who, in turn, sold them to scalpers, who sold them back to the tournament to satisfy celebrities who suddenly decided to do a brief drop-by. This meant the average fan stood little chance of buying a ticket that hadn't been marked up two or three times its face value.

Amid the myriad changes at the Italian Open, one thing had remained the same. Most of the umpires were ones I remembered from a decade ago, and their status was still that of amateur volunteers. They got their meals and a paltry amount for expenses.

When in the early 1980s I set out on the men's tour, I had assumed that umpires, like officials in other sports, were professionally trained men and women controlled by some autonomous agency. I assumed there were rules that forbade them from fraternizing with players, agents, tournament directors, and sponsors. I assumed the conflicts of interest endemic to the rest of tennis wouldn't be allowed to affect the officiating. But I was wrong on all counts.

Back then, on both the men's and women's tours, umpires were hired on an individual basis. Although national federations certified them, ultimate power lay with tournament directors, who alone decided whether to let an umpire work. Since these directors had a financial stake in their tournaments, they didn't care to put anybody in the chair who didn't understand that top-ranked players expected preferential treatment. As former Wimbledon champion and Davis Cup captain Arthur Ashe told me, "The stars are protected, and all the players know it. There's collusion between some tournament directors and some umps." Often this reduced itself to a single rule of thumb: The close calls went to the higher-ranked player.

Because top players were crucial to a tournament's success and because they were paid enormous guarantees, the last thing a tournament director wanted was to have a star upset in an early round or defaulted for a rule infraction. Already allowed to choose when and on what courts their matches were played, some male stars even got veto power over umpires.

Under the circumstances, one might wonder why anyone would want to be an ump. But there were compensations. Some simply loved tennis and enjoyed watching it from the best seat in the house. Others had an eye out for profitable opportunities.

Although the pay was poor or nonexistent, some umpires accepted lavish gifts and entertainment from tournaments, and they bought expensive products from sponsors at handsome discounts. As Arthur Ashe pointed out, it was interesting in those days to go to tournaments sponsored by Volvo or Saab or Mercedes and count how many umpires drove Volvos, Saabs, and Mercedes. What would happen to the owner of an American football or baseball team, Ashe mused, if he financed a car for an umpire or got him a ten-thousand-dollar reduction on a sponsor's product?

Umps also supplemented their incomes by representing clothing, racquet, and shoe companies, and they regarded tournaments as trade fairs. Whenever they weren't in the chair, they were keeping old clients happy and signing up new ones. In effect, these umpires were in business with the players they had to officiate.

Still other umps served as front men for special events, clinics, and tennis academies. Between matches at the Italian Open, they might recruit players for an exhibition in Asia or offer them guarantees to participate in a tournament in South America. Again they had financial links with players.

When I argued that these practices presented the appearance of evil, and perhaps much worse, authorities who administered pro tennis rejected any suggestion that there needed to be tighter controls. But soon after the publication of *Short Circuit,* the men's tour hired a cadre of paid officials who rotated from tournament to tournament and answered only to the Men's International Professional Tennis Council. In 1990, when the Association of Tennis Professionals assumed control of the men's circuit, they continued to employ an independent squad of umpires, and the International Tennis Federation (ITF) hired its own group to officiate at Grand Slam events.

In 1991 when I asked ITF supervisor Ken Farrar whether the umps in his group were allowed to accept gifts and discounts from tournament directors, serve as racquet and shoe reps, and act as flak men for special events and other tournaments, he said, "Absolutely not. Those were blatant conflicts of interest we just couldn't permit to go on any longer."

Yet the women's circuit continued to depend on unpaid umpires appointed by tournament directors. It took some doing, but I tracked down Pam Whytcross, a WTA tour director, who had been preoccupied for most of the day by what WTA employees described as "an emergency situation." When she had a free moment, Whytcross explained that much as the WTA would like to hire its own officials, there simply wasn't enough money, and so for the foreseeable future the WTA tour, which consisted of sixty-one events in twenty-two countries, offering a total of $23 million in prize money, would feature professional matches that were officiated by amateurs who were free to supplement their incomes in any way they pleased.

This wasn't the only information that resulted from my visit with Pam Whytcross. While waiting to meet with her, I cooled my heels outside the WTA office and it became apparent what the "emergency situation" was. None of the next day's quarterfinalists wanted to play at night. Seles, Sabatini, and Capriati all refused, and if none of these gimlet-eyed youngsters volunteered for night duty, then Navratilova wasn't going to either.

For three hours—from 6 to 9 P.M.—the women argued *alta voce*. When nobody budged, the WTA had little choice but to propose that they draw straws. At last they agreed on that.

Navratilova drew the short straw and lost in straight sets to Conchita Martinez of Spain. As if the defeat weren't annoying enough, Martina was forced to endure one of the Foro Italico's infamous blackouts. Afterward, a reporter asked a question of stupefying courage. "Would you rather have played during the daytime?"

Martina remained calm. Perhaps the previous evening's debate had left her spent of emotion.

"The courts are so different at night," she said. "They're a lot heavier, and it was cold and hard to see the ball. It doesn't help me, with the kind of game I have. It's difficult to play serve and volley. I'm not saying the outcome would have been different during the daytime, but I would have enjoyed it more!"

The longer she spoke, the better she seemed to feel. Asked for a quote on the crowd, Martina responded warmly. "I wanted to win this match just to go out there and play another one. They're great here. I hoped the match would be longer."

O O O

Monica Seles didn't share Martina's desire to stay on court longer. Moving with the brisk efficiency of a butcher, she massacred Leila Meskhi. After zipping through the first set 6–0, she didn't let up. She wanted to win love and love, wanted to dish out what people in tennis call a double bagel. When Meskhi hung on to win a game, you could hear the disappointment in Seles's grunt.

"What are your feelings after you win six–love, six–one, and you see your opponent burst into tears on court?" a journalist asked.

"I have lost matches six–love, six–one," Monica said. "There are just some days when nothing seems to go right and maybe your opponent is too strong, but you have to take each day as it comes and try to play your best. That's sport."

Indeed, that *was* sport. Weaker players and teams were slaughtered all the time. Usually this provoked no more than admiration for the victor and an admonition to the vanquished to buck up and get back to practice. But reporters, most of them men who routinely praised the killer instinct, seemed uncomfortable when one woman clobbered another and showed no remorse. They asked questions they'd never dream of asking a fighter who knocked out some stiff or a football team that trampled a pathetic opponent.

O O O

The Seles–Meskhi match had ended so swiftly—it lasted forty-one minutes—there was a long wait and a sweet sense of anticipation before the Capriati–Sabatini quarterfinal. Both girls were popular in Italy and had played a close match here last year, which seemed to promise better things this spring.

But in the first game, Jennifer double-faulted, then sprayed a wild backhand, giving Gaby a break to 0–1. Minutes later she dropped serve a second time. When Sabatini reached 5–0, the crowd began to murmur. They had witnessed one blowout and didn't welcome another. With her fans shouting, *"Vamos, Gaby!"* Sabatini served out the set 6–0, blanking Capriati for the first time in her career.

In the press section, journalists remarked on how heavy-legged and slow Capriati looked. Then they reviewed the list of women who had at some point in their careers run to fat—Billie Jean King, Martina Navratilova, Chris Evert, and dozens of less prominent girls. Now Capriati. With the dispassionate eyes of stockbreeders, these reporters were not unlike the coaches, agents, and sponsors who often ruminated on this touchy matter. If Jenny didn't watch it, they concluded, she'd wind up as portly as Papa Capriati. Worse yet, she'd wind up as a teenage has-been or never-was.

One couldn't help wondering how much of this had to do with genuine fears about Jennifer's future and how much with male notions of attractiveness and femininity. Even in their "fat" phases, King, Evert, and Navratilova had continued to win, just as did Monica Seles with her "widening caboose." Still, the assumption seemed to be that it was better for the game's image if the girls were thin and pretty.

When Jennifer won two games to start the second set, there was hope the match might turn into the kind of hard-hitting, hotly contested encounter the crowd had expected. But the long rallies tired her more than they did Sabatini, and she watched helplessly as Gaby came back for a 3–2 lead. Italian tennis writer Rino Tommasi remarked, *"Boccancini chiusi non aprono ancora."* Little mouths that close don't open again.

Actually, Capriati's mouth remained open as she gasped for air. But she never had a chance to do more than inconvenience Sabatini, who went on another six-game tear for a 6–0, 6–2 triumph.

"Equal prize money for what?" Tommasi demanded.

O O O

Jennifer seemed shell-shocked. "I'm more angry than disappointed," she murmured. "I didn't do anything today. She played great, but I made it easy on her. I wanted to change my game after the first set. I had opportunities to come to net, but I didn't. I was really eager for this match because I've lost to her so many times. I thought I was prepared."

"Do you feel farther from the top now? Farther away from being number one?"

"I still think I'm a level behind the best girls."

"Yes, but is it a shock to realize you're nowhere near them?"

Her eyes misted. "I knew I had a lot of work to catch up. But I guess it's a shock that she beat me so easily and I played so bad."

O O O

In victory or defeat, Sabatini's fellow Argentinean, Guillermo Vilas, used to gallop off court and into the press room with his shirt plastered to his chest and his legs caked with clay as if they had been batter-fried. But Gaby took a shower, shampooed her hair, dressed, and applied makeup before she appeared for interviews.

"Never have so many waited so long for so little," a journalist joked. Yet everybody stayed there debating whether Capriati's defeat signaled a temporary setback or the onset of the dread Thierry Tulasne syndrome.

A precocious French junior, Tulasne had burst onto the men's tour in 1980, when at the age of sixteen he stunned the defending Italian Open champion, Vitas Gerulaitis. Convinced that a new Borg had been born, clothing and equipment firms fell into a frenzy, offering contracts totaling the then unheard of sum of $200,000 annually for five years. Thereafter, every teenager who upset an aging champion or caught a star on a bad day demanded a million-dollar deal.

This not only bent the endorsement market out of shape, it was said to have had disastrous consequences for Thierry Tulasne. At the start of his career, just when he should have been improving, he felt no financial compulsion to work hard. Instead of liberating him, the money had crippled his game.

Whether Tulasne had had the talent to develop into a top player, nobody could say now. Still in his twenties, still on the circuit, he had spent the past decade drifting along with an anonymous pack of journeymen players. In fact, he was in Rome this year but had to play the qualifying rounds. He was beaten.

Although it sounded preposterous—from the age of eight Jenny had been labeled "can't miss"—people wondered whether it could happen to Capriati. Sure, she was good, but would she ever get better? Would her father's wheeling and dealing distract her? Would he burn her out with exhibitions? Would she, with all her millions, turn into another Thierry Tulasne?

○ ○ ○

I had moved out of the Hilton and into a friend's apartment in the historical center of the city. Each day on my way to the Foro Italico, I walked past the Quirinale, downhill through the throngs around Trevi Fountain, across Piazza di Spagna, and up Via del Babuino. It was the type of leisurely stroll a tourist might take, but one most unlikely to bring me into contact with anyone from the tournament. Although the circuit is referred to as "the tour," it has nothing in common with traditional notions of travel. While players used planes, trains, buses, and boats, their journey didn't lead to a place. It led to a condition, the claustrophobic existence of pro tennis.

Fatigue, nagging illness, homesickness, boredom, abrupt mood swings, a sense during the indoor season of living in a time capsule shut off from sun and fresh air—these are the hallmarks of the tour and they leave players with little opportunity or inclination to visit museums and landmarks, sample the cuisine, or meet local people. If a camera is the symbol of a tourist, then a Walkman headset is the symbol of the circuit. Whereas a traveler is open to what lies around him, a tennis player is interested almost exclusively in his own space, in creating through acoustical cologne a placid inner environment.

○ ○ ○

On Saturday, the day of the semifinals, the press box hummed with hot tips, fervent opinions, and slightly refined gossip. On the men's tour the main buzz was about money—who had jumped agencies, who had signed a million-dollar deal, who had pocketed a six-figure guarantee, then tanked. In women's tennis the buzz was all about sex. In the last five days I had listened to richly textured tales about lesbians. I had heard reputable reporters exchange bloodcurdling rumors about players they suspected of having incestuous affairs with their fathers. I had been told of teenage girls who had suffered breakdowns after being seduced by coaches or older players. A European player was reputed on good authority to share a live-in coach/lover with her mother.

Many of the most vivid stories dealt with Chris Evert, who, depending on the narrator, was characterized as a lady of healthy appetites or as a single-minded adventuress. Evert was also said to be an incorrigible teller of very dirty jokes. The only one people could remember was more in the nature of a quip, but it showed she had a salty side different from her prissy image. At a party, when asked to compare Jimmy Connors and Vitas Gerulaitis, Chris picked up a soda bottle that had a straw in it. She held the straw in one hand and the bottle in the other. "This is Jimmy," she said. "This is Vitas." (I'll leave it to Jimmy and Vitas to guess who was the straw and who the bottle.)

While Monica Seles and Mary Joe Fernandez warmed up before the first semifinal, clouds scudded so low over the court, the rain, once it came, didn't have far to fall. Fans fled under the bleachers and reporters raced back to a reverberating modular structure that served as a press center. There, waiting for the weather to clear, I spoke with Helen Scott-Smith.

Tall, blond, and attractive, Helen became a reporter after her athletic career ended with a terrible leg injury. "The knee exploded," was how she put it. As a young girl she had competed as a skier, first on a regional team, then at the national level. Since she had dual Swiss and British citizenship and knew how hard it would be to make her mark in Switzerland, she joined the British team. On the basis of her results, she should have been on the 1976 Olympic squad but wound up in Innsbruck as an alternate.

"The Olympic coaches," she said, "chose the girls they were sleeping with." Far from speaking with bitterness, she laughed at her naïveté in those days. "It's a perfectly normal thing," she said. "For many of the girls, especially the mature ones, it was natural to form an intimate relationship with a coach. And of course many of the coaches who were older were eager to have such affairs, even though they could be very hurtful and destructive to the girls.''

Depending on the season, Helen covered international ski meets or tennis tournaments, and she was convinced that what happened on ski teams occurred in women's tennis. Since so many players went on to marry their coaches, it stood to reason they had been sleeping together before that. She didn't moralize, she didn't judge. She simply described the reality of the situation. At a very early age, sometimes before they reached their teens, girls were put into the hands of older male coaches with whom they traveled the tour, living on the road for months at a time. Was it any surprise that some of them became sexually involved?

She mentioned coaches who had had a number of liaisons with players, then had married the girl who happened to be the highest ranked at the time. You didn't have to be a cynic, she said, to see these unions as exploitative and to wonder about their stability.

Although she was still an enthusiastic athlete, Helen observed that a woman, especially during adolescence, might be inclined to compete for the wrong reasons. "Girls, I think, start and go on with a sport to win someone's love—usually their father's. Then it may be a boyfriend. But they seldom get what they want, which is why a lot of them don't feel very beautiful. 'How can I be pretty,' they ask, 'when I can't get love from the one I want?' ''

In her opinion, fourteen, fifteen, and sixteen were critical years for a female athlete. "If a girl is already interested in boys, in a social and sexual life, she may have world-class ability, but the odds are fifty-fifty she'll quit rather than miss out on boys.''

For a man, sports are considered normal and healthy, she said, and people believe they make a boy more attractive. For a female, it's often the opposite. The more she does to improve as an athlete, the less conventionally attractive she may feel. Helen described her own reaction as a young girl the first time she was in the locker room after a ski meet and saw some older muscular women undress. She took one look and thought, I don't want to wind up like that. "Sports," she said flatly, "don't add to a woman's sex appeal."

Helen's views on sex and female athletes had been shaped not just by her experience as a skier and her journalistic knowledge of tennis. She had traveled the circuit with a friend, Christiane Jolissaint, then a top-ranked Swiss player, now the tournament director in Geneva. Because Christiane didn't like traveling alone—she felt it could create misunderstandings and affect her mood—she asked Helen to keep her company. But this itself had led to misunderstandings. Although Christiane had never been known as a lesbian, some players saw Helen and wondered whether she had changed. In Birmingham, England, at a restaurant frequented by players, some of the older ones "came sniffing around our table," Helen said. One of them touched Helen's face, testing her reaction. Helen told her she was interested in men.

Although she had no desire to exaggerate the significance of this incident, Helen Scott-Smith felt it showed what other girls must go through. The tour was so lonely and so competitive, players craved companionship, yet at the same time they needed to send a signal about their preferences. Perhaps, Helen said, some girls slept with their coaches to convince people, and themselves, that they weren't gay.

○ ○ ○

Two hours later when Seles and Fernandez emerged from the locker room, late-afternoon sun warmed the seats on the Tiber side of the stadium. Seats on the Monte Mario side were deep in cool shade. The moist clay was the color of smoked salmon.

"What a beautiful Caribbean maiden," a German journalist said of Fernandez.

Although an American, raised in Miami, Mary Joe (a translation from Maria-José) had been born in the Dominican Republic of a Spanish father and a Cuban mother. A mahogany-brown, imperially slim girl of nineteen, she had a cat's sinuous grace and slinky deceptive speed. Dark hair hung down her back in a single braid. Her sinewy legs were those of a dancer, her frail upper body that of a model. She was the fifth best woman player in the world, yet utterly unknown to the mass public. To redress the problem of her anonymity, she had recently left IMG and was now represented by Ion Tiriac.

Everybody in tennis thought it would take only one Grand Slam title for her to become as famous and marketable as Seles, Sabatini, or Capriati. In 1990, Fernandez had fallen just short, losing to Steffi Graf in the Australian Open final and to Sabatini in the semis of the U.S. Open. At this year's Australian she had a match point against Seles in the semis, but came up empty again.

Ernesto Ruiz Bry had been hired to teach Mary Joe a more aggressive game, but there were those who suspected that she was too sweet to break through to the top. Or else too intelligent. Tennis, it was said, was a game where you had to be smart enough to do it and dumb enough to think it mattered, and Mary Joe's education elevated her out of that category.

The subject of Mary Joe's education came up so often it had begun to embarrass her. "You should interview Mary Joe," WTA officials urged journalists. "She finished school." They didn't mean college. They meant she had a high school diploma, a rarity on the tour. Although Mary Joe played occasional tour events all during her adolescence—at the age of fourteen she was the youngest girl ever to win a match at the U.S. Open—she didn't go on the circuit full-time until after she graduated from the Carrollton School in Miami.

In the United States, where the low graduation rate of college athletes caused scandals, there was a curious indifference to the fact that tennis players received less formal education than any athletes in the world, with the possible exception of boxers or bullfighters. But, of course, the girls were prettier than boxers and toreadors, and few reporters or fans cared whether the stars had mastered plane geometry as long as they had learned to belt their ground strokes at acute angles.

At two games apiece in the first set, Mary Joe squandered a couple of break points, and as so often happens when a player lets a chance slide, she found herself in trouble in the next game. She lost her serve to 2–4, then watched as Seles held to 5–2 with an ace.

When Monica served for the set at 5–3, Mary Joe walloped a few inside-out forehands that caught her by surprise. After breaking to 4–5, Fernandez scrabbled to 5–5, but the running and retrieving had exacted a toll. Her thin shoulders sagged, her chest heaved. She took her time between points, trying to catch her breath. But Seles kept boring in and closed it out 7–5.

The set was a microcosm of Fernandez's career—stylish, close, and finally futile. With no strength in her sticklike arms, she was prone to injury and exhaustion. Belatedly, she had embarked on a fitness program and had been humiliated to discover that she couldn't do a single push-up. Still, she showed little weakness in the second set, and when she won 6–2, it looked as though she had turned the momentum in her favor.

In the third set, Monica leaped out to a 2–0 lead, only to have her serve desert her. As the temperature plummeted and spectators turtled down into their sweaters, Mary Joe broke Seles three times straight. The trouble was she couldn't hold her own serve.

At two sets and four games apiece, the clock on Campo Centrale indicated that the girls had been going at it for two hours, and the question was which one had the guts to raise the level of her game. Fernandez tried to take the initiative and the net, but Seles held to 5–4.

Serving to stay in the match, Mary Joe steered a tired forehand into the net and slipped to 0–15. At 0–30 she chipped the ball, charged, and got passed to 0–40. Fernandez saved two match points, but pushed an approach shot long and listened to the umpire intone another sad benediction on her ambitions. "Game, set, and match, Miss Seles."

o o o

In the interview room, an Italian reporter remarked that the crowd had been against Seles. How did that make her feel?

Monica's response would become a season-long refrain. She refused to accept that anybody was against her. "They were there when I needed them," she chirped.

Inevitably, someone asked who she'd rather face in the final. The only interesting answer I've ever heard to this question came from Ivan Lendl. He said he'd rather face the weaker player, the loser of the other semifinal.

As Seles rattled on about what she had done during the rain delay, she ran finger riffs over the green baize table as if it were a piano. "The locker room where they put us is pretty small," she said, "and we had to sort of sit squished up together. We never knew whether to eat or not." Mary Joe, "a great person," had been there with her and occasionally they talked. But mostly Monica fiddled with video games and her new portable keyboard synthesizer. In fact, she had played so much in the past week she was getting blisters on her fingertips. "But you can't just sit in your room at the hotel watching CNN," she wailed.

○ ○ ○

By the time the interview ended, Sabatini had crushed Conchita Martinez 6–1 in the first set and was on the way to shutting her out in the second. To few people's surprise, the two top women—Seles and Sabatini—would collide in the final.

○ ○ ○

Marty Mulligan rarely missed the Italian Open. For many years he had played the event as an adopted son, or lost child, of Italy. Although born in Australia, Marty had an Italian grandparent, which allowed him to claim citizenship and compete on Italy's Davis Cup team. This was a handy option to have during the Sixties, when Rosewall, Laver, Emerson, Newcombe, and a host of gifted Australians closed off opportunities for their slightly less talented countrymen. Always adaptable, Marty moved to Rome and became Martino Mulligano, winning the Italian Open three times.

Although he now lived in San Francisco, he returned to the Foro Italico every May to see old friends, participate in the veterans' doubles tournament, and take care of business. Marty represented Fila, an expensive line of Italian sportswear, and his two most famous clients, Monica Seles and Boris Becker, were playing Rome.

During the Seventies, when Guillermo Vilas and Bjorn Borg wore the Fila label, the company seemed ready to claim a major share of the market. Both players were handsome, popular champions, often featured in magazines and on television. As agents and accountants broke it down, if a magazine normally charged $20,000 for a page of advertising, then Fila was getting $20,000 worth of exposure every time Borg or Vilas appeared in a photograph wearing its distinctive label.

The same logic applied to television. Networks were then demanding $90,000 a minute from advertisers. That added up to $5,400,000 an hour. Since Borg and Vilas were on TV for hours every month, Fila received millions of dollars' worth of publicity free. Or if not free, then for no more than the fees they paid the players.

The problem was that publicity didn't necessarily result in sales. Spectators loved Borg and Vilas, but instead of buying Fila, they were more likely to go out and buy an Ellesse shirt and Cerrutti shorts or, worse yet, some cheap brand. And even when demand was great—for long periods it was no better than mediocre—Fila lacked the infrastructure and the delivery system to satisfy orders.

So in the Eighties, Fila, like a lot of clothing companies, fell on hard times and cut back. Later, as it recovered sufficiently to make a commitment to tennis, the company restricted itself to a select list of clients. When Fila approached Monica Seles, she was at Nick Bolletieri's and not yet number one. Because Nick had an endorsement deal with Nike, and Monica's agent, IMG, represented Donnay racquets and Adidas sportswear, Fila faced long, tough negotiations, but ultimately it won.

Seles won, too, signing a five-year, multimillion-dollar contract with escalation clauses that depended on her ranking and her results in Grand Slam tournaments. Marty Mulligan believed she was well worth it. "Now that she's number one, she gives us more exposure."

It didn't bother him that she wore promotional patches for Perrier and Matrix cosmetics on her Fila outfits. Although some companies insisted on exclusive contracts, they had to pay a lot more to get them.

Marty believed Fila had also benefited from the growing popularity of women's tennis, which he felt was in better shape than the men's tour. The WTA commanded the loyalty of its stars, he said, whereas the top men failed to give much back to the game. "They pull out of tournaments all the time, claiming injury. What a farce."

Even the new racquet technology favored the women, giving them more power and their game more excitement. But he feared that widebody racquets were on the verge of ruining men's tennis. The ball accelerated so fast and the points ended so abruptly, spectators couldn't follow the action.

This was not to say that Mulligan saw no problems in women's tennis. "Players are very very spoiled, and they get a warped view of life." The circuit had always been cut off from the real world, he conceded, but now girls were more cocooned than ever by entourages. "The top girls are making millions and can afford to take crowds of people with them. Even low-ranked players bring their coaches along, and there's less camaraderie on the circuit."

Although not opposed to coaches—"I think you need one today, somebody to organize your schedule and set up practices and hitting partners. A good one can do much more for a player than teach strokes and tactics"—Mulligan had serious reservations about parents who orchestrated their daughters' careers. "It's hard to get the proper distance from your child. I've tried to teach my son, and it's hard. And how can a girl say to her dad, 'You're just not good enough to coach me anymore'? At a certain point parents have to have the sense to let go. I don't know how Mr. Capriati or Mr. Seles can coach their daughters. Do they have the technical expertise? Monica needs to work on her serve and volley and smash. But is her father the one to teach her? When you have major surgery, you go to a specialist. These girls need specialists."

A moment later, Marty observed, "It may sound chauvinistic to say this, but there's still more pressure on men. If a girl doesn't make it on the tour, she can always get married and have her husband support her."

Marty was right. This did sound like male chauvinism. But before the month was out I would hear the same thing from several women players and from the WTA Director of Player Services, Joan Pennello, who volunteered that "more of the men see tennis as a career. I'm not sure that women know what they want to do with tennis. A lot of the girls, when they quit, they go back to school or try something else. The men don't."

Part of this was due to the youth of the players. A girl could be in the game for a decade and still be young enough to go back to school, young enough to postpone any decision about a career. This was all a dizzying change from the early days of women's tennis when Billie Jean King wrote: "That more women are making tennis their lifelong careers . . . is also measured by the interesting fact that the average age of the world's top-ten players had jumped from not quite twenty-three in 1962 to just over twenty-seven by 1971.'' Now, two decades later, the average age of top-ten women was down to twenty—and that figure would have been much lower if thirty-four-year-old Martina Navratilova hadn't been playing.

Although Marty Mulligan believed men were under more pressure, he harbored no delusions that women had it easy. "They do so much exercise, they get too muscular, and they're out in the sun so much, it ruins and ages their skin. A lot of the women you'll see have bad skin from playing outside. Of course, feminists may say this doesn't matter, but most women do seem to want to look good.''

He felt it was difficult for a girl to lead any kind of life on the circuit. How could she meet men? And if she met one she liked, when would she ever see him? "That's why a lot of girls make their boyfriends or husbands their coaches,'' said Marty. "Most guys can't give up a job to travel with a girl, so their job becomes traveling with her.''

Although it was a subject he didn't much care to discuss, Marty acknowledged that he had heard of an older coach who had started working with a girl when she was nine. By the time she was in her mid-teens they were, according to all accounts, sleeping together. The coach had a wife and kids, which not only created complications for him, but troubled the girl. She had enjoyed a meteoric rise into the top ten, then her career stalled. Eventually she and the coach suffered an anguished split, partly due to her dissatisfaction with her progress, partly because of her sense that he was smothering her and she couldn't grow as a player or a person until she asserted her independence. She was still on the tour, but no longer in the top ten or anywhere near her original goals.

Of coaches who slept with their players, Marty Mulligan said, "Once you cross the line, you've got problems. There should be ethical limits. But there's the professional issue, too. How can you be objective in a situation like that? How can you do what's best for the player?''

○ ○ ○

The day of the final was as gloomy and cold as the rest of this freakish Roman May. The best seats at courtside were empty, but up in the bleachers fans unfurled banners proclaiming themselves members of Gabriela's Praetorian Guard.

Seles had her supporters, too. After she survived a break point in the first game, a little boy held up a hand-lettered sign in English: "Monica, I'm impressed."

Gaby hit a double fault, giving Seles an early ad. But on a point that would come to seem symptomatic, Monica approached the net for an easy volley, hauled off with a big two-handed swing, and butchered the shot. Grateful to have gotten off the hook, visibly gaining confidence, Sabatini varied the spin on her ground strokes, smacking the ball with top, then hitting slice. Her strategy was to deny Seles the rhythm and speed that she fed on. In this, she got an assist from the wet clay, which Monica waded through as though wearing gum boots.

When Seles botched another big swing volley, Gaby broke to a 3–2 lead, held to 4–2, then tormented Monica with angled shots to her forehand. At times Seles had to stretch full-length and stab at the ball one-handed. To add to her misery, there was a soccer game in the nearby stadium, and as a clattering police helicopter hovered overhead checking the crowd for hooligans, Monica dropped serve and fell behind 2–5.

Still, she didn't give up. She had what Italians call *la grinta*, a grittiness that stiffened her resolve when the odds were stacked against her. She broke Sabatini to 3–5, but with the score 30–15 in her favor, the sky opened and down came the rain.

When the match resumed an hour and twenty minutes later, the court was a quagmire. Sabatini saw what she had to do. She slashed at the ball as if wielding a machete, then watched as it sailed to Monica's side of the net and dropped absolutely dead. It took her two minutes to finish off the first set 6–3.

It didn't take her much longer to leap ahead 3–0 in the second. Monica managed to win back a break, but she'd been knocked off kilter by the rain and by Sabatini's shower of off-speed shots. Seles had pounded her way to the top of the Virginia Slims computer by wielding her racquet like a sledgehammer, but today she was reduced to using it as a shovel, digging balls out of the dirt.

Serving at 2–5, Seles appeared to have put away a forehand. Sabatini protested that the shot was long. She asked the linesman to check the mark. He did so and signaled that it was good. Gaby appealed to the umpire, who clambered down from his chair, stooped for a closer look at the smudged clay, and signaled that Seles's shot had been out. The overrule gave Gaby match point, and she finished it with a drive down the line.

There were boos from the crowd, but not many, and Monica didn't protest. This was the second straight rain-interrupted final she had lost, and she was eager to get off the mud and into a dry, warm place. But first she had to endure the awards ceremony.

Lea Pericoli walked out in her dainty pumps to act as Mistress of Ceremonies. She introduced Paolo Galgani, president of the Italian Tennis Federation, a handsome fellow who had made no concession to the cold weather. Dressed in a creamy tan suit and a pair of sunshades as if he had stopped by on his way back from the Riviera, Galgani kissed Seles on both cheeks and handed her the runner-up trophy and a check for $40,000. Then he kissed Sabatini, who got a bigger check—$100,000—and a bigger trophy. As Gaby hoisted it overhead, the top of the trophy fell off and just missed beaning Galgani.

In her press conference, Seles was as cheerful as she had been after big wins. She congratulated Gaby and refused to complain about the overrule. "I felt the point was called wrong, but you can't change the umpire's decision. You just have to forget it."

In contrast, Gabriela Sabatini sounded lugubrious even though she claimed she was happy. She said she was looking forward to Wimbledon. She said she would celebrate her twenty-first birthday the following week in Berlin. She said, "I have a lot of confidence. I'm using everything on the court. I'm playing better and better."

Yet a few days later when she stayed out late the night of her birthday, then lost the next day to sixteen-year-old Anke Huber, she called into question whether she was, in fact, playing better and better. Or had she peaked too soon?

Teaming up with Jennifer Capriati, Seles seemed jubilant as they beat Nicole Provis and Elna Reinach for the doubles title. The sky had cleared, and by the time the match was over, the sun was casting the elongated shadows of umbrella pines over the field courts. Although it

was still cold, the dense golden light suggested that summer was near.
There was only one disconcerting sound to ruin this scene. At the end
of the day, Monica Seles stood outside the locker room crying. Stefano
Capriati urged her to go inside where no one would see her, but she
ignored him and continued sobbing. She'd cry if she wanted to wherever
she wanted to.

French Open

Les Très Riches Heures of Monica Seles

If a city the size and complexity of Paris can be said to have a microcosm, then the French Open at Stade Roland Garros fills that bill. For two weeks at the end of May and beginning of June, the tournament compresses into a twenty-acre enclave at the edge of the Bois de Boulogne the essential Parisian hallmarks—high fashion, high society, high-minded evocations of the nation's past, haute cuisine, copious wine, rampant commercialism, and pure artistry.

Each year the tournament's poster and program cover are the work of a celebrated artist. Many of the *affiches* from earlier decades have become collectors' items. In 1989 when the Museum of Modern Art in New York mounted an exhibition entitled "The Modern Poster," the catalog cover was an *affiche* by A. M. Cassandra, originally done for the 1932 French Open. The 1991 poster reproduced a watercolor by the late Joan Miró. And since this was the event's hundredth anniversary, Roman Opalka painted a mural on the wall behind Courts Three and Four, integrating into it the names of the 2,973 men and women who had participated at Roland Garros.

At other tournaments, fans show up in T-shirts and shorts, as if planning to sneak into the main draw and play. But in Paris, in the pricier seats on Court Central, spectators look as though they have arrived from a reception at the Elysée Palace. Regardless of the weather, which can range from glacial to torrid, many men wear dark suits, starched shirts and ties, and the women in their designer outfits have the half-starved, hollow-eyed appearance of couturier mannequins. Even the hired help is well turned-out. Hostesses in the VIP boxes and the Presidential Tribune are clothed by Christian Dior. Elsewhere, ushers wear pink ensembles by Galeries Lafayette.

Fashion shares a place of prominence with another Gallic obsession—food. An aroma of roasting meat laces the air, and the sounds of silverware on china and of hurried waiters shouting orders add a curious undercurrent to the cheering crowds. Fans who don't care to eat a sit-down dinner line up at stalls that sell crepes, *gauffres,* cheeses, strawberries and cream, pizza, and *pan bagnats.*

The press enjoys its own private dining room. At lunch on opening Monday, there was a choice of *steak frites,* roast veal, or fish in white wine sauce, all washed down with complimentary bottles of Beaujolais. A different *cru* was served with each meal, and during the fortnight sponsors laid on free samples of foie gras, oysters, champagne, and regional dishes.

This year, the Ministry of Sport circulated a communiqué reminding journalists that umpires would defend the sacred French language and call *"faute,"* not "out," *"filet,"* not "net," *"jeu décisif,"* not "tie-break." French reporters were supposed to write *"tir passant,"* not "passing shot," *"as,"* not "ace," *"brèche,"* not "break," *"lift,"* not "topspin," and *"Grand Chelem,"* not "Grand Slam."

The press's response to this directive was one long, loud raspberry. Of far greater concern to journalists was the state of Steffi Graf's health, the state of her mind, the state of her game. By the age of nineteen, the German star had won nine Grand Slam titles and seemed destined to dominate women's tennis for the next decade. She did hold the top spot in the rankings for a record 186 weeks, but then things—everything, in fact—went wrong, and it was impossible, in retrospect, to say where the trouble started.

Susceptible to flus, viruses, and allergies, Steffi had suffered a series of mysterious maladies. Several times she had to be treated for sinusitis so severe it prevented her from breathing. Then in a freak skiing accident in February 1990, she broke her thumb and was out of action for months. Tennis insiders wondered whether her ailments weren't psychosomatic and somehow linked to her thorny relationship with her father.

Brusque and overbearing, Peter Graf had encouraged Steffi to stay aloof from other players. Although he hired Pavel Slozil, a former member of the Czech Davis Cup team, to coach her, he continued to hold a tight rein on his daughter. Living through, as well as off her, he was one of dozens of fathers on the circuit who badgered their children to achieve what they themselves could never have hoped to accomplish.

In return, Steffi enjoyed the kind of connection with her father that some adolescent girls might secretly fantasize about. She was the center of Peter's life, the focal point of the whole family, and while he ran her career, she could in some sense regard herself as his rescuer. As reporter John Feinstein noted in his book *Hard Courts,* Peter Graf had a drinking problem and Steffi would sometimes remove the glass from his hand when she thought he had had too much. When Nicole Meissner, a young model best known for posing in the nude, alleged that Peter had fathered her child, "the real surprise among tennis people," Feinstein wrote, "was that a woman and not alcohol was the source of the scandal (although some people speculated that the two were connected)."

In an attempt to keep Nicole Meissner and fellow-extortionist Eberhard Thust from going public with accusations about his sexual indiscretions (which Peter didn't deny) and his love child (which he did deny) Peter Graf paid $484,000. But Meissner and Thust double-crossed him and sold their story.

Ultimately Graf passed a blood test, and the paternity suit was dismissed. But by then he had been tried by tabloid and convicted in the court of public opinion. (Meissner and Thust were later convicted in a different kind of court. She got two years in jail for extortion and Eberhard Thust got three years and a $121,000 fine.)

The innocent party who suffered most in this debacle was Steffi. She, not her father, had to play matches, then face the press. Hounded by questions about Nicole Meissner and the baby, Graf hadn't won a Grand Slam title in a year and a half, and the 1991 French Open offered an opportunity to gauge how far she had fallen. Or, as her fans hoped, how close she was to a comeback. True, her first-round opponent, Magdalena Maleeva, youngest of three tennis-playing sisters, was barely sixteen, but on clay, against a player groping to regain her confidence, the Bulgarian girl had a chance.

Graf got off to a 4–0 lead, then took a nasty spill and had to hobble to her chair to wipe the clay from her hands and legs. She resumed play sucking a wounded thumb.

Maleeva held to 2–5, then broke to 3–5. Although Graf broke back to win the first set 6–3, Maleeva seemed to have found the range, and in the second set Graf's play turned erratic. Her forehand started to sail long; her backhand landed shorter and shorter. Maleeva forced the match into a tie-break—excuse me, a *jeu décisif*—where an extraordinary thing occurred. In the middle of a rally the ball went dead and dribbled into the net. Steffi felt the point should be replayed. The umpire decided otherwise.

Still, Graf reached 6–3, giving her three match points. Maleeva saved the first, then smacked a service winner to save the second. With Graf serving, Magdalena cracked a crosscourt backhand to even the score 6–6. Although Steffi scraped through the tie-break 8–6, neither she nor her supporters could have been encouraged by her performance.

She arrived at her press conference in a pair of blue jeans and a long-sleeve jersey. Her straw-colored hair hung to her shoulders. She had applied mascara, but no lipstick. As she answered questions in a faraway voice, she swung back and forth in her chair and kept her eyes fixed on the floor. She said she hadn't suffered any recent sinus trouble and was eager to play well here and prove something to herself. "I don't really care about being number one. I just care about my game."

When a reporter asked whether she had undergone therapy to improve her attitude, Graf glanced up, narrowing her eyes. "Therapy?"

The man made it clear that he meant psychotherapy.

"No." Steffi sounded horrified and swore she'd never do that.

○ ○ ○

Like Graf, Mary Pierce advanced to the second round with a tie-break. There all resemblance ended. While the German girl was world-renowned and had won more than $8 million in prize money, the sixteen-year-old American from St. Petersburg, Florida, had labored in obscurity to scratch out fifty thousand in her two years on the tour. Insofar as the public was aware of her at all, they knew her because of a *Sports Illustrated* article that can best be described as a cautionary tale. If the Capriatis embodied the American Dream, then the Pierces were the nightmare.

When Mary was fourteen, Jim Pierce had sold his house, packed his family into a 1979 Cadillac, and hit the road. For months they drove from tournament to tournament, pursuing a goal—stardom for Mary— via a route that could most kindly be called circuitous. Behind them lay miles of heat-distorted highway, burned bridges, and bad vibes.

Like a lot of tennis fathers, Jim Pierce had bounced around in his early life and had no background in the sport. Then he met and married a Frenchwoman named Yannick who was working on a doctorate in linguistics at the University of Montreal. After Mary was born, they moved to Florida, and when she took up tennis as a kid, Jim, then well into middle age, took it up too and became her self-taught coach and manager. In many respects he wasn't all that different from Stefano Capriati, Peter Graf, or Roland Jaeger.

But then Jim jumped the tracks. As he tells it, when the United States Tennis Association failed to provide the sort of financial and instructional assistance Mary deserved, he decided to strike out on his own. As the USTA tells it, Jim refused to step aside and let professional coaches train his daughter. He insisted on running the show, interfering at practices and dictating what should be done. During matches he sat in the stands screaming at Mary, at umpires, and at her opponents. On the junior circuit, he had been known to bark obscenities and brawl with other parents. His idea of encouragement was to scream, "Kill the bitch, Mary!" Now he had taken his turbulent show onto the tour and couldn't comprehend why Mary wasn't winning and why the tennis community winced whenever his name was mentioned.

Searching for the sort of arrangement the USTA hadn't provided, Jim had shopped his daughter around. Because she had been born in Montreal, he contacted the Canadian Tennis Federation, but when they didn't have the money or resources to meet his demands, he moved to France. Since his wife was French, Mary could claim citizenship there.

Settling near Nice, in the town of Villeneuve Loubet, Mary had become a member of the French national team.

On court, she wore glasses that gave her the appearance of an ugly duckling, but she had only to remove the horn-rims to metamorphose into an exquisite swan. When I interviewed her at Roland Garros, the glasses were off, her long blond hair hung straight to the middle of her back, and huge heart-shaped earrings dangled from her lobes. She had a caramel-colored tan, and her arms were lightly downed with golden hair.

Of her change in countries and cultures, she said, "I adapt easily. At home"—by which she meant Florida—"we were living half French, half American. We'll stay in France six months this year and six months in the States. We'll go to Miami in winter."

What about technical changes? Was it different to train in France? No, she trained the same way. "My father is always the coach."

"Is that what went wrong with the USTA—your father wanted to coach you?"

Her answer had the canned quality of a recorded announcement. "When I asked for coaching, the USTA couldn't provide it. I waited. Then someone who came along after me asked for coaching and got it right away."

When I mentioned the *Sports Illustrated* article, her pretty face darkened. She said she had been told it was going to be a piece about her, not her father, not her family. "Some of the things they wrote were true, some weren't."

"What wasn't true?"

"The picture of my father wasn't accurate."

"In what way was it inaccurate?"

She shook her head. She didn't care to discuss it.

"Have you tried to correct the inaccuracies?"

"I can't be bothered with that." Her voice had flattened; her eyes fled mine.

○ ○ ○

In contrast to his wary, close-mouthed daughter, Jim Pierce had the brash, florid face of a fellow who had never ducked a question, a challenge, or a punch in his life. When I caught up with him several days later, he was watching matches on the outside courts. Mary was with him and so was his wife, who hovered in the background carrying her daughter's bags.

Mary gave no sign that she remembered me or our conversation. Neither did she react when her father gestured toward her. "Here she is, my girl, a goddess."

He hadn't missed the mark by much. She was an impressive specimen standing there in a pastel tennis outfit by Ellesse.

"I think as soon as she reaches her full mental maturity," Jim said, "she'll bury Seles and Capriati. I'm not in this for the money. I'm putting it all where Mary will have it. When she turns fifty, I want her to know it's there and she'll have nothing to worry about."

Gruff and good-natured though he seemed, Pierce was so outspoken, it was easy to understand how he often put his foot in his mouth. He said IMG represented Mary. "But I don't think we'll renew when our contract is up. All they care about is Capriati and piling up contracts and promotion deals for her. They might as well throw a bag over Mary and pretend she doesn't exist."

Most tennis interviews are like dentist chair torture; a reporter is always pulling teeth. But talking to Jim Pierce was like lifting fruit out of Jell-O. His personality was like the game he had given his daughter— strong and straightforward, but with only one gear. "I've taught her I don't even want her to have a second serve," he said. "Just burn that first one in."

He claimed that the *Sports Illustrated* article "didn't hurt me. It helped me. I thought they were a sport magazine, not the *National Enquirer*. But if they want to make me out to be a bad guy, that's all right with me. It's like General Schwarzkopf. You're in the desert, you're in battle, and you gotta give the guys a kick in the ass and tell them to move out or you'll kick them in the ass again. It's kill or be killed out there. If you don't have the balls to do it, the other guy will. So like I said, if they want to make me out to be the bad guy, that's all right by me."

Mary tapped his arm. She had something to say. I expected her to object that she wasn't a guy, she wasn't out to kill anybody, and she didn't need a coach to kick her in the ass. Instead she said she was hungry. She asked her father for money for ice cream.

OOO

Monica Seles dispatched her first-round opponent, Radka Zrubakova, 6–3, 6–0, then scurried into her press conference to feed journalists more grist for their mill. Reporters had yet to recover from a pre–French Open interview that Seles attended braless, in a one-piece nylon see-through outfit. Today someone asked if she had read a recent article comparing her with Madonna and Suzanne Lenglen.

"I haven't had time to read all of it, but I have run through the captions. It was very funny. I love both of them a lot."

"Who would you prefer to be?"

"I really can't choose. If I could go back in time, then I'd be Suzanne Lenglen. She was a great star and a great player. But I would also love to be Madonna."

Someone asked whether she would participate in the Federation Cup, an international event for women comparable to the men's Davis Cup. Teams from fifty-six countries were scheduled to compete in Nottingham, England, at the end of July.

"I haven't decided yet," Seles said. "It depends who the other player on the Yugoslavian team is. It would be a total waste of time to go there for one day and lose. I'm going back to the U.S. after Wimbledon and I have to play in San Diego. It isn't worth coming back for one day. If we had a really good second player and had a chance to get to the quarter- or semifinals, then maybe I'd do it. But we'd probably run into Germany in the first round and get blown over."

OOO

According to International Tennis Federation regulations, any woman who failed to participate in the Fed Cup would lose her eligibility for the 1992 Olympics. As it looked now, three of the world's best women— Seles, Sabatini, and Navratilova—might miss out. But there were rumors that the rules would be waived and the stars would be granted wild cards in Barcelona. The ITF categorically denied this.

Although the ITF had set aside a $500,000 bonus pool to entice top-ten players to the Fed Cup, that wasn't enough to tempt some stars. According to *Tennis Week,* Seles demanded a $250,000 guarantee. Navratilova claimed she was committed to play Team Tennis in the States. Gaby begged off, saying she would be too tired after Wimbledon.

Whether these players had foolishly frittered away a chance to qualify for the Olympics was a question that popped up every day in Paris, and since the French Open paid women half a million dollars less in prize money than the men, each press conference became a forum for that debate as well. Publicly the International Tennis Federation professed to be above this battle, but privately it spread information that buttressed its case. As one ITF official put it to me, "In strictly financial and commercial terms, the women don't deserve equal prize money. They don't draw spectators like the men and they don't command the same money from sponsors. At Roland Garros the only day that isn't sold out is the women's semifinals. Maybe women should receive equal money as a matter of principle or as a symbolic gesture, but in business terms it doesn't make sense."

Some felt it didn't make sense in any terms. Whether viewed as sport or entertainment, women's tennis was, its critics complained, an inferior product. That's why *L'Equipe,* the French sport newspaper of record, devoted three or four pages to the men and only half a page or less to the women. That's why television was saturated with coverage of the men.

Women might argue that these were self-fulfilling prophecies. They might contend that they couldn't hope to attract fans unless they received equal press and television coverage. But no matter what they said, the men who controlled tennis seemed to believe that the debate could be reduced to a single issue: As long as men could beat women, men deserved more money. Thus at Roland Garros the story of Harold Solomon circulated like a saga chanted by misogynist fathers to misogynist sons.

Now thirty-eight, the diminutive Solomon had emerged from retirement and announced his comeback. Since he no longer had a ranking, he couldn't enter tournaments except via the qualifying rounds. In fact, he needed a wild card to play the qualies at Roland Garros.

An implacable baseline player who had once reached the French Open final, Sollie flew to Paris thinking that if nothing else, he'd enjoy himself and see friends. But he didn't have time to do either. An unknown Spanish boy bounced him out of the qualies in the first round 6–3, 6–0.

As Harold was coming off court, Ernesto Ruiz Bry asked if he'd like to hit with Mary Joe Fernandez. Sollie had gone straight back on court and, as the tale tellers recounted, even at his age, even after the merciless, morale-destroying drubbing he had just endured, he cleaned her clock 6–0, 6–1. End of anecdote, end of issue, end of debate—at least until the next day, when somebody brought it up again.

Although it's not, strictly speaking, relevant to whether men and women should receive equal prize money, it's worth pointing out that pro tennis does pay female athletes far more than any other sport. No female track star, skier, skater, or gymnast, no golfer or basketball player has won anything remotely approaching the $8 million Chris Evert and Steffi Graf have pocketed in prize money, and they themselves fall far behind Martina Navratilova, who has earned $17 million along with her slew of titles. Most stars can double or triple their prize money with endorsements and exhibitions. And it's not just lucrative at the top. Tennis affords an opportunity for hundreds of women athletes to support themselves. That they don't make as much as men may be regrettable, but that they make so much more than other world-class female athletes is still remarkable.

○ ○ ○

Two very different tournaments take place at the French Open and at other Grand Slam events. There's a tournament for top-ranked players, and a second—some would say a second-class—tournament for everybody else.

The tournament for stars is the one most fans know. At Roland Garros it's set on Court Central, Court One, and Court Eleven, where matches have full complements of officials, including net cord judges. Spectators aren't allowed to leave the bleachers except during changeovers, and every effort is made to maintain silence and order.

The second tournament is staged out on the field courts, and the farther a player is exiled from Court Central, the worse the conditions. Skeleton crews of six officiate the matches, and fans wander back and forth, an arm's length from the sidelines. Noise and confusion are so constant, players don't waste their breath complaining, and since there are no ushers to enforce order, umpires don't bother calling for it.

On Court Thirteen, located in a clamorous angle formed by Le Buffet public restaurant and the private Club des Loges, Bettina Fulco, the game Argentinean who had once again had to survive the qualies, was struggling against Elizabeth Smylie, an Australian with a net game honed by dozens of doubles titles. While Smylie wanted to end points quickly, Fulco attempted to prolong them, but this required a precarious balance of patience and stamina. Having played three matches over the weekend, Bettina risked exhausting herself as she painstakingly maneuvered her opponent into mistakes.

At 4–4 in the first set, Smylie suffered the frustration of an aggressive, fast-court player trying to adapt to clay. Rushing in behind an ill-advised approach shot, she got passed and could do no more than wave futilely as the ball flew by. When Fulco held serve to win 6–4, the contest was over. Fed up with the slow pace, Smylie lost her heart and head at the same time, and Bettina reeled off six games in a row to win the second set and the match.

On Court Fifteen—one had only to swivel around to see it—Renata Baranski, née Marcinkowski, a resident of Rock Hill, South Carolina by way of Szczecin, Poland, had a break point to go up 5–3 in the third set against Maider Laval of France. Wearing a baseball cap on this sunny day, Baranski resembled a scrappy shortstop as she gobbled up a second serve, sliced it to Laval's backhand, and knocked off a volley. She made quick work of the final game and jubilantly smacked a ball into the air. Laval shook the victor's hand, stomped on her racquet, breaking it, screamed at the blue indifferent sky, picked up her equipment bag, slammed it down, picked it up again, and stalked off in tears.

O O O

Someone tapped me on the shoulder. A big-boned, sun-freckled fellow, he said he had heard I was doing a book about women's tennis. He introduced himself as Dennis Van der Meer.

Originally from South Africa, Van der Meer ran a center on Hilton Head Island where he trained coaches as well as players. Billie Jean King had called him "the best tennis teacher in the world." For years he had served as an Instruction Editor of *Tennis* magazine.

Van der Meer explained that he was in Paris with one of his young protégées, Christina Papadaki. At one time or another, he had worked with many of the players in this year's French Open, but he feared that the coaching profession was about to "move more toward the European model of national schools. I prefer the entrepreneurial approach," he said. "This is an entrepreneurial sport. I don't want a kind of tennis socialism. We showed it works, the entrepreneurial approach. Look at the champions we produced."

While Van der Meer acknowledged that a few national federations produced good results, he felt champions required a continuing relationship with the same coach. Too many national programs overlooked that fact, and they failed to consider a player's needs as they evolved over the course of a career.

"In the beginning," he said, "a girl has to learn to deal with her nerves. Then she reaches her peak, and her need is to maintain that level. As she gets older, curiously, she comes down with a case of bad nerves again. Look at Martina. Last year she lost four matches on double faults on the final point.

"But it's not just the girls. Did you see McEnroe lose to Cherkasov yesterday? He was guiding the ball, not hitting it. That's when you know there's trouble, when they start steering the ball."

As we strolled among the field courts, Van der Meer veered from subject to subject, reminded by a match or a player of something else he wanted to discuss. "So much of this game is in the mind," he remarked. "Steffi Graf is the same girl she was last year, physically the same. But she's fifteen percent or twenty percent less as a player because of the mental part."

Everybody on the circuit had an opinion about why the best female players were now so young. Some claimed it was the racquets. Some credited new training techniques. But Van der Meer maintained that young girls also concentrated better; an adolescent had less on her mind than a mature woman.

Of course, he conceded, there was always the potential disruption of boys. He cited the example of Christina Papadaki. "She's eighteen and beautiful. Right now her life is all tennis. But next year or the next, who knows, a boy could come along, and her attention could wander and her game go away. Once you lose the mental part it doesn't come back."

Not only were women tennis stars getting younger. Van der Meer pointed out that they were also getting bigger. "Steffi's big. Seles is big. You've got to be big to play the power game."

But the trick was to produce strong girls, not fat ones, and that wasn't easy. Too many of the women were overweight and out of shape, he said. Rather than eat and exercise sensibly, they fasted after binges or became bulimic and forced themselves to vomit. Other girls went on fad diets.

"A lot of match results are skewed by these diets and eating disorders," said Van der Meer. At his tennis center, "We weigh the girls every week—we don't weigh the boys—and if a girl has gained weight, we measure her body fat content. If the body fat is low, then it's muscle she's gained and that's all right."

He asked whether I had read an article in the *Herald Tribune* that dealt with homosexuality among female athletes and the problems this posed for sponsors. Based on his experience at organizing clinics and exhibitions, Van der Meer said that corporations were leery of what they suspected was the high incidence of lesbianism on the WTA tour. "Some say fifty percent of the girls are lesbians. Some say it's much less. Others say the higher figure is accurate and some girls just aren't out yet."

The exact number, in Van der Meer's opinion, mattered less than the general perception that a significant portion of the women were gay. This not only affected the game's image, its media coverage and marketability; Van der Meer felt it affected the day-to-day operation of the circuit.

"You've got to handle this subject sensitively," he stressed. "We're men talking and it's hard to be objective, hard not to sound prejudiced. You can't be judgmental. But the practical consequences have to be looked at. You go to the WTA and meet the women [who run the tour] and some of them are lesbians and if you're a player and you're not a lesbian . . . well, there's the thought that they'll give the lesbians a break because they don't get breaks in the rest of their life.''

Van der Meer went on to say, ''You're sixteen and you're out on the tour and Billie Jean or Martina start paying attention to you, watching your matches, offering advice and coaching tips. Well, a girl may decide to go with them. Who knows whether they change her, or she would have done it anyway at some point. But the girl who doesn't go that way may feel disadvantaged, shut out.''

Again he stressed, ''I don't want to sound prejudiced.'' He had coached lots of girls and never favored straights or gays. He had coached Billie Jean King during a crucial period of her career and had been her trainer for the famous Battle of the Sexes against Bobby Riggs. After Billie Jean ground Riggs into the carpet in three straight sets, she ran over to kiss Van der Meer in gratitude. So Dennis didn't feel he was a sexist or a gay basher. Still, he believed that lesbianism had caused problems for women's tennis.

For an outsider—i.e., anyone outside the locker room—and for a male, it may be impossible to do more than report what informed sources said about this issue. While most men on the circuit seemed to feel that, whatever their precise number, lesbians constituted a critical mass, the players themselves assured me that there was no problem; they claimed they had never noticed gays making advances that weren't welcome. As Hungarian veteran Andrea Temesvari told me, ''Okay, sometimes a girl is fourteen and doesn't know what she's interested in. She may talk and be nice, and the gay girls might misunderstand, but mostly they go with the ones they can see are interested.''

Don Candy, who spent years in women's tennis coaching Pam Shriver, put the matter in a broader context by comparing it to his days on the men's circuit. ''There's no doubt about it,'' Candy said, ''there were gay guys who I mingled with and traveled with and played against, and there were no problems in the locker room. It's the same with the women. They stay with their own kind.''

Still, there existed a group, many of them retired players, who felt that lesbians had had a powerful, positive influence on the tour. They compared this influence to that of homosexuals in fashion, the theater, and other arts. Something of the same sensibility, they said, had shaped women's tennis, and the sad thing was that this created a lot of fear, snickering, and denial, instead of pride.

For all his talk about difficulties brought on by lesbians, Van der Meer admitted that heterosexuals caused problems, too. "Most coaches and their players, I think you'll see the relationships are sexual." He decried cases where much older men were sleeping with adolescent girls or where an ambitious hitting partner used sex to insinuate himself between a girl and her father, or between a girl and her coach. "They travel together more than forty weeks a year. A lot of the low-ranked ones stay in the same room with a coach to save money. At the start maybe they have separate beds. But then after a bad loss he moves over to comfort her." Dennis made a hugging motion. " 'This is nice,' " she says, and there you are."

He compared a coach sleeping with a player to a psychiatrist who had sex with a patient and rationalized it as part of therapy. "You can't be objective with someone you sleep with. They have a bad time in bed, and the coach says, 'That's why your backhand is bad.' It confuses the personal and the professional. It's a conflict of interest. How can the girl change coaches without losing her lover? What if she wants to keep him as a coach and stop being a lover?"

Later I asked if he thought the WTA was aware of these problems and was taking steps to deal with them. Van der Meer didn't answer directly. Instead he described a WTA meeting he had attended. The topic of the day was a new multimillion-dollar sponsorship deal. While it was being discussed, Dennis glanced around the room at "teenage girls chewing bubble gum, cracking jokes, laughing. The scene was ludicrous—big business based on a kiddie corps."

○ ○ ○

Each morning I bought *L'Equipe,* the *Herald Tribune,* the *London Times,* and *La Repubblica,* and settled into a café on Place de la Contrescarpe to read what my colleagues had written. Then after a croissant and a couple of *cafés crèmes,* I strolled down to Rue Cardinal Lemoine and caught the Métro.

On those warm mornings, Roland Garros had a freshly laundered look. The red-clay courts were ironed smooth and the lines had been bleached white as a shirt collar. *Smashez la vie,* the Perrier signs exhorted spectators, and most of us did as instructed. We had a smashing time watching tennis, working on our tans, talking with friends, trying not to overdo it with the midday bottles of Beaujolais. But for some players, Paris was a less than gleeful occasion.

In the second round, American Kathy Rinaldi was ahead 4–2 in the first set when she seemed to become the personification of a passage in the Koran that poses the question "Does there not pass over every man a space of time when his life is blank?" Rinaldi's blank space lasted ten games and cost her the match, 6–4, 6–0.

When no one called Kathy for a press conference, I requested a one-on-one interview.

According to the vast compendium of computerized statistics at Roland Garros, this was Rinaldi's tenth French Open. Although not the oldest player—she was twenty-four—she had played here more often than any other woman. Once touted as potentially "the best woman player of all time," Kathy had skipped her eighth-grade graduation and knocked off two seeded players to reach the quarterfinals of the 1981 French Open. A couple of weeks later, at the age of fourteen, she became the youngest player to win a match at Wimbledon. That same summer, a profile in *Sports Illustrated* struck all the familiar notes in the dreamy song about the latest teenage sensation, the successor to Evert, Austin, and Jaeger.

At the age of four, she had learned the game from her mother and father, and was eventually placed into the hands of Frank Froehling, an ex–U.S. Davis Cup ace. By the age of twelve, she had put away childish things, giving up her other interests—Girl Scouts, cheerleading, and the piano—to concentrate on tennis. When she was thirteen, her father, a dentist, took over as her coach without informing Froehling. Predictably, there had been hard feelings. Predictably, Mr. Rinaldi had no real background in tennis. And, almost as predictably, Kathy's career never came close to fulfilling people's extravagant expectations.

She had gotten to the 1985 semifinals at Wimbledon and had again reached the French Open quarterfinals in 1986, but by the time she was twenty, she had won only three minor tournaments. Then she fell on a staircase in Monte Carlo, fractured her right thumb, and couldn't play for a year. Now ranked eighty-two, Rinaldi seemed to provide yet another example of the way the women's tour was reputed to chew up, break down, and burn out talented young players.

Fine-boned and pretty enough to have been a model, Kathy had wide blue eyes and the slightly glazed expression of a doe that had been frozen in the headlights of a truck. Yet despite her tender, vulnerable appearance, her hand when I shook it was dry and rough. This was the identity badge of a tennis pro—a palm with a thick crust of calluses acquired from years of holding a racquet.

When I reminded her that she was the grande dame of the French Open, Rinaldi smiled and said she was just happy to have kept going and had a career. "When I was fourteen, I heard so much about burnout, burnout. It was something I didn't want to happen to me. I tried to find a happy medium between tennis and a quote normal life unquote. Maybe if I had concentrated solely on tennis, I would have burnt out. When I turned nineteen, I remember Bud Collins said, 'Congratulations. You've survived burnout.' "

But had she? Given what had been expected of her, was she satisfied?

Sliding off the question, Kathy talked in general terms about people's expectations. Once they had centered on her; now they fell on Capriati. "They expect her to be number one. That's only normal. I was compared to Chris and Tracy. But in the end you've gotta go out and play and please yourself. I'm enjoying myself. I don't have any time limit on my career. Since my injury in 'eighty-seven, I feel I'm still coming back. I'll keep playing as long as I enjoy it."

What about the girls today? Did she identify with them and what they were up against?

Rinaldi said she wasn't like so many young players whose entire lives revolved around tennis. Again she insisted she had had a normal life—"quote and unquote." "I went to football games, I hung out with friends, I went to movies. And I've been able to keep on in tennis because of my outside interests. Some people do better when they're totally focused. Not me. I finished school." She meant high school.

Were American girls at a disadvantage when they competed against

Europeans and South Americans who dropped out of junior high to hone their games?

"I wouldn't want to give up my education. I couldn't imagine that," Kathy exclaimed. But she hastened to add that she didn't want to criticize girls who left school. "The tour is an education in itself—the travel, the people you meet. I think you grow up quickly because you're around older people. You're dealing with the press. You're dealing with pressures. You're putting yourself on the line week after week. You're learning to handle the ups and downs."

Although she didn't travel with a coach, she said, "The game's getting so competitive, it's a help to have someone with you, someone to support you." It was tough being away from family and friends, and although she called the players "a great bunch of girls," she admitted, "It's hard to get close with them because the next day you may have to compete against them." It would be nice, she said, to have someone behind you a hundred percent.

Was there anybody in her life who filled that bill?

Rinaldi said she had dated the same boy since high school. "He's pretty good at understanding my life. He's in business. It's refreshing to me that he has nothing to do with tennis. He doesn't care whether I win or lose."

But Kathy made it clear that she did care. "I like to win for my family, who love me a lot."

Despite today's disappointing loss, she was a positive and upbeat person who claimed she liked everything about her life. "I like running, biking, jumping rope, running sprints, doing the Stairmaster. But it's difficult on the road. You get out of your normal habits."

Lest this suggest that she didn't like being on the road, she assured me, "I like the travel. During the off-season, I'm itching to get on the go again. When I stop having that itch, then I'll know it's time to quit."

Much as one couldn't help admiring her spunkiness, it seemed that her tendency to punctuate each sentence with a happy face prevented her from casting a cool eye of appraisal at her game. Today she had lost 6–4, 6–0, not to Seles or Sabatini, but to Tami Whitlinger, a girl who wore a leg brace and was ranked even lower than Rinaldi. She hadn't gotten beyond the second round of a Grand Slam event in four years. Yet rather than turn introspective, rather than express regrets, Kathy just kept on plugging along.

○ ○ ○

Unlike Rinaldi, Andrea Temesvari had her regrets and it wasn't in her nature to deny them. Tall—she was nearly six feet—blond, and stunning, Temesvari, a Hungarian, was a year older than Kathy Rinaldi and she, too, had burst onto the scene as a teenager. The summer she was seventeen, she won the U.S. Clay Courts Championship, crushing Zina Garrison 6–2, 6–2. Earlier that spring, she had taken the Italian Open, blitzing her semifinal and final opponents 6–0, 6–0 and 6–1, 6–0. *Sports Illustrated* proclaimed her ''the best natural athlete to emerge in women's tennis since Navratilova,'' and Ted Tinling bestowed his blessing: ''Andrea sustains my faith in grace and beauty in the future of tennis.''

Daughter of a fashion model and an ex-Olympic athlete, she had grown up in Algeria, where her father, Otto, coached the national basketball team. Once Andrea blossomed as a tennis player, Otto quit his job to travel with her. He financed her first year on the tour, but she was soon in a position to pay him back with her prize money and endorsement contracts.

As *Sports Illustrated* described them, ''The Temesvaris are the toughest father-daughter act to hit the pro tennis circuit since Roland and another Andrea, Jaeger. Roland, a former boxer, is the prototypical tennis father pounding the game into his daughter, but he says, 'Otto is worse than I am.' ''

All during his daughter's matches, Otto ranted and screamed at her. Some who spoke Hungarian said he called her foul names. Others claimed he was shouting instructions, but in a voice everybody agreed was far too strident. Soon Andrea started suffering inexplicable losses.

Players and reporters gossiped that boys, not Otto, were the reason for her fall. Andrea liked to party, they said. She liked attention and she liked to tweak Otto's nose by staying out late. She was more worried about her makeup, the catty rumors ran, than about keeping in shape. She just wanted to get on court and show off her legs.

But there were more plausible explanations for her decline. During her glory years, she played a lot, and had a taxing baseline style that depended on topspin shots hit at terrific velocity. In March 1987, she dropped off the tour for twenty months. Although this too caused scurrilous rumors, the truth was she had two ankle operations and arthroscopic surgery on her right shoulder. Except for brief flashes of brilliance, she had never been the same player since.

Now ranked 104, she faced a second-round encounter with Jennifer Capriati, whom some believed was destined to inherit Chris Evert's crown and others feared might follow in the footsteps of Rinaldi and Temesvari. In the warm-up, Andrea looked great. Still a striking figure, her golden hair held back by a headband, her eyes highlighted by mascara, she wore several layers of socks that sagged around her ankles like a ballerina's leg warmers. Her power was as impressive as her appearance. She thumped her ground strokes and threw her buxom body into each serve.

But then the match started. Capriati was more mobile and could hit with as much power and far more accuracy than Temesvari. In a mere fifty-three minutes, Jennifer won 6–2, 6–1.

Capriati came to her interview in a pair of cutoff Levi's and a peach-colored shirt. With much giggling she recounted how she and her father had gone jogging in a park the day before and a thief had stolen their bags. They had lost their passports, some money, and a computer gadget she couldn't quite describe.

A reporter, perhaps planted by Walt Disney Inc., asked if next year she'd like to visit the new EuroDisney outside of Paris.

"Sure," she said, "if it's not too far." Between questions she bobbed her head as if plugged into a Walkman, listening to music and keeping the beat.

I mentioned that Andrea Temesvari, at the age of eighteen, had been ranked seventh in the world. Today Jennifer had beaten her two and one. "Did that give you any pause for reflection, the fact that a few years ago she was in your position?"

Capriati murmured that she'd heard Temesvari used to be good. "Maybe she got injured or something. I don't know. I've never thought about it."

As the room cleared, John Feinstein said, "You can come back in

seven years and Capriati still won't have thought about it." He attended
Jennifer's press conferences just to count the "you knows" and "I
means." "Last year her act was fresh," he said, "but it hasn't changed
and probably it never will. Most kids develop. They read books, they
meet new people, they have new experiences. But kids in tennis keep
doing the same things. Nothing new happens to them, so they have
nothing to say."

He compared Capriati to Sabatini. Feinstein had interviewed Gaby
at the age of fifteen and found her no more interesting now than he had
then. He said he had talked to other Argentinean players and they told
him Gaby was just as boring in Spanish as she was in English.

Mary Carillo, a commentator for ESPN, was strolling past and heard
Feinstein mention Sabatini. She burst into laughter. "I watched people
coming out of Sabatini's press conference today. The first couple of
them were yawning. It was so funny."

○ ○ ○

After she lost, Temesvari didn't linger at the courts. For the past three
years she had been married to Andras Trunkos, a Hungarian rock singer
with hair to his shoulders. When I arrived at their hotel to interview
Andrea, Andras was there waiting to be introduced. Impeccably correct
in an old-world manner incongruous with his appearance, he shook my
hand, then left us alone.

Andrea wore tight jeans, a black T-shirt, and a black leather jacket.
Pale and smooth with makeup, her face had a mole on the left cheek,
like a blemish a Renaissance artist had applied to a portrait to prove
that no earthly creature was perfect. Her bangs hung down over her
eyes and from time to time she blew them back. In each ear she had
three tiny earrings.

"My mother started modeling very early," Andrea said, "and she
always liked beautiful clothes. She's maybe a little too perfect, too neat.
She even ironed my headbands. She encouraged me to be the same—
to be neat, to shower fifteen times a day. When I went on the circuit,
I cleaned my own clothes and my father's.

"Many of the other girls didn't try to look normal, much less good.
You don't have to wear fancy clothes to look good. Just ironing your

clothes before a match isn't a big deal. When people said I cared more how I looked, it bothered me. I worked very hard. I practiced all the time. I don't think it's a crime to be a woman and to look like one on the court. Still, the older women made fun of me, and it hurt.''

Temesvari noted that the press chided her for worrying about her appearance, then turned around and wrote cruel articles about girls for not caring how they looked. "It's unfair," she said. "You see these women waiting in the lounge for the men players. Everybody thinks they're beautiful. But they had all day to get ready, to make themselves up. They don't have to train or practice. They have no pressure in their lives. I'd like to see them wake up one morning and realize they have to play the first match. You know, it can even change how you look, the pressure. Put women players in the right clothes, and they'd look just as good as those people the men think are so beautiful. Don't call a player to a press conference without letting her change clothes and put on makeup, don't show her sweating on TV or print a photograph of her face all twisted when she's hitting a shot, then say, 'Where's the beauty in women's tennis?'

"The top-ten women have the time and money to worry about their looks. Sabatini cares, Steffi cares, Seles cares, Martina cares—there are different kinds of beauty. Many other girls care, but . . . well, it's like Agassi. If he was ranked two hundred and fifty and he dressed like that, people would make fun of him.''

Andrea's reputation as a boy-crazy party girl infuriated her far more than catty comments about her looks. ''A man can go out and get girls and if he sleeps with a lot of them, that's macho. But if a girl sleeps with two men''—she jabbed two fingers in the air—''she's a bitch. A man who makes money in tennis can pay to bring a girl with him on the tour. But it's hard for a girl to invite a boyfriend to travel with her. What guy wants to do that? The ego is very important, and men don't like to think a woman is paying all the bills.''

Still, she said, ''There are a lot of weird relationships on the tour. A girl gets lonely or in a mood, and she meets a man and goes with him. But she can't be sure it's love. It may be the situation, the isolation of the circuit.''

A waitress brought us coffee and dishes of potato chips, peanuts, and olives stuffed with pimentos. After drinking down her coffee in one gulp, Andrea nibbled nervously as the talk turned to parents.

"Many, many younger kids are playing," she said, "and their parents push them to go into tennis as a business. Parents take advantage, I think. It's always the ones that never had money or success that want success through their children.

"It's good at the beginning to have your parents behind you. But at a certain point they have to look into the mirror and be honest and say, 'I've done all I can. I'm going to get a coach who's better for her.' Instead, parents start to get too strict. They make rules. They demand the kids to concentrate. But if the parents are too strict, it kills a relationship. If they can't stop hurting each other . . . Well, they have to realize, 'I can't treat her like a baby.' "

Temesvari had finished the chips and the peanuts, and was pressing the pimentos out of the olives and eating them one by one.

"If I have children," she said, "I don't want to live through them. I want to help them, not force them to do what I like. These parents in tennis, they're wearing Guccis and carrying Vuitton bags. Then they won't let their daughter buy anything. You see it all the time on the tour."

When I asked about Otto, Andrea stared at her fingers and squeezed out another pimento. "We don't have a relationship anymore. He feels he lost me. He feels he lost his golden girl, and I betrayed him and didn't become the person, the player, he wanted. When I telephone him, we can't talk without him bringing up tennis or something I'm doing wrong with my game, and that sets my hair on end, so I'm right away looking like a punk. I don't think he'll ever see me, I mean see what and who I am, because I'm not what he wanted—what he thought he had made me. It's sad, but you have to talk about it because it happens to a lot of girls on the tour. You just can't have parents there all the time telling you, 'Don't do this,' 'You can't do that,' and worrying that their daughter will go off with boys at twelve or will lose her virginity or whatever you call it, the way Mr. Seles worries about Monica."

Seeing her husband coming back to join us, Andrea said, "Being married makes life easier on the tour. It's ninety-nine percent positive.

The one percent that isn't positive is when he gets bored or when he's rooting for me and I lose. He feels sorry for me sometimes. Because, yes, I do a lot of crying. You know, he's never seen me at my best, winning matches and tournaments.''

○ ○ ○

By the end of the first week, the weather remained clear, but a few clouds had intruded on the women's tournament. Coverage of their matches had dwindled to a fourth of a page in *L'Equipe*. The *Herald Tribune* devoted a single sentence to the women, buried deep in a long piece about the men.

Then Steffi Graf broke ranks and rejected the official WTA line that demanded equal prize money. Having won two matches by identical scores of 6–0, 6–1, she said she thought the women got enough for what they did. After Graf's next match, a 6–2, 6–3 romp over Sabine Appelmans of Belgium, a journalist asked, "Has the women's competition begun yet?"

"I think it wasn't that tough today. It will begin next week."

"Is it difficult to keep concentrated when you are so far ahead?"

"I wasn't one hundred percent in it, especially when I was up five–one. It was too easy." So easy, Steffi admitted, her mind had wandered.

"Do you feel pity for opponents who are so much lower than you?"

"No. I know quite a few players who have the ability to do more. I have worked hard to be where I am. They need to work harder. I cannot be sorry for them—although maybe sometimes I am."

"About equal prize money, you said women made enough. Did you get a reaction to that?"

"Yes, some people were upset. They weren't happy with my answers. As I say, women's tennis has risen so fast recently and the prize money has gone up, I don't think we should force things too quickly. I am sure it will eventually equalize. Why is this question so interesting? There are more important things to talk about."

○ ○ ○

Petra Thoren of Finland had come through the qualies and reached the third round of the main draw, where she shocked Mary Joe Fernandez with an inside-out forehand that she swung like the hammer of Thor. After four straight service breaks, both players settled in for a slug fest.

With the score tied at four games apiece, Conchita Martinez, a Spanish player seeded number seven, entered the area reserved for the press and players' guests. She was with two girls. She sat behind the younger one and massaged her shoulders and neck, watching Fernandez break to 5–4, then hold serve to take the first set.

In the second, the battle continued—and so did the massage. Martinez and the girl had reversed positions, with Conchita sitting in front enjoying a rubdown.

Journalists looked on askance, grumbling among themselves that it was her own business what Conchita or any girl cared to do in private. But it struck them as stupid to do this in public and not expect people to gossip.

Barely nineteen, her teeth still fitted with braces, Martinez had had a career plagued by rumors of lesbianism. Her own coach had accused her of leaving him to go off with a gay girl. This had prompted splashy headlines and a lurid story in *Interviu,* a Spanish magazine.

The massage was down to fine strokes. Conchita let her head droop on the supple stem of her neck as the other girl kneaded her scalp and the base of her skull. Then she leaned back between her friend's spread legs.

Martinez hailed from a small town and a poor family, a Spanish reporter told me, and she was much less popular than Arantxa Sanchez Vicario, who was a city girl from Barcelona. ''Conchita left home very young,'' the journalist said, ''and I think on the tour it's always lonely and she looks for a friend.''

She seemed to have found one. For many fans the match—Mary Joe had just executed an audacious drop shot to break Petra Thoren— was now of secondary importance. Martinez had stretched out full length on her back. Her friend leaned forward, letting her long hair brush Conchita's face. She swayed back and forth tickling Martinez until she giggled and sat up in time to see Fernandez close out the second set.

As Dennis Van der Meer remarked, a man commenting on these matters had to exercise sensitivity. The incident wouldn't have merited a mention if it hadn't occurred in front of thousands of spectators and if it hadn't provided insight into a nettlesome problem that confronted the press. Whereas on the men's circuit a reporter had to decide how much he wished to divulge of the financial skulduggery that frequently determined when, where, and how well players performed, in women's tennis he had to determine how much to write about the personal matters that affected a girl's game, image, and marketability.

○ ○ ○

Gerry Smith, the WTA's executive director and CEO, was a newcomer to women's tennis. A pleasant-faced fellow in his late forties, with a thatch of gray-flecked hair, Smith had previously been publisher of *Newsweek* and, before that, a senior vice president and marketing director at Ogilvy and Mather. But he had always been interested in sports. At Belmont Abbey College in North Carolina, he had been on the basketball team—a bench warmer, he admitted, but an eager player nonetheless. While at *Newsweek* he had committed the magazine to a $1 million sponsorship deal with a men's tennis tournament in Indian Wells, California, and he leased a $250,000 tent at Wimbledon. Then he became a director of the International Tennis Hall of Fame in Newport, Rhode Island. After Smith was let go by *Newsweek*, the job at the WTA opened at the end of 1989, and he was an applicant.

"I was looking for a breath of fresh air," Smith said as we sat on the terrace of the press restaurant at a table strewn with bread crumbs and stained with red wine. Behind us, the crowd on Court Central cheered for the Jimmy Connors–Michael Chang match. Toying with an empty Evian bottle, Smith told me, "The time couldn't be better to get into women's tennis. The sport has gotten so strong in such a short time. I really looked at what the product was. What's the share of market? Could it improve? Could I contribute? That's how I looked at it.

"I preach that we're totally in a service business. We're serving players, agents, coaches, and staff. A group of very dedicated individuals got together and made it work. That tradition has carried us till today."

When I summarized what I had seen in the past few days—poor attendance at women's matches, sporadic press coverage, disagreement among players about the prize money debate—he maintained that this was a matter of perception. Resistance to women's tennis, particularly in Europe, was "cultural more than anything else. The disparity between the men and women is overstated. It's more a feeling. People see Graf win one and one, but they forget Patrick McEnroe losing to Agassi today two, two, and zero. In the last three years at Wimbledon and the French Open, over thirty percent of the women's matches have gone the full three sets. But only twenty percent of the men's matches have gone the full five sets. Would you rather see a boring two out of three match or a boring three out of five?"

I told him I'd prefer not to see any boring matches.

He said he couldn't have agreed with me more. "Tennis is the entertainment business and the women's game has more marquee value. There's more identification and familiarity with women players. The press refers to them on a first-name basis. It's Chrissie, Martina, Steffi, Monica—not Lendl, McEnroe, and Becker. People claim there are more upsets among the men, but if I'm a promoter, I want the top-rated players to make it to the weekend when matches are on television."

Since men received legal guarantees at certain tournaments, did he think women should demand them just as they were demanding equal prize money?

"Guarantees mislead the public," Smith insisted. "They result in a lot of questionable matches among the men. I'm not saying men are tanking. But sometimes the effort isn't there. So we're just not going to accept guarantees."

On the other hand, he didn't want to appear naive. He granted that guarantees were hard to police because they were often paid in the guise of promotional contracts. "We all know the Pan Pacific Open in Tokyo gets the best women's field every year. The players all have endorsement contracts that require them to play there."

Another thing that made it difficult to police guarantees, Smith said, "was players from poor and disadvantaged backgrounds. They want to maximize their earnings in a short time. As in any sport that relies on young athletes, there are parents and coaches out to maximize their earnings. But eventually they get more secure and think long term."

Were there other problems with young athletes? I asked. Didn't their immaturity make them a tough sell?

Not at all. Smith maintained that they attracted adolescent fans around the world. "The buying potential of teenagers is flabbergasting. That's why Capriati signed such incredible contracts—because of her appeal to young people. Jennifer is one of their peers. They identify with her."

"But what about their lack of education? The fact that so many of them drop out of high school and junior high must trouble you."

"Personally I'm a firm believer in education," Smith said. "I would hope that the parents of these kids are cognizant of the value of education. But they're getting a different kind of education." He gave me, virtually verbatim, the line I had heard from Kathy Rinaldi. "There's the exposure to the world, exposure to the media, the interaction on the tour. It doesn't take the place of a formal education, but it does some good."

Since Smith had played college basketball, I asked whether he would buy that line of reasoning from an apologist for American intercollegiate athletics. Many people believed it was unethical for universities to recruit eighteen-year-old boys, keep them on campus for a few years, then cut them adrift without a degree. While no one denied that these fellows got to see a bit of the world and learned to deal with game pressures and journalists, the fact was that when their careers ended, they had no job skills and little ability to cope anywhere except on a playing field or a court. Didn't Smith feel that tennis could be accused of the same exploitative behavior? And wasn't the women's tour worse since so many of the girls were barely in their teens when they quit school?

Smith replied that much as he might personally regret the situation, we shouldn't impose our values or an American point of view on people. "A lot of players come from different cultures, different socioeconomic backgrounds. There's a broad mixture out there. That's not to say I don't believe in education. Maybe there's a way—a player suggested this—maybe we could have players teach languages to one another." He smiled. "Maybe we could do a deal with Berlitz. Get them involved in a contract."

Among the many changes in women's tennis, one that was as striking as the youth of the players was the growth of entourages. Even low-ranked girls now traveled with coaches, and at some tournaments the players were outnumbered by trainers, hitting partners, and assorted hangers-on. Had this forced the WTA into any adjustments or rule changes?

"Coaches are very beneficial," Smith said. "We're trying to provide them with more amenities, make sure that they have a locker room and have access to the players' lounge, see that they'll be available to the press."

"That wasn't what I meant. My question was whether the WTA had a code of conduct for coaches?"

Smith said he didn't believe the WTA had any right, or any reason, to impose rules on anybody except players. Coaches and entourages weren't really part of the tour.

"Then why provide them with amenities?" It seemed the WTA was trying to have it both ways—establishing a relationship with entourages, but refusing to accept responsibility for any problems they caused.

Smith smiled and shook his head. He didn't see how coaches could cause problems.

There were any number of hypothetical scenarios I might have described, but I stuck to historical fact. In 1983, Ion Tiriac was Guillermo Vilas's coach and business manager. When the ABN Bank Tournament in Rotterdam suffered the last-minute withdrawal of a top-ranked player, it asked Vilas to fill in. Tiriac demanded a sixty-thousand-dollar guarantee, to be delivered to his hotel room in hundred-dollar bills. Tournament officials withdrew sixty thousand from ABN Bank, signed a receipt for it with a forged signature, and brought it to Tiriac. A Dutch journalist stumbled onto the story and reported it to authorities in men's tennis. Although Vilas denied he knew anything about any deal his coach might have made, he was found guilty of accepting a guarantee, fined twenty thousand dollars, and suspended from competition for a year.

In the course of Vilas's appeal, Tiriac kept in touch with the tournament director in Rotterdam. They talked on the telephone, and Tiriac recorded some of their conversations. Depending on whom you believed and how you interpreted the tapes, Tiriac was offering the fellow a

$300,000 bribe to confess he had never delivered the guarantee. Or else the tournament director was trying to extort $300,000 from Tiriac.

Forgery, embezzlement, bribery, extortion—all these accusations became part of the testimony in the case, bringing a batch of unprecedented bad publicity to tennis. It ruined Vilas's career and cast the sport into ill repute. Now Ion Tiriac was contractually linked to Mary Joe Fernandez. With no rules or controls on entourages, how could women's tennis prevent history from repeating itself?

Once again Gerry Smith smiled and shook his head. "That's one advantage of being new to the game. I don't have to be burdened by— I don't even know about—what you're describing. My premise is you don't need to control coaches."

o o o

In celebration of Monica Seles's rise to number one, Perrier was throwing a party, and the press was invited. To put it more accurately, Perrier was throwing Monica a party *so* the press could be invited. Our role was to record the event for posterity and snap pictures of Seles receiving what was described in the English-language publicity release as "a special rock crystal golden necklace . . . truly fascinating, pure magic, astonishing splendour with mysterious uniqueness."

Always suckers for "astonishing splendour with mysterious uniqueness," not to mention free booze and food, we assembled in the Perrier tent and waited. It was a dry hot day, and we were thirsty. Clustered around TV monitors, we watched the Connors–Chang match and marked time, murmuring that this was a bloody bore.

An IMG agent arrived with Goran Ivanisevic, who, like Monica, hailed from Yugoslavia and wore a Perrier patch on his sleeve.

"Five minutes," Goran growled as he was led to the far end of the tent. "Five minutes, that's all I do."

A grinning MC greeted Ivanisevic as if neither he nor the rest of us had heard Goran hollering. Photographers flooded forward.

"Please, please, not beyond the line," the MC warned them. Then as a few frantic ushers set up a barrier of chairs, he barked, "Not beyond the chairs." But Seles had slipped in through a back flap of the tent and the paparazzi crashed forward.

"Here she is," the MC announced, "our ambassador all around
the world—drinking Perrier and wearing our patch. Diamonds stand for
innocence. Gold stands for purity and success. Congratulations, Monica,
and have much happiness on your Saturday-night fevers."

As the man handed her the necklace, photographers pushed and
shoved, and chairs clattered to the floor. Seles smiled, waved to the
cameras, and backed out of the tent without a word.

"This is really stupid," said Goran Ivanisevic, the voice of wisdom,
as the IMG agent led him away.

O O O

In response to every inquiry about drugs on the tour, the official position
was that tennis players didn't do them. Period. End of discussion.

Much as it defied reason to think that hundreds of young people
with millions of dollars of disposable income wouldn't dabble with dope,
pro tennis officials insisted that theirs was the one sport that remained
immaculate. Basketball, baseball, football, soccer, cycling, track, and
even cricket have acknowledged that numbers of their most famous
athletes have tested positive for drug use. Yet although some tennis
players have openly admitted smoking marijuana—Chris Evert was the
latest on the list—and some tournament directors, Gene Scott prominent
among them, have discussed cocaine and amphetamine use on the circuit, tennis authorities refused to give an inch of ground on this subject.

Perhaps they were right. Perhaps all the rumors, rational guesses,
and anecdotal evidence to the contrary notwithstanding, tennis enjoyed
the great good luck of being the world's unique drug-free game. Still,
since it was now an Olympic sport, it had had to institute a drug-testing
program, and the Kraft General Foods World Tour book of Rules and
Regulations contained more than four pages of information about prohibited substances, testing procedures, and penalties.

According to the handbook, "The prohibited substances subject to
the provisions of this Program are Narcotic Analgesics (e.g. heroin,
morphine and codeine), Stimulants (e.g. cocaine, amphetamine-like
compounds), Anabolic Steroids, Masking Agents and Diuretics." There
followed a list of eighteen substances banned as steroids, and more than
fifty substances categorized as masking agents.

The WTA's drug testing, by means of "random, unannounced and observed urinalysis," took place at least once a year. Violation of the ban on steroids and masking agents carried a nine-month suspension from tournament play. Reinstatement depended on compliance with "a supervised outpatient program." A second offense brought permanent disqualification.

To compare the WTA's drug program with the one governing international track and field, when sprinter Ben Johnson was first found using steroids at the 1988 Olympics, he was stripped of his gold medal and his world records, and banned for life—a penalty later reduced to a two-year suspension when Johnson submitted himself to treatment and stayed dope-free. A violation of the ban on stimulants would have carried similar penalties—i.e., loss of medals and records, followed by a lifetime ban.

The biggest difference between the WTA's drug program and those in other sports was the absolute confidentiality that tennis imposed on the entire procedure. The rules forbade any revelation of test results, positive or negative, or of the identities of players tested or of those penalized for violations. In short, a woman could drop off the tour and enter a rehabilitation center, or could be suspended or disqualified for life, and the public would never know. Although this might be humane and commendable in some cases, it was hardly a deterrent or an adequate punishment for a player who used performanceenhancing drugs. What's more, it risked spawning rumors that might stigmatize players who took a break from the game or retired without explanation.

When it became clear that players were being tested at Roland Garros, *L'Equipe* demanded, "Who controls the anti-doping controls?" It was foolish to pretend that such tests, conducted in secret with results that were never revealed, could "assure public confidence in the integrity of this sport." Without any proof to the contrary, it was possible, *L'Equipe* pointed out, that no tests were actually being conducted. The only satisfactory solution was for an independent organization to handle this matter and make its findings public.

○ ○ ○

Despite her disappointing play in Rome, Jennifer Capriati remained popular at Roland Garros, where she had reached the semifinals last year in her first French Open. So it surprised fans, and distressed the Capriati clan, when she and Conchita Martinez were relegated to Court Eleven. Because seating capacity was limited, spectators had to scramble for places, and because the backcourt was shorter than on Court Central or Court One, Jennifer had less room to maneuver.

It didn't console the Capriatis that Nathalie Tauziat, the last French-woman in contention, was scheduled on Court Central. Nor did they care that her opponent, Naoko Sawamatsu, gave Japanese television an opportunity to broadcast a match that would appeal to fans in Tokyo. They felt Jenny had been slighted and, worse, that she was vulnerable.

The section reserved for the press and players' guests was packed. I stood wedged next to Stefano Capriati and USTA coach José Higueras. Nearby sat IMG agents John Evert and Cino Marchese, and USTA coaches Stan Smith and Tom Gullikson, who had helped train Jenny. None of them looked happy when Martinez broke in the first game, then held serve at love for a 2–0 lead.

Decked out in a lime green outfit by Diadora, his daughter's primary sponsor, Stefano Capriati was fizzing with tension and firing bursts of Spanish, English, and Italian. "Brava!" he hollered as Jenny broke to even the score 2–2. But almost immediately she was in trouble on her serve. She hated heavily topped balls to her backhand and had a bad habit of retreating and playing them defensively. Half the time her shoulders were pressed to the fence.

"No, no!" her father shouted. "Come in, come in. Take the ball early."

But she either didn't hear him or couldn't heed him. Galloping after Martinez's clever placements, she dropped serve again.

"When she plays off her back foot, she goes wrong," Stefano complained.

"It's a question of experience," Higueras assured him.

"Up, up, up!" Stefano yelled at Jenny, who drifted back, back, back until she bumped into the windscreen. On one point, Martinez's shot nicked the baseline, spun into the air, and sailed in a smooth parabola over the fence.

Papa Capriati clapped his meaty palms, clenched them into fists, and signaled for her to move forward. "Come on, Jenny, she's tired."

Jennifer got to double break point. Another winner and she'd level the score at four games apiece. Cino Marchese slapped John Evert on the shoulders, relishing his client's comeback. "Yeah, she's tiring," Tom Gullikson said of Martinez. "We can sit down now," Stefano said.

But he stayed on his feet, and as Martinez resumed smacking topspin backhands, he cursed in Italian, "Oh, fuck this." Conchita clawed her way to deuce, and Stefano fumed, "Come on, Jenny, she's taking her time." But on the next shot, Conchita didn't take any time at all. She cracked a clean forehand winner, and Papa Capriati conceded, "They're playing good," even as his daughter lost the first set 6–3.

At the start of the second, Mrs. Capriati slipped through the crowd with her ten-year-old son, Steven, and stood beside her husband. Dressed in white shorts and a white blouse, her eyes shielded by sunglasses as if to guard against the glare of her gold bracelet and gold Rolex, Denise Capriati carried a bottle of Volvic mineral water from which she took jittery little sips.

"Hey, guess what," Steven said. "Jennifer should have been on Center Court. I just heard the truth. The Japanese paid to get their girl on Center Court."

"Shhh!" said Denise. "People here speak English."

"Is it Jenny's ad?" the little boy asked.

"Are we watching the same match?" Stefano growled at him.

Capriati wasted two break points, then dropped four games in succession. Conchita was chasing her from side to side, and Jenny looked exhausted. But as Martinez served for the match at 5–1, she tried to finish it off too quickly. Tossing up a lob, Jennifer broke to 2–5, restoring her father's hope. "Come on, Jenny, one point at a time."

In the next game, Capriati slowed the rhythm; she wasn't going to give away any more cheap points. Martinez would have to earn them. So the Spanish girl returned to what had worked best. She whacked slow rolling backhands. When Conchita held for game, set, and match, Stefano predicted to everyone within earshot, "Martinez will play like a dog tomorrow. She played well today, but Seles will kill her."

O O O

On Court Central Tauziat and Sawamatsu were in the third set and the
crowd was whistling and clapping. It wasn't applause. Spectators were
impatient for the girls to clear off so that Boris Becker could come on.

As Gerry Smith said, it was a matter of perception. Becker would
batter his Spanish opponent into oblivion in three boring sets while
Tauziat and Sawamatsu played a match as quirky as it was exciting. At
5–3 in the third set, the Frenchwoman had two match balls, but the
eighteen-year-old Japanese girl was like one of those Oriental martial
arts masters who wave their hands as if flicking away flies and wind up
breaking down brick walls. She appeared to have no power at all, yet
every time Tauziat rushed the net, Sawamatsu smacked a winning shot.
From the same position and same preparation, she could hit a passing
shot, a drop shot, or a lob.

The Japanese girl's racquet was strung at twenty-eight pounds, by
far the lowest tension in the tournament. As the ball snuggled into the
loose strings, it lost its zip and came wobbling back like a wounded
canary. Sawamatsu broke, then held to five games all, and the two of
them dug in for a duel of nerves. Because the French Open didn't allow
tie-breaks in the final set, it took Tauziat three hours and five minutes
to close out the match 12–10.

That put her into the quarterfinals against Steffi Graf, who had
whipped her twelve times straight. Unhappily for Tauziat, Graf continued her jinx, prompting a French journalist to ask why Nathalie didn't
forfeit the next time she played Steffi. True to Stefano Capriati's pre-
diction, Seles had an easy time with Martinez. And once again, Mary
Joe Fernandez fell short. That she lost to Arantxa Sanchez Vicario, a
former French Open champion, wasn't especially surprising. That she
did so 6–3, 6–0, was a shock.

O O O

Ernesto Ruiz Bry, Mary Joe's coach, loitered in the players' lounge,
which, this late in the tournament, had no players in it. A tan, handsome
Chilean with a shock of black hair and high cheekbones, Ernesto had
played briefly on the men's tour before he started coaching. Guillermo

Vilas had been his most famous pupil. More recently he had worked with Ronald Agenor, a Haitian who had spent much of his life in France and had reached the quarterfinals of the 1989 French Open. In early April 1991, Ion Tiriac asked Ernesto to train Mary Joe.

After two months on the job, Ernesto felt they were making progress. While Fernandez hadn't won a title, she hadn't lost any ground either. Her defeats here and in Rome had been to talented girls—Seles and Sanchez Vicario—and it took time to change a player's mentality so that she could then change her game. Against top competition, she had to realize she couldn't wait for her opponents to make mistakes. She had to beat them. There was, Ernesto emphasized, a big difference.

There was, also, a difference between coaching men and women. "With a woman," he said, "you have much more work to do on the technical side. Normally a top-thirty player on the men's tour is technically complete. Not the women. I can have more satisfaction working with a woman because I can teach her more both technically and in terms of strategy."

But what they lacked in technique, the women compensated for with superior concentration. "Mary Joe listens," Ernesto said. "She learns very fast. She's on time and she's disciplined. They are more into tennis, the girls. The men have other interests. I used to have to drag Vilas away from his music to get him to practice. Agenor, too, is a singer and has made an album. And, of course, the boys are thinking about going out, thinking about girls. They go to a disco and get to bed at three in the morning. But Mary Joe, I don't ever remember her going to bed after midnight. She never goes to discos. Her parents are very strict, and she's obedient. She's intelligent, but she's a simple person with simple tastes. She's beautiful, but she dresses simply, not in designer clothes. The only difference between her and the girls she went to high school with is she drives a Porsche—not even the best Porsche," Ernesto added in amazement.

Mary Joe's simplicity and niceness were not, however, what prevented her from breaking through. Ernesto insisted, "She's very competitive. And being nice you can be a champion. Gabriela's nice. Steffi's nice. Mary Joe is very intelligent," he repeated, then mentioned, as everyone did, that she had finished school. In his opinion, girls who had no education were headed for trouble. "No culture," he said, "and you lead an incomplete life."

As for himself, he was "very involved in art. I paint. I have had exhibitions. At one time I stopped coaching for a year and a half and just painted. When I'm alone in the hotel room, I'm painting. But I know for a player the tour gets boring. When I see Mary Joe closing herself in her room, I know she's lonely. A guy can go out, can go look for girls, look for sex. But a girl looks for love and you don't find that in two days at a tournament. To survive on the circuit you have to accelerate your feelings. Some men meet a girl for a weekend and next week they're traveling together. But Mary Joe wants to marry and have many babies. That's in five or six years. Right now she's not interested. She wants to finish her career."

Although he had spoken of Mary Joe's loneliness, her father traveled with her, and Ernesto thought this was a good idea. "Other girls travel alone and they're never relaxed. I see them at breakfast and they frighten me, they're so tense. I've been doing this a short time, but from what I see I don't think it's good for a girl to be on the tour alone.

"The low-ranked players, I don't know how they can even afford to pay coaches," Ernesto said. "Some of them I think are just with boyfriends. She teaches him to play, then makes him her coach. It's a way to justify things. When a girl doesn't have enough money, she hires a good friend instead of a good coach. And he can help her arrange practice courts and airplane reservations. At that level, perhaps it's more important to have a boyfriend. Later on, when she has more money, she can afford a boyfriend *and* a coach."

He viewed the fact that girls in their teens got sexually involved with middle-age coaches as unsurprising, perhaps inevitable. "Sometimes with an older man, a girl gets more stability. We see this not just in tennis, but elsewhere in life."

Ion Tiriac, looking rumpled and grumpy as a bear wakened prematurely from hibernation, strolled over to where Ernesto and I sat. His trademark mustache, woolly as a caterpillar, had turned white at the tips, and he had taken to wearing the sort of tinted prescription glasses you used to see on Eastern Bloc strongmen. Otherwise, the advancing years had left Tiriac unbowed. With no time wasted on pleasantries, he broke into the conversation and told Ernesto that they had to talk. Ernesto asked me to come back in fifteen minutes.

When I did so, he was alone and looked as he had before—like just another tan, healthy fellow in jeans and a faded chambray shirt kicking back in the players' lounge. But his tone had changed; he spoke with an edgy directness. He said it was hard to understand Mary Joe's defensive mentality, and thus hard to convert her into an offensive player. "I hit with her, but I can't get close to her off the court. That's when you get to know somebody. That's when you learn about their confidence and their psychology. But Mary Joe, whether she's happy or sad, how her mind is before a match, I don't know because she's always with her family whenever we're not practicing. To see matches together, to talk tactics, that's what we need."

He crossed his legs and folded his hands on his knees. He appeared to be locking up, trying to keep his answers short. Yet he blurted, "A lot of parents want to coach their daughters. This tennis tour, it's not the real world."

"How's that?"

"In the real world nobody lives all year in five-star hotels and travels by limo. But on the circuit even journalists and parents and low-ranked players live like movie stars." After a pause, he said, "These girls, they don't really have any experience. They are very naive. They think they know a lot. But since twelve years old they're hitting a ball. The circuit takes a lot out of them."

As he fell silent again, I thanked him for his time and said I'd see him at Wimbledon.

Ernesto said he wasn't going to Wimbledon; he wasn't coaching Mary Joe any longer. The words came tumbling out of him with amazingly little emotion. Tiriac had just told him he was finished. He had expected to stay with Mary Joe through the grass-court season. He had thought they were making progress.

"The only problem was Mary Joe's father. He was always there at practice, always making a remark. I tried not to answer back, but not to answer a sixty-five-year-old man can be impolite, too. I was afraid it could be ugly."

Occasionally he had handed the racquet to Mr. Fernandez, as if to tell him, Okay, you do it. Instead Mr. Fernandez had hired Juan Avendano, a former player on the men's tour, a baseliner who had rarely come to the net in his career.

Ernesto complained that he could have helped Mary Joe. He could hit with topspin or slice, he could impersonate any player's style. The trouble was he never had a chance to develop a close rapport with her. In his opinion, some of the most important coaching occurred off court while talking to a player, watching matches and discussing tactics, learning about a woman as a person so he could help her more as a player.

"Maybe that's what Mr. Fernandez didn't want," I said. "For you to develop a close personal relationship with his daughter."

Ernesto mulled this over for a moment. "Yes, a lot of players and coaches wind up in bed. But that idea, that thought that people have, makes me mad. Already an umpire told me when I first started coaching Mary Joe, 'You'll end up in bed with her.' I wanted to hit him in the face. Maybe that's what Mary Joe's father was afraid of. I don't know." And now Ernesto Ruiz Bry was tired of talking about it. Tomorrow he would fly to Monte Carlo and try to arrange an exhibition of his paintings.

O O O

During the quarterfinal between Gabriela Sabatini and Jana Novotna, the sky clouded and the temperature plunged. For both women the weather must have seemed an evil omen. Novotna had beaten Gaby at Roland Garros last year, and it was that loss that had convinced Sabatini to change coaches. Since then, Novotna had twice held match balls against Gaby—at a tournament in Zurich and at the 1990 Virginia Slims Championships—but had seen sure victories turn into the kinds of defeats that caused a player to question her character.

Meanwhile, Novotna's choice of coaches caused tennis insiders to question her wisdom more than her character. With the exception of Martina Navratilova, who employed Billie Jean King on a part-time, per-diem contract, Novotna was the lone top-ten player to be trained by a woman. She worked with fellow Czech Hana Mandlikova. As was often the case when a woman coached a woman, this was assumed to be a personal as well as a professional relationship.

All during her career Hana had alternated between being called a marvel and a mystery. A graceful, leggy, all-court athlete, she had reached the finals of eight Grand Slam events and won four. But she was best known for her erratic temperament. Charming one day, abrasive the next, she rarely had had any better idea than her fans what she would do during matches.

Mandlikova wasn't any more predictable off court. In 1986, while participating in the Federation Cup in Prague, she astounded the press by announcing that she had just married an Australian restaurateur. Apparently a shy guy, the bridegroom didn't show up for the wedding reception that evening at Hana's parents' house. Nor did he show up later. She spent her wedding night without her husband.

A year later Hana received Australian citizenship, established residency in Queensland, then revealed that she and her husband were divorcing. In pre-perestroika Prague, this was viewed as a way of defecting without jeopardizing her family.

In 1990, Hana retired at the age of twenty-eight, but stayed on the tour with the twenty-two-year-old Jana. Thus, the uncoachable Mandlikova had become the coach of a player who herself was notorious for high-strung nerves and inconsistent play.

Her short blond hair hanging straight in the damp air, Jana Novotna started like a woman on a mission—a search-and-destroy mission. Alternating deep inside-out forehands with sliced backhands, she got off to a 3–0 lead, then survived two break points to hold for 4–2.

But Gaby got to 3–4, broke Novotna, and held again to go up 5–4. For the Czech girl this reversal of fortune must have been freighted with nightmarish memories of other leads she had let slip through her fingers. But then she had a bit of luck. At 30–30, Sabatini believed a Novotna forehand would float long and didn't bother to hit it. When the ball landed well inside the baseline, Gaby's shoulders sagged and Jana squared the score at five games apiece.

Still fretting about the ball she should have put away, Sabatini lost her serve and had to break Jana to save the set. Gaby got her chances at 15–40 but hit a short approach shot which Novotna nailed at her with enough weight to snap Sabatini's strings. After Gaby changed racquets, it took Jana three tries to do it, but she held for 7–5. The first set had lasted an hour and twelve minutes, longer than many a women's match this week.

At Roland Garros, photographers stand in bunkers behind the court shooting through narrow camera slots in the windscreen. As the second set started, they must have felt as if they were under siege; balls came buzzing through the slots like hand grenades. Novotna had found the range and again launched herself to a 3–0 lead. Then she broke to 5–2 and served for the match.

Unfortunately, Jana had ninety seconds during the changeover to sit and think. An intuitive athlete, she was fine when playing by reflex, but any pause for reflection left her flustered. Burned by a double fault and a limp-wristed backhand, she dropped to 5–3, then turned into a listless spectator as Gaby reached 4–5.

For the second time Jana served for the match, and at 30–30, she appeared to have hit a winning volley. But Gaby chased it down and passed her. On the next point, Novotna fumbled a ball into the net and was broken.

At 5–5, Sabatini blew a forehand volley every bit as bad as Jana's. She screamed, bounced a ball, and angrily grabbed it. Then she hit a backhand that faded out, followed by a drop shot that Novotna shoveled over the net. Sabatini stretched for it and did the splits on the slippery clay. She lost the next point and the game, giving Jana her third chance to serve for the match.

Both girls appeared to be trapped by a repetition compulsion in which past mistakes were relived in a public ritual that demonstrated that character is fate. Although it made for a compelling spectacle, it was too painful to be enjoyable. Gaby's father, Osvaldo, buried his head in his hands and couldn't bear to watch.

Fighting against the ratlike gnawing of her nerves, Novotna staved off two break points but lost her serve again and limped into a tie-break. Even after Sabatini zoomed to a 6–2 lead, giving her four set points, Jana kept fighting and managed to reach match point in her favor at 8–7, then again at 9–8. But she couldn't capitalize. Finally she cracked and lost the tie-break 12–10.

The third set lasted twenty minutes. Sabatini might as well have been alone on court. A ghost floating through the foggy scene of her own death, Novotna never won another game.

○ ○ ○

Sabatini's coach, Carlos Kirmayr, was as pale and wiped out as Jana Novotna, but he hoped today would help Gaby. "She was in a deep, deep hole and it builds confidence to come out of it," he said.

Dick Dell, Gaby's agent, had given his client up for dead. "I can't say much for Gaby's strategy. She kept hitting to Jana's backhand and approaching to her backhand. I think Novotna's weaker when you make her run wide for her forehand. But today wasn't about great tennis. It was about winning on guts."

○ ○ ○

Jana Novotna fled in tears and had to be fetched to a press conference under the threat of a fine.

"You had two match balls," a journalist said. "What happened on those points?"

"I don't know. I'm trying to remember. Maybe I hurried too much. Or maybe I played too safe. I wanted to win so badly. I'm very disappointed."

Against all evidence, she insisted she'd played with a positive attitude and hadn't thought of her past catastrophic lapses against Sabatini.

"Why six–love in the third set?" someone hollered.

"I gave everything I had in the first two sets. Mentally I had nothing left. It was too hard to go on fighting."

○ ○ ○

The day of the semifinals was cold and gray, with intermittent drizzle. The temperature rose no higher than the mid-fifties, and perhaps that explained why Court Central remained half-empty for the Seles–Sabatini match. Or maybe people were still at lunch. As Yannick Noah once lamented, "Parisians like tennis, but they love *la cuisine* more."

Seles was leading Sabatini 3–2 when gusty wind began to swirl the chestnut trees in the Bois de Boulogne into a green froth. Umbrellas popped open. Despite the umpire's call for quiet, fans darted for the exits and play stopped.

After a sixteen-minute rain delay, the match resumed and as the advantage shifted back and forth, the sky darkened and spat more rain. As soon as Gaby held to 4–4, play was suspended again.

This delay dragged on for twenty-eight minutes, and when the girls returned to warm up for the third time, Monica was in her third outfit. She had gone from fuschia to purple and back again. With little effort she held to 5–4.

Gaby seemed hesitant. Her first serve was undependable, and Monica was jumping on her second. As Sabatini's shots landed shorter, Seles advanced, swatting the ball at hellacious angles. Gaby couldn't hold her back and was too busy retrieving to go on the attack herself.

Although she was doing no more than spinning in her serves, Gaby double-faulted to give Monica set point. On an exchange of ground strokes, the linesman—actually, a lineswoman; the whole crew was female today—signaled that Sabatini's shot was good. Seles gestured with her racquet. The lineswoman checked the mark and conceded that she had made a mistake. Gaby's ball was long. First set to Seles 6–4, on an overrule.

Sabatini's lovely face pouted, the sky lowered, and her game crumbled as Seles swung her from side to side like a toy on a string. The score was 5–0 in Monica's favor before Gabriela held serve. Then Seles closed out the match, taking the last point on another overrule.

"This year on clay whenever there's been a rain break it has been against me," Monica said afterward. "I tried not to think about that. It was cold and it wasn't going to be easy to go back out on court. You're always tight in the first game. If I lost the first game, she'd be serving for the set. That first game after the break was the key game. I just said to myself not to be too superstitious."

"How about meeting Steffi in the final?" a journalist asked, jumping to conclusions.

"What happens will happen," Seles said.

○ ○ ○

What happened was enough to astonish even Arantxa Sanchez Vicario's most ardent fans. Although Arantxa had beaten Graf to win the 1989 French Open, that was regarded as a great upset. Steffi had been weakened by menstrual cramps, and she resented reminders of the match. "I don't ever look back. I look forward."

Perhaps that was her problem today—she was so busy looking forward, she couldn't focus on her forehand. She thumped the first one long, and that unleashed an avalanche of unforced errors. At times, Steffi did no more than swat halfheartedly at Arantxa's shots, and even on questionable calls, she didn't bother checking the clay for a mark.

Incroyable, murmured the French press, sending up thick clouds of smoke from their Gauloises. Arantxa ran away with the first set 6–0 in twenty minutes. Steffi had won only eleven points. Since she was a wee sprout of fourteen, Graf had blanked her opponents 143 times, but she hadn't lost a set at love since 1984.

Up in the stands, Peter Graf stormed out of the players' box and into an altercation with a gray-haired, mustachioed man. In full view of a worldwide TV audience, Peter appeared to belt the guy on the crown of his head. Peter later claimed it had been a friendly tap, but the fellow didn't take it like that. He scrambled after Graf, whacked him in the back, then shouted at Steffi's coach, Pavel Slozil, "Wait until Wimbledon. I'll have a bodyguard and he'll break Peter's legs!"

The gray-haired gent was James Annenberg Levee, the nephew of billionaire Walter Annenberg. Levee used to be Steffi's second most fanatical fan. Her most fanatical one was a deranged German boy who slit his wrists in front of her to prove his love. Levee proved his love by bleeding money rather than bodily fluids. He claimed to have given Steffi two Porsches, $200,000 in cash, and $80,000 worth of jewelry.

In return he craved her friendship, a guest badge, and a prominent seat at courtside. But according to Levee, the Grafs were ingrates. They accepted his gifts, called him at all hours to demand private planes and limos, yet invited him to sit in the players' box just once. "All I ask is for a little appreciation—a thank-you, a phone call on my birthday."

Peter Graf insisted that his family had felt overwhelmed by Levee's attention and thought his generosity was excessive. The Grafs didn't relish it when Levee shouted, "I love you!" during Steffi's matches.

When they let the relationship cool, Levee switched his allegiance to other players. He gave them money, paid their coaches, contributed to their favorite charities, and in one case leased a Lear jet to fly an injured girl, Patty Fendick, to California. These days the primary object of his affection was Monica Seles, and that seemed to rankle Peter Graf. When Seles beat Steffi for the 1990 French Open title, Levee taunted both father and daughter by pointing to Monica and yelling, "Number one!"

In the following weeks much would be written and whispered about Levee and his motives, but the more immediate questions concerned the players who courted his favor and the WTA officials, like Gerry Smith, who saw no reason to formulate guidelines for the tour's growing number of squirrelly entourages. As Curry Kirkpatrick observed in *Sports Illustrated,* "A rich guy can spend his money and time any pitiable way he wishes, but what does it say about the Grafs and the Seleses that they accepted such largesse or embarrassing backing or whatever it is?"

○ ○ ○

In the second set, Sanchez Vicario broke to a 2–1 lead just before a cloudburst interrupted play. After forty-three minutes, the match resumed at 7:15 P.M., but Arantxa was still as spry as a rooster at the first light of dawn. At 4–1 in the Spanish girl's favor, Graf had three chances to break back, but she blew each one, and Arantxa served out the set 6–2.

Total playing time was fifty-four minutes—which was how long it usually took Steffi to dispatch an opponent. One school of thought held that that was part of her problem. She encountered so little resistance in the early rounds, she had lost the ability to deal with competitors who kept the ball in play. Whenever she couldn't win quickly by overpowering a girl, she began to flail wildly with her forehand.

Reporters pressed Graf to explain what had happened between her father and Jim Levee. Haltingly, Steffi started to formulate her version of events, then gave up and snapped, "I don't know what happened and I don't care."

She said she hadn't bothered questioning line calls because "things weren't really going my way. I've never felt such a sense of power-lessness. I can't remember when I played that badly. I couldn't feel the ball. And Arantxa was hitting incredible shots."

In stunning understatement she said of the disaster: "It wasn't my day."

It was, however, Sanchez Vicario's day, and she didn't care to hear anything about Steffi's problems. She preferred to believe the difference had been her sterling performance. Although Arantxa sounded more than a little pleased with herself, she came across as the soul of diplomacy compared to Andre Agassi, who after beating Boris Becker announced to the press, "I'm as happy as a faggot in a submarine."

○ ○ ○

John Lloyd, who coached Chris Evert during their marriage, once upset his wife's colleagues by commenting that 50 percent of the women on the circuit were too fat. By 1991, things had improved, Lloyd told me. Now only 30 percent were overweight. Still, Canadian journalist Nora McCabe wisecracked that there was more cellulite on the WTA tour than at the Canyon Ranch Spa.

Don Candy scoffed at the notion that improved conditioning had added depth to women's tennis. "Forget it," he said. "Just because they're eating spaghetti, they think they're eating right. There's more depth today because there's more money, not because of better conditioning."

Candy believed that conditioning on the women's tour often amounted to little more than cosmetics. He told of a player who made it to the third round of a tournament but seemed exhausted after easy matches. At first he suspected she wasn't training hard enough. Then he discovered she was overdoing it, going to the gym every day and spending hours on the Stairmaster "because she felt she was too heavy in the legs. It wasn't to help her tennis. It was just that she didn't like how she looked."

While a lot of women didn't like how they looked, and this resulted in fad diets, self-defeating exercise programs, and serious eating disorders, it should be noted that poor conditioning and nutrition also plagued the men's circuit. At Roland Garros, half a dozen men had to abandon matches—no woman did—and many others limped along in pain. Two on-site French trainers explained to *L'Equipe* that most of these injuries occurred because the men played too many tournaments, spent too little time stretching and warming up, tended to eat the wrong foods at the wrong time, gave scant attention to minor ailments that turned into major ones, and devoted too many hours to hitting tennis balls and too few to drills that would improve their stamina, strength, and coordination. "The majority of the men players are too careless," one trainer said. "But that's normal. They are all twenty years old and are deprived of a normal life for nine months a year. When they have a few days off, they go to a restaurant or a nightclub" instead of resting and recuperating.

Hoping for a similarly candid assessment of the women's tour, I interviewed Kathleen Stroia, a WTA physical therapist. Stroia wore a pair of horn-rimmed glasses that gave her a studious appearance—which was only fitting since she had earned B.S. and M.S. degrees in athletic training, and a second B.S. in physical therapy. As an undergraduate at Purdue, she had treated players in various sports, including men's basketball and football, and believed she had a broad base of experience which allowed her to judge by a person's physiognomy and personality what sport he or she practiced. With tennis players, she said, "round shoulders are perceptible. They have lower-body symmetry and nicely developed legs." As for their personalities, Stroia felt that since tennis players "have to be so focused on themselves, they're more poised. They have to be self-absorbed, but they're fragile. What it takes to be a champion is a healthy ego. If it's not healthy, you're not a champion."

Much as these remarks might suggest otherwise, Kathleen Stroia was reluctant to generalize and she pondered my questions before responding. When I asked her to compare players on the women's tour with female athletes she had worked with in other sports, she warily circled the subject and worded and reworded her answer with such care she might have been speaking in code. Finally, she said that the best women tennis players were comparable to girls on the Purdue track team. Although it may simply have been her equivocating manner, this seemed to suggest that the game's greatest stars were in no better shape than intercollegiate athletes on a track team of no particular distinction.

When I mentioned what coaches had said about women players being overweight and out of condition, Stroia's response evolved in stages, like features emerging on a developing photograph. "Diet's always difficult when you travel. We have a health column to explain the proper way to eat on the road. My focus is not on what the women weigh, but on whether they're eating well. A lot of players don't like to drink water, and that's important, too. If you're talking about young players, some of the changes [in weight] are just natural development. A lot of times you're just looking at a girl becoming a woman."

But other times, I pointed out, you're looking at a girl becoming anorexic or bulimic. Canadian player Carling Bassett Seguso had openly discussed her battle with anorexia. Her weight had dropped to ninety-eight pounds and she had to be hospitalized. Zina Garrison had spoken of her periodic binges and purges. Still suffering from bouts of bulimia, Zina had confronted her problem. But there must have been other players who suffered in silence.

"Compared to the average college sorority house, there's no problem with eating disorders on the circuit," Stroia insisted.

Many experts were in profound disagreement with this claim. Six months earlier, Cindy Hahn of *Tennis* magazine quoted sources who contended that although only 1 percent of the U.S. female population suffered from bulimia or anorexia, a much higher percentage of tennis players did. According to Hahn, "Julie Anthony, a former touring pro who holds a Ph.D. in clinical psychology and advises many top pros, says: 'I wouldn't be surprised if around 30 percent of the women on the tour have some form of an eating disorder. I know a number of women in the top twenty [who do].' "

In the growing body of literature on the subject, Canadian sociologist Helen Lenskyj has written, "A high proportion of competitive female athletes resort to dangerous weight control behaviors to maintain an edge over their opponents and to satisfy coaches', judges', and spectators' standards of heterosexual attractiveness."

It sounded to me, I said to Kathleen Stroia, as if she believed the WTA tour was free of problems.

No, she did concede that women could be unreasonable about their conditioning programs. "Sometimes even though they're hurt, they feel they have to run. We have to convince them to do alternative exercises to keep up their cardiovascular fitness. A lot of them are driven. To ask them to take off two weeks to recover from an injury—that to them is a long time. It's a fast pace on the tour. You're always thinking, Where did the season go? Where did the year go?"

She volunteered that in promoting fitness, "we emphasize prevention. But prevention is a hard sell. It's difficult to get girls to stretch. They get bored. And it's difficult to convince a fourteen- or fifteen-year-old to strengthen her back. She just says, 'I don't have back problems.' Whereas players in their late twenties will have an ache and immediately ask me to check it out, younger girls might let it slide."

She added that fifteen, sixteen, and seventeen were key years for bone growth and formation. "There are conditions and problems that come from the extreme youth of the players. Like Monica—she's grown a lot in the last year and her muscles aren't as flexible as they should be. Part of the remedy is increasing her flexibility and using orthotics in her shoes." All during the French Open, Kathleen Stroia said, Seles had been hobbled by very painful shin splints.

○ ○ ○

It was cool and overcast for the final, almost too nippy to enjoy the oysters from Languedoc that were laid on for the press out on the terrace. In the players' box on Court Central, Jim Levee and his fiancée, Jill Genson, sat with Mr. and Mrs. Seles. Nearby Marisa Sanchez Vicario, Arantxa's mother, cuddled her daughter's pet Yorkie, named Roland in memory of Arantxa's first and only Grand Slam title. Still, that was more than her brothers had won. After taking this year's Italian Open title, Emilio had seemed ready to challenge for the French crown, but he had been upset in an early round and Javier hadn't lasted much longer. Now the whole family pulled for Arantxa, and she responded by breaking Seles and holding for a 2–0 lead.

A short, thickset, nimble-footed girl of nineteen, Arantxa hailed from Barcelona and now resided in tax-free Andorra. Her game used to resemble that vest-pocket principality. She had had a fortress mentality founded on the cautious hoarding of assets. Lately, though, she had begun to hit the ball harder and deeper, and to take the net, as she did in doubles and mixed doubles.

But there was a thin line between efficient aggression and self-immolating belligerence, and Arantxa tripped over it in the fourth game when the umpire overruled and gave a point to Monica. *"Hombre! No!"* Arantxa screamed, demanding that he climb down from his chair and check the mark. He refused to do it, which made her furious. A moment later she was broken, knotting the score at two games apiece.

As Monica started to take charge of the exchanges, Arantxa fell into her old role of retriever. Seles broke to 5–3, then blasted an overhead to win the set 6–3.

In the second set the rallies lasted twenty and thirty shots, and it took six minutes for Arantxa to survive the first game. Seles also had to struggle on serve, and as soon as she squared things at 1–1, she toweled off her hands and arms. Despite the goose pimply weather, she was bathed in a sweat.

Sanchez Vicario held to 2–1, then blanked Seles for a 3–1 lead. When she got another bad call, she bellowed, "No, no, no!" and this time the ump agreed with her. With a cleverly placed drop shot, she sucked Monica to the net, then lobbed, only to have Seles run it down. Arantxa executed another drop, and Monica scooped this one long, giving Sanchez Vicario a commanding 4–1 advantage.

But once again her pugnacity appeared to derail Arantxa. After Seles reached 2–4 on a disputed point, the Spanish girl blew an easy overhead and was broken. In a long game, with both girls challenging the linesmen, checking for marks and appealing for overrules, Seles clawed her way to 4–4. Then she broke Arantxa's serve at love.

Monica came off her chair after the changeover like a prize-fighter rushing out for the final round. When she got to 30–0, it looked like the match was over. But Sanchez Vicario wouldn't quit. She bravely came to net, she brashly chipped drop shots, she miraculously kept the ball in play with desperation lobs. Three times she staved off match points. But Monica got a fourth, and Arantxa poked a final backhand into the net.

A carpet was rolled out and a stairway unfolded to allow access to the presidential box. The two finalists climbed up for the awards ceremony, and Monica was in mid-babble by the time the microphone hit her hand. "This is great. This is just great. I'd like to thank Kraft Foods for sponsoring the tour. I'd like to thank my dad. He's the greatest coach ever. I'm the one on the court, but he knows so much about the game. He's my coach and always has been, it's our victory, we pulled it off."

Spectators were screaming, "Shut up, shut up!" but she kept on foaming like Perrier. "I'd like to thank my mom. I'd like to thank you all for coming and making this such a wonderful week. I just can't believe I won two titles in a row and I just can't wait to come back next year."

Fans were filing toward the exits. The last game, all sixteen minutes of it, had been worth the price of a ticket. But they weren't in the market for Monica's Valley Girl monologue.

O O O

Seles showed up at her press conference in a black sheath with gold and crystal accessories. Reporters remarked that it was hard to remember she was only seventeen—perhaps because she resembled a twelve year old who had raided Mommy's wardrobe. A journalist posed the question that had sports fans all over the globe hanging by tenterhooks. "Would you talk about your earrings?"

"I got them from Perrier a few days ago. I think they are very pretty. I like the style and I thought today was the perfect occasion to wear them."

Now that that had been cleared up, someone asked if she felt that having won the Australian and the French opens, she had a shot at the Grand Slam.

"The key will be Wimbledon and the U.S. Open. I have never got past the fourth round at the U.S. Open. I will concentrate for Wimbledon. I need to be able to serve and volley to do well at Wimbledon."

○ ○ ○

In the players' lounge, Karolj Seles sipped a celebratory beer and transfixed several reporters who were trying to paw through the briar patch of his syntax and pluck out a printable quote.

"I am not realist," Karolj said. "I am not fan. I am parent. I tell Monica, believe chair. Me good friends Arantxa family, Capriati family, Steffi family, Mary Joe family. This is sport. Steffi is fantastic person. Monica like her."

It was easier to understand Mansour Bahrami, Monica's hitting partner. Bow-legged and barrel-chested, his body swathed in a shag carpet of dark hair, Mansour, an Iranian, sported a handlebar mustache big enough to hang your hat on. His tennis was boisterous, powerful, and improvised. Regardless of the surface, he was apt to experiment and produce shot patterns that imitated the arabesques on a Persian carpet. A fun-loving fantasist, he had been known to return let-serves with his head.

The joy had gone out of his life during the Iranian revolution when the Ayatollah Khomeini decreed that tennis was another invention of the Great Satan. In his teens, Bahrami had been ranked in the top hundred, but then he was trapped in Iran, and by the time he escaped to Paris, he had fallen off the computer. It wasn't until 1985, just before he turned thirty, that he began playing the circuit again. Making his mark as a doubles specialist, he once got as far as the final of the French Open.

Monica Seles had seen his matches and asked her father to arrange for Mansour to hit with her. They had started three weeks ago in Hamburg and had continued through Roland Garros.

"I didn't think a girl could play that well or hit the ball that hard," Bahrami said. "I was stupefied. Monica makes you run. She can't hit as hard as a man, but she can swing you off the court, then hit to the open spot. She doesn't have a fast serve, but it's well placed. Sometimes that's better than a hard serve. A player can use a hard serve against you."

He had enjoyed this coaching stint, and Karolj had asked him to sign on full-time. But Bahrami wasn't ready to give up his own career.

"It's not a huge career," he conceded, "but I play a lot of exhibitions. I make good money all over Europe. Even when I play qualifying events, people come to watch me. When the people stop watching, I'll stop playing."

"Will you coach her at Wimbledon?" I asked.

"I'm in the doubles. So I'll coach her—if she plays."

"*If?*" That single word set off alarm bells.

"She might not."

"What do you mean?"

Immediately Mansour regretted he had spoken. He hadn't meant to mention this. He begged me not to print it. I explained that my book wouldn't come out until more than a year after Wimbledon. What was wrong with Monica? I pressed him.

"She's hurt," he said. "She's having trouble with her feet and her leg. She needed treatment all during the tournament. Don't tell anyone, but I don't think she'll play Wimbledon."

Wimbledon

Martina's Dark Tea Time of the Soul

Wimbledon lasts for two weeks, but the British press begins pounding the drums months in advance, building expectations, speculating about the prospects of this player or that, airing disputes and petty squabbles, publishing the ghosted memoirs of top-ranked stars. So the fortnight expands into a season, a sort of theatrical run with its cast of characters and distinctive themes. Among the men, the leitmotiv in 1991 was whether Andre Agassi would shuck his flamboyantly colored clothes and wear white, as stipulated by the rules of the All England Lawn Tennis and Croquet Club. Among the women, the hottest topic looked to be equal prize money. But then Judy Nelson filed suit against Martina Navratilova, demanding half her fortune, and instantly a more provocative story line was struck.

While tabloids had no compunctions about gloating over the seamiest details—"Wild Sex and Sin With Martina; What Went on in Her Gay Love Nest," screamed a typical headline—reputable newspapers tried to have it both ways. As they analyzed Martina's chances of winning a tenth Wimbledon title, they insisted that one really couldn't comment on her current form without reference to her legal and emotional torments. And how could one convey to readers the devastating effects of those torments without—oh, how it pained them to do so—without repeating every calumny printed by the Beastie Boys of the bottom-feeding press?

As if hell-bent on keeping the story in the headlines, the two litigants held dueling press conferences. Tearfully, Judy Nelson explained that Navratilova had signed a Non-Marital Cohabitation Agreement, which provided for a settlement in the event that they split up. The contract called for Martina to pay Judy half the assets she had accumulated during their relationship. After all, Judy argued, she had supplied valuable personal and professional services during that period. They had had a business partnership and were developing a clothing line. But now Martina refused to abide by the agreement, leaving Judy without the means to support herself and her children. Nelson's suit alleged "that Martina Navratilova, acting alone and through International Management Group (IMG), has committed actual or constructive fraud against Judy Nelson."

In her defense, Martina said she had supported Judy and her sons for years, lavishing gifts on them and picking up their travel expenses on the tour. While she didn't deny signing the Non-Marital Cohabitation Agreement—since there was a videotape of her doing so, she couldn't deny it—she did insist that she hadn't read it and hadn't understood it. But she had submitted a financial statement describing $5 million in assets which she had accumulated previous to the agreement, and she had initialed every page, including one which stated that she had waived the right to consult her own attorney, had "freely and voluntarily" signed the contract, and "acknowledged that [she] understood [the] consequences and benefits of this agreement."

In a televised interview with Barbara Walters, Martina talked like a moonstruck ingenue who had rashly accepted terms she hadn't had time to reflect on. When Walters asked if the agreement amounted to "money for sex," Martina said it was more like "money for love." Sad and pathetic as this sounded, it was an accommodation to reality that was common on the women's tour among straight girls as well as gays. To sustain a romance the girl always seemed to have to pay.

Navratilova sounded less like a victim of her impetuous heart when she observed to Walters that since homosexual relationships were illegal in Texas, where Judy and she claimed residence, she didn't see how a contract that formalized such an arrangement could be legal and binding. She conceded that she had reached a financial settlement with basketball star Nancy Lieberman whom she had lived with and who helped her

with her physical fitness. She wasn't asked what arra[ngements]
she had made when she split up with novelist Rita Mae [nor was]
there any discussion of the end of her relationship with [Nancy]
Haynie. But she stated without challenge from Barbara W. [that she]
couldn't afford to pay Judy what the agreement called for. A settlement
of $2 million would wipe her out, she protested.

As for the new Nelson, her friend Cindy, Martina said, "I'm very
close to her." But she maintained that Cindy wasn't the reason she left
Judy.

In the face of massive publicity about Navratilova and Judy Nelson,
the tennis establishment, insofar as it reacted at all, treated the matter
as though Martina were the lone gay player on the tour. In this respect,
women's tennis hadn't made much progress in the last decade. In 1981,
Marilyn Barnett, Billie Jean King's former hairdresser and traveling
secretary, filed suit, forcing one of the greatest players in the sport to
admit that they had had an affair. Billie Jean later wrote a book about
the episode, but neither she nor the press, much less other players,
addressed the most obvious issues about lesbianism and women's tennis.
Instead, Billie Jean said that "Marilyn and I were only having an isolated
homosexual experience, and . . . we were not participating in a full homosexual lifestyle"—whatever that was.

The impression she left was that she hadn't previously had sex with
women and didn't foresee doing so in the future. She admitted, "I knew
well enough there were lesbians in tennis," but she downplayed their
number even though during her heyday more than half the top players
were gay. While one could understand her desire not to subject herself
to more vilification and could sympathize with her discretion about her
friends, a bit more candor about the subject might have saved women's
tennis from these periodic convulsions that result in so much anguish
for a solitary scapegoat.

○ ○ ○

It took a howling hurricane—actually, it was more a tempest in a
teapot—to knock Martina Navratilova out of the headlines. Seventy-
two hours before play was scheduled to start, Monica Seles withdrew
from Wimbledon, explaining through Stephanie Tolleson, her agent at

IMG, that she had been injured in a "minor accident." A fax received by the All England Club quoted Monica as saying no more than "I am very disappointed to miss Wimbledon this year but look forward to returning in 1992."

When Alan Mills, the tournament referee, demanded additional information, IMG replied that Seles didn't care to elaborate. At which point the earth under Centre Court buckled and heaved, the heavens split wide open, and the moon, sun, and stars were stayed in their courses. Or so one would have assumed from reading newspapers. Journalists, no less than the All England Club, demanded to know why Monica wasn't playing, and when she wouldn't give them what they regarded as a good reason, they leaped to the conclusion that there must be a bad one. Maybe her injury was more serious than she admitted. Was hers another case of terminal teenage burnout? Had she suffered a mental, not a physical, breakdown?

Those of a more cynical frame of mind claimed that Seles's endorsement contract called for her to receive a $1 million bonus if she remained number one on the Virginia Slims computer after Wimbledon. Unsure of herself on grass, had she skipped this event to preserve her ranking and her cash bonanza?

Other conspiratorial theorists surmised that Monica's maneuvering might relate to the Olympics. Since she refused to play Federation Cup for Yugoslavia, as ITF rules required, maybe she was laying the predicate for a claim that she had been available for the Fed Cup but was forced by injury to withdraw. Thus, she met the qualifying conditions for Barcelona.

One notion never occurred to journalists. They never wondered whether Seles was simply treating the All England Club with the same disdain as it treated everybody else. Its officials rarely felt compelled to respond to questions, much less ultimatums, so they had little room to complain when Monica declined to do more than fax her curt regrets.

But most people didn't see it this way. They saw only one side of Wimbledon, the lovely mauve and green side. Manicured lawns and trellised roses, ladies in Liberty dresses and gents in regimental ties, the steeple of St. Mary's Church, champagne and Pimm's cup, strawberries and Devonshire cream, schoolgirls in straw boaters and knobby-kneed schoolboys in short pants—all these charming touches blinded spectators to the less pleasant realities of the place, which were summed up, in the words of the *Sunday Times*, as "a whole tradition of English blank-faced absolutism." Here a long history of arrogance and class consciousness had combined with self-interest to produce a sporting event that depended upon fans and players for whom the Club felt little except thinly veiled contempt. Yet when a player responded with similar contempt, Wimbledon professed to be shocked.

Although the All England Club preferred to regard the Championships, as they're called, in a more flattering light, Wimbledon was essentially a lucrative fund-raiser which covered the Club's annual expenses, kept the dues low, and contributed a sizable surplus to support British tennis. (In 1990 the surplus was 10 million pounds sterling.) Wimbledon liked to boast that, unlike other Grand Slam events, it had kept Centre Court virginally pure of advertisements, but it could afford to do so because it had transformed the entire tournament into a highly successful advertisement for itself. Entrusting its commercial interests to IMG, it franchised a Flying W trademark in 1978 and ever since then had fronted for a long line of products, many of which had nothing to do with tennis.

Although the Club made $50 million a year by marketing its logo, it wasn't always careful about the parties to its contracts. During the 1991 championships, a deal to put the Flying W imprimatur on a line of fragrances and cosmetics unraveled amid claims of unpaid royalties and troubling improprieties. The All England Club believed its licensing agreement was with Indol Inc. of Palm Springs, California, but Indol was wholly owned by Craven Ventures of Vancouver, British Columbia. According to the *Sunday Times,* the marketing executive of Craven Ventures, one Gino Cicci, had been jailed for eighteen months in 1979 "along with Joey Romano, a prominent Vancouver underworld figure, for defrauding a publicly quoted company."

Wimbledon refused to comment on this matter with a resoluteness that Monica Seles would have admired.

○ ○ ○

The first Monday of the tournament it poured rain all morning. It was the coldest June in England since 1659, and there had yet to be a single dry day that month. Still, a sellout crowd waited for the matches to begin. Even after an announcement over the public-address system predicted two more hours of heavy showers, few people left. In dim tunnels under Centre Court and Court One, thousands huddled miserably as if awaiting rescue from a disaster site. Wet and shivering, they slumped against the walls. Some seemed to be unconscious—perhaps sleeping, perhaps bored stiff. "It looks like the London Underground during the Blitz," said Australian writer Alan Trengove. "I almost expect them to break into a chorus of 'Land of Hope and Glory.' "

At 5:30 P.M. Gerry Smith called a press conference to announce that he had imposed a six-thousand-dollar fine on Monica Seles for her late and unexplained withdrawal. During a question-answer session, he said he had requested a doctor's certificate and a full accounting from Monica, but he admitted he hadn't spoken to her directly; she never responded to his phone calls. Asked whether Seles's injury—if that's what it was—had convinced the WTA to reconsider its policy of letting girls play so often at such a tender age, Smith said the question was too speculative for him to answer.

At 7 P.M. play was canceled without a single ball being struck. Since Wimbledon was the only Grand Slam event that didn't give rain checks, more than 27,000 fans trudged home having spent $500,000 for nothing. The road to London ran hubcap-deep in water, and traffic advanced so slowly the driver of the press courtesy van worked on a crossword puzzle as we inched along.

○ ○ ○

Tuesday the meteorological center predicted "another problem day with more rain forecast. The difficulties are: (1) Will there be any rain before the main rain belt arrives? (2) How persistent will the rain be when it arrives? (3) How heavy will it be? (4) When will it clear?" With admirable scientific detachment, the report concluded, "At this stage all of the answers are uncertain."

Still, play started, and Martina Navratilova marched onto Centre Court, commencing her campaign for a tenth Wimbledon title. She appeared to be at the ragged edge of control. Dropping the first point on a double fault, she was soon down a break to Elna Reinach, the awkward South African whom she had beaten so handily in Rome, earlier in the year.

A few knowing British reporters attributed Navratilova's scratchy play less to nerves than to "the green condition" of the grass. Although it might look more attractive in its pristine state, the grass gave an inconsistent bounce until it was worn down and broken in. Whatever the reason, Martina's timing was atrocious, her footwork sloppy, and she lost the set 6–4.

In the second, although she continued to play far below her normal standard, Navratilova won 6–2 and seemed to have too many weapons for her opponent to handle. But Reinach, a tall girl, got a lot of torque on her serve, and whenever she put her first ball in, she won 80 percent of the points. In the third set, she broke for an early 3–2 lead, lost that advantage, then broke again to 4–3. When she went up 30–0 on her serve, it seemed that Martina had deposited herself deep in a hole from which she could never dig out.

Reinach tossed the ball high, uncoiled her arm, and snapped her wrist. The serve rocketed toward Martina, who blocked back a short floating return. To Reinach the ball must have looked the size of a balloon, the size of her huge and growing hopes. But somehow she pushed it into the net. Although the score was still 30–15, Leslie Allen, a former top-twenty player and current Kraft General Foods event manager, said, "That's the match."

Sure enough, Reinach lost the next point, then the next and the next. With the score four games all, Leslie Allen got up to leave. "Well, that's it," she said, and it was. Martina held, then broke to win the match.

This scenario often unfolds at Grand Slam events. An unknown girl with nothing to lose races to an apparently insurmountable lead over a top seed. But just when the match is hers for the taking, she suffers a lapse not so much of technique as imagination. Suddenly she cannot conceive of beating a star, of upsetting the sport's hierarchy. Subconsciously that idea may be more threatening than the specter of defeat.

Afterward, Elna Reinach confessed that she'd suffered the fatal disease of underdogs. "When it came to the punch, I guess I was scared."

"Scared of winning or scared of losing?"

"Scared of going for it," she said. It had been her first time on Centre Court, and she had had difficulty coping with the enormity of the place, of the crowd, of the situation. "Even up a break at four–three in the third set, I never thought I was beating Martina. At most I thought I was giving her a run for her money."

Navratilova felt she had gotten more than a run. "I felt like I was in a final. My adrenaline was pumping big time. I came up with the shots when I had to, so I'm happy about that. But it was an uphill struggle."

Then she made a literary allusion that flummoxed many listeners. "I felt like Sisyphus," Martina said. "You have to keep pushing the stone uphill. As soon as I got close to the top, it came down again."

Reporters whispered back and forth. "She felt like what?" The transcript of the press conference had her saying, "I felt like Epyphyces."

"Are you able to keep the legal problems in your life out of this championship?"

"I don't see lawyers hitting the balls out there," she drawled. "Elna may be studying law, but I don't know."

"Do you feel like those problems with your personal life are affecting your game?"

"So far, so good. I've won two tournaments coming into Wimbledon, so maybe I should have more problems in my life."

O O O

At 4:30 P.M. the rain came down, the rubberized court covers went up, and I retreated to the press tea room with Italian correspondent Lea Pericoli, who described her playing days when her biggest wins had been over Billie Jean King and Virginia Wade. On three occasions she had reached the round of sixteen at Wimbledon. But her fondest memories were of Teddy Tinling and the outfits he had fashioned for her. In 1967, when Lea wore a feather dress, the *Evening Standard* had done a special photo feature. In other years she had worn a dress trimmed with mink and an outfit confected of flowers.

"I checked the draw," she admitted. "If I was up against a strong player, I wore plain white. When you wear feathers on court, you have to win. So I picked my spots.

"Now women have a contract with Nike and Nike makes a horrible shirt, and they wear it anyway. I would never have done that. Some of these designers have no sense of design.

"I find it funny," Lea said. "Today everybody is talking about Agassi and what he'll wear. In my day they talked about the women. We'd all have a new dress every day. I would never go on court without makeup. Now they make fun of a girl if she does that. 'Look at Temesvari,' they say. 'Look at the eyeliner, the lipstick.' But so what? It doesn't hurt her backhand to look pretty."

She didn't understand why so few girls had a sense of style, especially when there were men who knew all about clothes and camera angles and makeup. She recalled her first encounter with Andre Agassi when he played the Italian Open at the age of seventeen, and she had taken a film crew to interview him at the Excelsior Hotel on Via Veneto. Before going on camera, he had insisted on putting powder on his nose so it wouldn't shine and applying gloss to his lips so that they would. Even back then, he had sported an earring and had had his hair dyed and moussed. Why, Lea wondered, was it all right for Agassi, but not for the girls, to worry about clothes and makeup?

"Maybe the girls are trying to redefine what constitutes feminine beauty," I suggested.

Lea burst into laughter. "Oh, come on!"

O O O

A few days later, over dinner with George Vescey of *The New York Times,* I recounted my conversation with Lea Pericoli, and he said that in his coverage of last year's Wimbledon final between Navratilova and Zina Garrison, he had described how they were dressed. But the passage had been deleted by editors in New York. They claimed that it was insensitive and sexist to discuss what female players wore. Men were a different matter. Vescey was free to say what they wore.

○ ○ ○

By Day Three, only 28 out of 128 first-round matches had been completed. In an effort to catch up, play started at 11 A.M., but by noon another rainstorm raked the grounds, interrupting matches for more than three hours.

During the break I attempted to contact Billie Jean King, who served as a commentator for Home Box Office, which, along with NBC, was beaming Wimbledon back to the States. When my phone calls failed, I hiked over to the HBO trailer. The rain diminished to a drizzle as I strolled through an unmanned gate into a warren of alleyways formed by vans, cars, and equipment cases. A snake's nest of wires and cables snarled the footpaths. Few people were about, but at yet another gate there was a helpful guard who gave me directions.

At the HBO trailer I learned that Billie Jean had returned to London. There was nothing for her to do here. Larry Merchant, another commentator, was caught in the same limbo. The weather was so foul, he couldn't even find a dry spot to shoot a feature about the rain. The camera lenses kept fogging over, and the backgrounds were all a whiter shade of pale.

Like everyone else, Merchant was reduced to ruminating about Monica Seles. The *Sun* had run an article reporting that she was pregnant. Enrico Cocchi, her hitting partner during the Italian Open, was alleged to be the father. Cocchi denied it, but a couple of Yugoslavian newspapers quoted an unidentified family friend who said, "Monica has put on eighteen pounds in the last six weeks. Her bosom is much bigger and she's added a lot of weight around her hips."

In my opinion, the weight gain was the result of Monica's slathering butter on her pizza and French fries. Merchant agreed, but said cholesterol was less sexy than . . . well, than sex.

On my return trip through the labyrinth of TV trailers and equipment vans, a different guard nabbed me and demanded my pass. I flashed my press credentials, but he claimed they wouldn't do. I needed a special permit to enter the TV area.

"No problem," I said. "I'm leaving."

For him there was a problem. How had I sneaked in here? There had been bomb threats. Who could say what I was up to?

It had started to rain heavily, and my tolerance for his nutty interrogation was wearing thin. But the guard wouldn't let me leave until he notified "the authorities."

"The authorities" were, if anything, more inflamed than the guard. "The authorities," in the form of a frazzled woman and a bull-necked man, ordered me to backtrack to the HBO trailer, cross a parking lot, slog through the muddy fields of Aorangi Park, and reenter Wimbledon by a gate more than a mile away.

"You have to understand," the woman said, "we're all fraught because of the rain. We've only broadcast three hours of tennis in three days and we're simply fraught."

Fraught, that was the word for it. By the time I returned to the press area, I was fraught, not to mention sopping wet. Other journalists were also fraught, and they jabbered about Monica Seles, who was fraught with child. Or maybe with drugs. That was another rumor making the rounds. She was fraught with drugs, and had tested positive in Paris. Or she hadn't tested positive there, but feared she would at Wimbledon. Or during her drug test, they discovered she was pregnant. Naturally, none of these conjectures could be refuted or confirmed for the simple reason that pro tennis refused to reveal any information, positive or negative, about drug testing.

Bud Collins, who despite the wintry weather wore a flowery Hawaiian shirt, said, "It's ridiculous. Seles should be suspended for a year—or at least until she comes out with an explanation. You can't let these stories and rumors build. England is a country where gambling is legal. You can't let people think gamblers got to her or there's some kind of fiddle taking place."

○ ○ ○

At 7 P.M. play resumed, and I settled down in my damp duds in the video room to watch adjacent monitors featuring Jennifer Capriati versus Shaun Stafford on Court One, and Gabriela Sabatini versus Monique Javer on Centre Court. The matches appeared to be running at radically different speeds. Capriati fast-forwarded through the first set 6–0 in twenty minutes, while Sabatini moved in slow motion for a 6–4 win in forty-three minutes.

In the second set, the speeds reversed. Shaun Stafford reined in Capriati's headlong rush, while Monique Javer faltered, much to the disappointment of the crowd, which had applauded her as a British competitor. Although she held an English passport through her mother, Javer was American on her father's side, resided in Hillsborough, California, and had attended San Diego State for two years. Her game had a Made-in-America label.

With only slight exaggeration, the same might be said of Gabriela Sabatini, who had moved to Miami at the age of twelve to train with Patricio Apey. She owned a home on Key Biscayne and, like a lot of girls on the tour, she spent substantial time in Florida. There were thirty-three American citizens in this year's women's draw and almost as many foreigners who had established a port of convenience in the States.

Stafford served for the second set, only to have Capriati bounce back and win 7–5. Meanwhile, Sabatini had hung a bagel on Javer.

o o o

The fourth day dawned. . . . Actually, it didn't dawn. Morning looked like late evening, and afternoon resembled a winter's night. Mist prevented play until 12:45 P.M., at which point a downpour struck and the courts had to be covered again.

The Monica Seles rumor *du jour* revolved around her brother Zoltan, who had committed her to participate in a special event the week before the Federation Cup. She was said to be receiving a quarter-of-a-million-dollar fee. But who knew whether to trust that figure when more basic information had been erroneous. Early accounts maintained that the special event would take place in Maui, and this had ignited ardent jeremiads about the shortsightedness of a young girl who would skip Wimbledon, then go winging all the way to Hawaii for a meaningless exhibition match. It turned out, however, that the exhibition was in Mahwah, New Jersey, not Maui. Still, the question remained: If Monica was well enough to play when the money was right, would she show up for the Fed Cup and preserve her Olympic eligibility?

At 1:31 P.M. play started on Centre Court, but nowhere else. At 2:02 P.M. play stopped because of rain. At 3:30 P.M. matches recommenced on Centre Court and Court One. Although matches hadn't gotten under way elsewhere, the covers had been peeled off the damp grass, umpires perched in their chairs, and ball boys and girls in green and purple uniforms stood ready to retrieve errant balls. Finally, by 4:30, there was the happy, cork-popping sound of tennis on every court, and when the sun appeared, it seemed that summer had arrived. But then the horizon darkened with a mass of clouds as black as a slate roof. At 5:10 P.M., the slate liquified and play was canceled.

On the return trip to London, the courtesy van smelled of wet wool, damp socks, and ruined shoes, of wilted newsprint, beery breath, and grease from the press dining room's invariable midday meal of beans, sausage, bacon and eggs, and fried bread. A journalist in the back was chatting disconsolately on a cellular phone, contacting his home office in some faraway city where it was summer.

O O O

Donna Faber of Hilton Head Island, South Carolina, had begun her first-round match on Monday morning. During the next few days, she won the first set and held two match balls in the second. But Cathy Caverzasio of Switzerland evened the score, and in a tie-break that transpired during brief dry intervals over two days, Caverzasio squeezed through to the third set. On Friday, Faber finally advanced to the second round with a 6–3, 6–7, 6–2 victory.

Nineteen and looking forward to her twentieth birthday the following week, dark-haired and short, Donna had started playing tennis at the age of seven, coached by her mother, Ofelia.

"She's really good with juniors," Donna said. "She has a good eye and the ability to communicate, and little kids like her." But Donna felt she and her mother had gone as far as they could. "We're so close and we were together all the time. It's easier for another coach to be objective."

Still, Faber admitted it was a difficult adjustment. "You get used to it. But everything has to change."

Now she was working with Billy Stearns in the States and sharing

Ola Malmquist as a road coach with Shaun Stafford and Tami Whitlinger. "I have a lot of technical things to iron out. Like with my footwork. I'm pretty quick. I get to the ball, but sometimes I'm off balance and the shot flies."

She was also learning to travel alone. "I always went places with my mother. Now I'm going to some tournaments by myself. For me it's harder to get going when I'm alone. I need someone to push me"— to practice and to eat a sensible diet. "My favorite snack is cereal. At home I eat Cheerios and Shredded Wheat. Over here my favorite is Weet-a-Bex. A lot of times on the road, you're tired and just eat junk."

The biggest decision of her career had been whether to finish high school and go to Princeton, as her father, uncle, and cousin had done, or turn pro and complete high school by correspondence. She chose the latter course and didn't regret it. "I know with my grades I can go to college later on. I can see myself doing that."

Meanwhile, she didn't delude herself that the circuit was an educational experience. "I like to see things when I can. Sometimes it's frustrating not to see more. But I have to remind myself I'm there to play tennis. People don't realize how much work goes into tennis. I train six or seven hours a day."

She described a time on Hilton Head when she sat in the stands watching Martina Navratilova whip Amanda Coetzer. Behind her were two men. "They didn't recognize me," Donna said, "but they were talking about me and Amanda and saying that girls like us—unseeded players—we were just along for the ride. They didn't think we took the game seriously and they sure didn't take us seriously. That hurt. Whatever they did for a living, I wanted to ask whether they're in the top hundred in the world. I doubt it. I really doubt it."

O O O

Years ago the Competitors' Lounge at Wimbledon had, in theory, been the sacrosanct preserve of players and their guests. But, in practice, it had always been a throbbing hive of hustlers, racquet dealers, clothing reps, agents, tournament directors, assorted groupies, gofers, and camp followers. Now journalists had access to this sanctuary. Flashing a special forty-five-minute permit, I passed the guard at the door and, during yet another rain delay, climbed the stairs to the third floor and stopped at the Prize Money Office, where a woman cheerfully explained her job.

Once a player lost, he or she popped in here to pick up a check. A player's agent or manager could collect prize money, but only with written permission. "Even though we know, for example, that Ion Tiriac is Boris Becker's manager, we have to have it in writing before we'll hand over Becker's money," the woman said.

"What if players want cash?" I asked.

"Then they carry the check to the bank here on the grounds."

"Do you deduct U.K. taxes?"

Indeed she did. Foreigners paid a flat 25 percent on their winnings, but they received a £150 per diem exclusion before British taxes bit into their purse. The Prize Money Office also deducted WTA dues and fines for code violations. Although it sounded complicated, she assured me that "because of computers, we can get a player in and out in thirty or forty seconds. That's a lot different from the old days." She smiled sweetly. "Now I'm afraid I can't say anything else."

"Do you ever get any strange requests?"

The smile never faltered. "Lots, but I'm not allowed to tell you."

O O O

As rain fell in straight lines, like gray pencil strokes on a color field of green, dispirited players and coaches congregated in the buffet of the Competitors' Lounge. Tiburce Darou was leaving England tomorrow and that wasn't soon enough for him. He had hair like a bronze Brillo pad and a body that called to mind a boxer, not a tennis player. His face was seamed with wrinkles and his eyes had a weary cast, as if they had witnessed disappointments other men couldn't imagine. A Rumanian, Tiburce had trained a constellation of French and Italian stars—Noah, Moretton, Benhabiles, Panatta, Ocleppo—and now coached Ronald Agenor, the Haitian Sensation, and a French woman, Isabelle Demongeot.

"I have a girl," he said, "who lost today like a shit, and I told her she play like shit." Catarina Lindqvist of Sweden had decimated Demongeot 6–1, 6–0.

"Men and women . . . " Tiburce shook his head. "It's not the same game. The woman is so emotional. Men can drive away the emotion. The women can't—except the top ones, and that's why they win. Women practice, but the big difference is between practicing and playing. Women practice like top ten—my player practices like that—then she plays like nothing.

"The girls don't have a great condition," Tiburce continued. "Okay, Martina does and she needs it because she has a man's game. When you see the others—Gigi Fernandez, Capriati . . . '' He puffed his cheeks like a blow fish. "They don't have a good physical shape. But in the women's game you don't need to be in great shape. The girls win such easy money for nothing. Between thirteen and one hundred fifty on the computer, there's no difference physically. It's psychological. The woman wants to work, but they don't do it during the match because of the emotional."

As we sat in a booth talking, Tiburce sounded as though he weren't entirely free of the emotional himself. On the tour, he said, "You take many things in your mind. It's too much. It's an artificial life here." He waved his gnarled hands at the crowded room. "The reality is on the court. This relationship isn't normal. You cannot stay with a twenty-year-old girl all the time. It's sick. Sometimes the girls want to play for the coach, and that's bad. The women have to be more professional. Mary Joe Fernandez, she take a coach like she take a T-shirt. She changes every week."

He was shaking his head again. "It's a big show, the women's tour, a bluff. With men, we coaches have a business relationship. With women the business comes after. I have a girlfriend and she can't understand this life. Who can?"

The thing he could least abide was family interference. "I am no Bocuse, so I don't talk cooking. If you're not a tennis player, I say, 'Don't talk tennis, don't coach.' The girl does what she wants with her parents, but I don't want to talk tennis with the father. I tell Jim Pierce, Mary's father, 'You can't put one ball into the court, so don't tell me how to coach.'

"Then I see Stefano Capriati on the court when Tom Gullikson coaches his daughter. How can he do that? Who is he in tennis? Nobody!"

Although his candor was at the expense of his own profession, he
swore that some women needed a psychiatrist, not a coach, and much
of what a coach did at tournaments amounted to no more than baby-
sitting.

"Steffi don't need a coach," he claimed. "She need a sparring
partner and that's it. She need to stay alone and learn. She has to open
up.

"The problem of Seles," he ran on, "I don't know how long she
can play like that. She uses so much of herself, I don't know how long
her body can last. Tennis is a very hard sport for a woman, much harder
than basketball or volleyball. It hurts so much the body. The racquet,"
Tiburce Darou concluded his discourse, "don't give a shit about the
body."

O O O

At quarter of eight that evening, Steffi Graf came on for her second-
round match against Peanut Harper, an American woman of Oriental
descent whose father ran a kung fu academy. It seemed a silly hour to
start playing, especially since Peanut was famous for her slowly moon-
balling opponents and spectators into a stupor. Some players are said
to be as solid as rock, but Peanut was more like rubber. She just kept
bouncing the ball back. Or that is, she normally did. Against Graf she
never had a chance.

As Steffi cycloned through the first set, she seemed to be breathing
fire. But it was a trumpet of condensation that formed every time she
exhaled the cool evening air. She won 6–0, then tore through the second
set, too.

Afterward, the All England Club announced that the backlog of
matches had grown so long it would break 114 years of tradition and
allow play on the middle Sunday.

O O O

Saturday was a first of a different sort—the first dry day of the tournament, the first and only dry day of June. Players and spectators blinked
at the sun in disbelief.

Of Pam Shriver it has been said that she's more than just a tennis player. In fact, she so frequently said it of herself, John Feinstein suggested it should be incorporated into her name—Pam "Not a Tennis Player" Shriver. Smart and sassy, she hailed from Baltimore, Maryland, and still lived there, which was odd in a sport where everybody, it seemed, settled in Florida, Texas, or California. In addition to keeping her close to her roots, Baltimore, Pam believed, had saved her from sun-damaged skin, a common scourge on the tour.

If this weren't enough to set her apart from her peers, Shriver was serious about politics. She had supported Reagan, was honorary chair of Athletes for Bush/Quayle during the 1988 campaign, and had done nothing to discourage speculation that she intended to run for elective office herself someday. Meanwhile, she concentrated on tennis politics, serving for more than seven years on the WTA Board of Directors, twice as vice president.

Pam had also worked as a TV commentator and once kept a year-long journal which was published in book form as *Passing Shots,* a reasonably candid portrait of women's tennis and herself. The diary was especially astute about rapacious parents—some of whom weren't above stealing food from the locker room—and prickly stars like Chris Evert, who, contrary to her Olympian image, was sensitive to every real and illusory slight.

The most touching passages in *Passing Shots* dealt with Shriver's first faint suspicions that she would never achieve her goals. A U.S. Open finalist at sixteen, she had seemed destined to win many Grand Slam titles but had never done as well again. For years she had been stymied short of the top. First, Evert and Navratilova had blocked her path, then a batch of younger girls—Graf, Sabatini, and Seles—had jostled her aside.

Now Pam was approaching her twenty-ninth birthday, which fell on July 4, and viewed herself as in the process of a comeback. Others saw her in the terminal stages of a career which had earned her more than $4 million in prize money and twenty-one Grand Slam doubles titles. The year before, she had had arthroscopic surgery to "correct a loose and unstable shoulder with a torn posterior glinoid labrum"— or so said the Kraft General Foods Media Guide. Since then her results had been mixed and her ranking had drifted into the nether reaches of the computer. For the first time, she hadn't been seeded at Wimbledon, but thanks to an easy draw, she was into the third round against Mary Joe Fernandez, a player more than capable of testing her recovery.

A reporter from the Baltimore *Sun,* Bill Glauber, and I arranged to meet Pam in a one-on-one interview room, an austerely lit cubicle with carpeted walls and a couple of uncomfortable chairs. I preferred to sit on the floor.

Shriver showed up in a pair of cutoff Levi's and a Yonex T-shirt. She had one ice pack on her shoulder and another attached by an Ace bandage to her elbow. She said Don Candy wasn't at Wimbledon, but she intended to call him in the States to discuss strategy for the Fernandez match.

This surprised me. After describing in her journal her anguish at breaking away from Candy and going it alone—Pam confessed she couldn't bear to think of him coaching another girl—why would she ask his advice? Why would a woman of her maturity and competence remain so dependent?

Weeks later, I asked Don Candy if he was coaching Shriver, and he said, "When the dark clouds gather, Pam still acknowledges me. But when the sun shines, well, then sometimes she may not know me." Which only showed how intense and complicated many coach-player relationships continued to be long after they had supposedly ended.

Bill Glauber brought up Pam's rehabilitation program, remarking that she now had more definition in her leg muscles. Almost at once he apologized, uncertain of the appropriateness of his comment. "I hope that doesn't sound sexist."

Pam laughed. "Thanks for noticing my legs."

Time after time I had witnessed this delicate adagio of male reporters and female players. I had danced the dance myself, wondering whether teenagers preferred to be called women, worried that questions I wouldn't hesitate to ask a man might offend a woman. But the reaction was invariably the same. Women on the tour didn't set much stock by feminism or political correctness. As Shriver had written, "Women tennis players call themselves girls. . . . If we go to a party or a function where we have to get all dressed up, we're women, but if we're at the tennis club wearing track suits, we're girls—except when we're bitches, of course.''

Asked about the condition of the courts after a week of rain, Pam said she wasn't in any position to pass judgment. She had played way out in the cow pastures, where the grass, not to mention the atmosphere, bore little resemblance to Centre Court. ''I've never been on the back row before.''

She had also been bumped from posh Dressing Room One to humbler Dressing Room Two. But she insisted it didn't bother her. She made it sound like an adventure to be rubbing elbows with low-ranked girls after years in the rarefied air of the top ten. ''They told me in Beckenham that I'd be in Two. If they hadn't, I might have gone upstairs and had egg on my face. I guess my five doubles titles here don't carry much weight.''

''What's it like,'' I asked, ''out there with all the young girls?''

''It's not young girls,'' she corrected me. ''The young ones are in the top ten and they go to Dressing Room One. It's players my age in Two.''

○ ○ ○

Like Shriver, Mary Joe Fernandez had suffered from injuries. In 1990, she dropped out of the Pan Pacific in Tokyo with tendonitis in her right shoulder. At the Virginia Slims of Florida, she had to withdraw because of a pulled hamstring muscle. In Berlin, a back injury forced her to retire. Then she missed Wimbledon with a torn knee cartilage. But this year she was feeling confident about her chances.

Wearing floral pattern shorts, a T-shirt and earrings, she entered the interview area and kissed Fred Stolle, the former Australian star whose son, Sandon, had won his first-round match.

Once we were alone I asked, ''Who are you hitting with here?''

Mary Joe said Tim Gullikson, Tom's twin brother, was around. He was on the USTA coaching staff, and sometimes she worked with him. But she now traveled with Juan Avendano. ''He knows I want to come to the net, and even though he never came to the net, he knows that's how you win.''

''What happened to Ernesto Ruiz Bry?''

''He was painting,'' she said. ''He had a big exhibition coming up. He wanted to take a break. He was asking permission to take off other weeks for his painting and exhibitions.''

''That's not what Ernesto told me. He said your father didn't like him and decided to get rid of him.''

Mary Joe crossed her long brown legs and wagged her foot back and forth. Her pretty face was as smooth as a pond into which one small pebble had been dropped. There was just the slightest ripple of a reaction. ''No. Dad was disappointed Ernesto wanted to take time off. I had a lot of fun on court with Ernesto. It was a little difficult, though, because he hit with a lot of spin and I'd rather hit with someone who hits flat. I couldn't get grooved on his strokes.''

This not only contradicted Ernesto's version of events, it conflicted with what a few Hispanic players had told me. They too had asked what happened to Ernesto, and Mr. Fernandez explained that when he didn't agree with certain drills and had suggested different ones, Ernesto responded by holding out the racquet and saying, ''You coach her, you show her, if you know how.'' Offended by what he saw as insolence, Mr. Fernandez had dropped Ernesto.

But Mary Joe wouldn't budge. Ernesto had quit because of his art, she insisted. Still, she didn't deny that her father played a major role in her life. She was close to him, to her whole family. ''My foundation has been very good. That's why I stayed in school. I'm different from other girls not because of my education, but because of my family. You see other girls on the tour. I wish they talked more or knew more. They dropped out of school at an early age and all they did was bang tennis balls. This is a short part of your life. What are they going to do later? I don't want to judge people, but it's sad.''

I asked her, as I had Gabriela Sabatini in Rome, whether it was fair to expect a world-class athlete to be a world-class beauty.

''A woman should be feminine, on court and off,'' Mary Joe answered, echoing Gaby. ''I wouldn't like to look muscular or masculine.

Some players think that's what you have to do to win and they don't care if they look masculine. But in my opinion, if you're a woman, you should look like one.''

On the other hand, she acknowledged that she had gone too far in the opposite direction. "But I'm working with weights now. I'm not doing it to get big, just to get stronger. I have no upper-body strength, and I want to guard against arm and shoulder problems. After the French Open I got a postcard. I don't know who it was from. It said, 'You played great, but don't you think you'd do better if you had a few muscles in your arms?' I thought, jeez, even fans know it.''

The conversation swung back to coaches, and Mary Joe Fernandez remarked, "It's very important, the relationship between a coach and a player. You have to have a lot of faith in a coach. But you click with some people and not others.''

I repeated Ernesto's assessment of the problem: Since he couldn't get to know her off court, he couldn't teach her as well as he wanted to.

"Yes, that might have helped," she blandly replied and let it go at that.

o o o

Martina Navratilova's press conference lasted almost as long as her second-round match. Gregarious after an easy win, she said she was delighted to be playing again. "I hit outdoors yesterday, but it was slippery to run, so I hit serves and overheads just to see the sky, which was blue for a change. I felt like I hadn't played in months.''

During Wimbledon, she was working with Billie Jean King as well as Craig Kardon. "I think it says a lot for the kind of person Billie Jean is that she's actually helping me try to break her record here. I don't think you would see too many people doing that.''

As she closed in on Chris Evert's record for tournaments won, Martina said Chris "apparently is not too happy about it—if I can believe what I read in the papers. She's been saying for the last couple of years that I'm very conscious of records, but she's just as conscious, if not more, than I am.''

"Martina, how would you assess Jennifer Capriati's progress in the year since last Wimbledon till now?"

"That's too long to answer," she begged off.

"How about a shorty?" the reporter persisted.

"I don't have enough time for that."

"How about a summation?"

"I really haven't seen her play. I have only played her once and that was a year ago at Hilton Head."

"Are you surprised she's not ranked higher?"

Most players wouldn't have touched the subject. But Martina didn't have it in her to duck the question a fourth time. "No, I'm not surprised. The hype isn't winning her any matches."

○ ○ ○

Flying blind as it inaugurated its first middle Sunday of tennis, the All England Club agreed to sell tickets for a flat price of ten pounds, on a first-come, first-serve basis. It regarded this extra day of play as a bonus for nearby Wimbledon residents, who, having endured the annual influx of spectators, would get a chance to see some matches themselves. But the Club feared a calamitous crush of a hundred thousand fans, the sort of riffraff that had ruined the reputation of British soccer.

Instead, a small crowd streamed down Church Road that damp gray morning. Bobbies with loudspeakers urged them to walk, not run, but there was no stampede, no unruliness. True, they didn't fit the traditional Wimbledon mold. They weren't, as Ilie Nastase once characterized members of the All England Club, "somewhere between sixty-five years old and dead." They didn't congregate in the Debenture Holders' Lounge like an affinity group of lock-jawed ladies and stiff-upper-lip gents. They fizzed with excitement and gave loud voice to their feelings.

When Gabriela Sabatini and Andrea Strnadova of Czechoslovakia came on Centre Court and curtsied to the Royal Box, they were greeted with boisterous cheers. Fans wolf-whistled as the players removed their warm-ups; they counted out loud as the girls exchanged strokes; they created witty sound effects as Sabatini tossed up lobs and Strnadova practiced overheads. They even did the wave, or a fair approximation of it.

"I can't believe it," a British journalist told me. "There's been a total social class breakdown."

On Court One, there were far fewer people—the stands were 80 percent empty—and milky clouds cast wan light over the Pam Shriver–Mary Joe Fernandez match. The one source of color was Jim Levee, who wore a dashing blue and maroon scarf wound around his neck. He backed Mary Joe all the way, and when she broke Shriver's serve in the first game, he shot her the thumbs-up sign, showing on his wrist a fat gold watch, the talisman of the tennis tour. Since players, coaches, and hangers-on spent so much time in warm-ups and sneakers, they had few opportunities for conspicuous display and could proclaim their wealth and status only through dazzling accessories—watches, necklaces, earrings, bracelets, nose studs, rings, and chains.

Nursing that lone service break, Mary Joe was urged on by Juan Avendano, who called, *"Vamos, María!"* and *"Bueno!"* and *"Venga!"* Levee limited himself to "Come on, baby," until she reached triple set point. Then he turned to the Fernandez entourage and broke into Italian. *"Fortissimo!"* he hollered.

After Mary Joe took the first set 6–3, it was Shriver who shouted, "Come on!"—at herself. She broke to a 1–0 lead and sat on her chair during the changeover, spitting between her spread knees.

Jill Genson, Levee's fiancée, a high-cheeked blonde with straight, shoulder-length hair, joined him at courtside, and once Mary Joe had evened the score at 1–1, he clowned for a photographer taking his picture.

Jill nuzzled close to Levee and mugged for the camera. "Put your arm around me," she said. He did so and joked, "For the first time in history I'll put my arm around her. Don't ask me to kiss her."

But then it was back to business. Shriver and Fernandez stayed on serve until 5–4 in Fernandez's favor when Pam fell behind 0–40. In these desperate straits, a club player might double-fault his way to defeat or patty cake the ball into the court and pray for a miracle. But down three match points, Pam attacked. She smacked a service winner, then twice served and volleyed to bring the score to deuce and go on to hold to 5–5.

When Mary Joe got to 6–5, Shriver again served to stay alive. She double-faulted, and Juan Avendano shouted, *"Ahora!"* Now! He wanted Fernandez to break now. Up in the bleachers a baby was crying. "Take him out," Levee muttered. "Put a gag in his mouth." But Mary Joe didn't mind. She got Shriver down 15–40 and finished her off with a crosscourt backhand.

○ ○ ○

Once again Bill Glauber and I met Shriver in the one-on-one interview room, which was lit like an interrogation chamber. Before leaving, a press liaison switched off one of the blinding lights.

"Don't turn off the other one," Pam wisecracked. "I don't trust these guys in the dark."

But she didn't joke about her disappointment at the loss. "I had trouble with her backhand down the line. She also has this crosscourt lob off her backhand. It's tough to cover both. I just couldn't win a big point. If I played well today, I could have made it to the quarterfinals. Throughout the Eighties, I was the one making the big points. Now I'm a little tentative."

Still, she insisted, "I'm making progress. Hopefully I'll keep building on my fitness program, keep strengthening my arm. I may go to the gym tonight."

Meanwhile, she was happy to have played on this unprecedented middle Sunday. The scene on Centre Court, she said, had been "one of the neatest things I've ever witnessed. I was there with Alan Mills, the tournament referee, and he had this big grin on his face and I gave him a high five. Then John Curry [chairman of the All England Club] came along and he said he had goose bumps. It was a real snapshot of grass-roots tennis."

But as for whether Mills and Curry would decide that this should be an annual event, a way to broaden the popularity of the game in Great Britain, Shriver said, "I don't know. It's hard for them to change."

○ ○ ○

Martina Navratilova had played and won on Court Two. She envied the girls on Centre Court. "I wanted to be out there. I told Gaby, 'You are one lucky woman.' "

A journalist popped a question out of the bonzo zone, asking whether she had liked Argentina when she played there ten years ago. Maybe the guy was a plant from the Chamber of Commerce scavenging for a quote to put in tourist brochures. But Martina was her usual blunt self.

"I found it had too many policemen with machine guns walking around. It reminded me of Czechoslovakia in the old days."

"How long ago was that?"

"You just said it. Ten years ago. So maybe it's changed."

Who were her all-time favorite players? someone asked.

"Well, growing up I always looked up to Rod Laver and Billie Jean King and Margaret Court." Martina paused a beat. "She was my role model."

Reporters laughed at the wicked way she twisted the knife, taunting Margaret Court, who had remarked after the previous year's Wimbledon that Martina was a poor role model because of her sexual orientation.

○ ○ ○

Having interviewed her coach, Tiburce Darou, I had a chance a few days later to talk with Isabelle Demongeot. A slender, shapely French-woman with ash-blond hair, Demongeot had the sporty good looks of a beach girl from her hometown of St. Tropez. She had taken up tennis at eleven and hadn't gone on the tour until she was nearly eighteen. "That's late," she said. "But I worked a lot and came through. Sometimes when you start very young, you play too much and get bored or injured."

Lately she herself had suffered injuries and seen her ranking slide. Ranked number 35 as recently as March 1990, she had tumbled to 161 and had to qualify for every tournament. "To come back is difficult," she said. "I would like to play one or two more years. But I don't want to have to keep playing qualies. I've had a lot of troubles in my career and I don't need more. I'm very emotional. Women are more sensitive than men, that's normal. Some players are strong even when they lose. The Americans have a different mentality. But in France once you start losing, they don't care about you."

Like Mary Joe Fernandez, she knew she needed to train harder. "I never worked physically. Tiburce is just getting me to take care and improve my body. You can't just play tennis and hit the ball. I don't know if I can have a body like Martina's." The very idea struck her as droll. "But there's something in between. I would like to be a little bit more muscular and stronger."

Her family was far from the prototypical tennis brood, and Isabelle was grateful for that. Her father manufactured and sold lampshades and lamps. One brother was an architect, the other managed a fashion shop.

"Sometimes the parents on the tour make too much pressure on the girls," she said. "Maybe because they want money. You can see Capriati, she's surrounded by her family. It's too much. You can see the father of Mary Joe even on the practice court. It seems the parents need more the player than the girl needs the parents."

No matter whether a girl traveled alone or with an entourage, Isabelle believed "it's hard to have a normal life and it's difficult to get married. The man cannot wait around for the woman. A man needs to work. He cannot just stand on the side of the court."

I asked if she would like to have a coach for a husband, and she drew back in disbelief. "My feeling is if my husband is my coach, it would make me crazy. Our life is just wait, wait, wait, then play, play, play, then travel, travel. You know, we cannot live like other girls our age. People our age want to go out, go to disco, and we can't always do that."

The constant travel and training were enough to destroy a player's personal life, and Isabelle complained it was impossible to have any privacy. "On the tour if you're sleeping with someone, everybody knows. Always everybody is talking. You go crazy. You're always seeing the same people, yet it's a lonely life."

If she herself had a daughter, would she want her to play professional tennis?

"I don't think so. It's a tough life and it's getting tougher. It's such a business now. Look around." She gestured at the crowded room. "All these agents and wheeler-dealers. It's all about money. At the U.S. Open it's even worse."

Then she caught herself and reconsidered the question. She was twenty-five and had already won more than $400,000 in prize money. She also made a sizable amount playing club matches in France. Even here, where she had lost disappointingly in the first round of singles, she had had better luck at doubles and would take home almost $8,000. One had to think of that. "I suppose I should say it's the life I chose and," Isabelle Demongeot concluded, "it's better than sitting behind a desk all day."

○ ○ ○

James Levee was much in the news and on people's minds. The English simply didn't know what to make of the multimillionaire American. Nobody, including players who benefited from his largesse, could understand why he did it—why he spent half the year following the tour, handing over huge hunks of the money he had inherited when the Annenberg family sold Triangle Publications.

One recipient of his support, Meredith McGrath, told *Tennis Weekly*, "A lot of people wonder what the deal really is. Sometimes I feel weird about it, but Jim never asks for anything."

McGrath accepted his money with the excuse that she wasn't highly ranked and it was expensive for her to travel the circuit. She had made *only* $110,000 in 1990. Many of Levee's favorites—Monica Seles, Mary Joe Fernandez, Conchita Martinez, Arantxa Sanchez Vicario—were wealthy in their own right. Yet according to Levee, Gabriela Sabatini and Jennifer Capriati were the lone players to reject his generosity.

A graduate of the University of Minnesota Law School, with a Ph.D. in comparative literature and a masters in creative writing from Syracuse University, Jim Levee offered a variety of explanations for his obsession with women's tennis. He said he was a frustrated athlete who would have loved to play pro hockey. He said that he contributed to many other causes and charities. He insisted he wasn't a groupie or dilettante; he was a "tennis expert." As Jill Genson, his fiancée, told the *London Independent*, "The way I see it, tennis is Jim's business and, hey, don't presidents of corporations give gifts?"

But there was a personal component that far outweighed any other consideration. Levee acknowledged that the deepest desire of his life was to have a daughter and "the players are daughters to me. Jill and I keep the same schedule; we are at the courts all day between practices and matches. We wanted to get married in Paris but did not have time."

Yet the more Levee explained, the more uneasy people became. There was something over the edge about his enthusiasm and it seemed to be contagious. Jill confided to the *Independent* that she loved the girls almost as much as Jim did. "It's great because I can help them with some of my knowledge and experience. Yesterday, for example, I saw that Arantxa's game was just a tiny bit off and I just *knew* what was wrong. It was her woman's time—even Jim didn't know. And when I spoke to her, it turned out I was right and she couldn't believe it. She said, 'You are unbelievable, Jill.' So you see, all of this gives me some purpose in life as well as Jim.''

O O O

In other pro sports "super fans" have caused problems. Gamblers, con men, convicted criminals, and dubious characters hoping to curry favor have hung around locker rooms, and sometimes they have euchred athletes into illegal deals and troubling endorsements. They have paid for inside information and fixed matches. They have sought legitimacy by association. An Argentinean journalist told me of a recent case that had brushed dangerously close to Gabriela Sabatini.

A gentleman from Buenos Aires began showing up at tennis events, living in the reflected glory of the top-ranked girls. After Gaby won the 1990 U.S. Open, he was part of the group that welcomed her at the airport and formed a motorcade back into Buenos Aires. He was eager to be seen with Sabatini, eager to appear in photographs with her.

Then the man got swept up in a drug-smuggling scandal and was accused of importing cocaine. He defended himself with the alibi that he worked for the U.S. Drug Enforcement Administration. Whatever the truth of the matter, Gaby had experienced a bout of awkward publicity that left her gun-shy. It showed, the Argentinean journalist said, why star players and their families had to be wary of outsiders who might have hidden motives.

O O O

On the second Monday, Sabatini had to survive an unexpectedly tough test against Nathalie Tauziat of France. Wimbledon was supposed to have been the perfect forum for her new, adventurous serve-and-volley style, but for the past week she had played like the old, pensive Gaby still ironing out the mistakes she had made at Roland Garros. She treated grass as though it were red clay, planting herself at the baseline and praying to outlast her opponents.

After squeezing through a tie-break in the first set, Sabatini got a 3–0 lead in the second, then let the fiery French redhead back into the match. Although Gaby finally won 6–3, she looked vulnerable.

o o o

To listen to tennis insiders, the circuit is a cemetery of love affairs and marriages. When writing about the men's tour, I had interviewed a couple who agreed to talk if I granted them anonymity.

The player, an American, had been married and divorced, and now lived with a European woman. Although coping with defeat had once been a problem, the fellow had made peace with that and set realistic goals for himself. The greatest difficulty of traveling the circuit, the couple said, was waiting—for planes, for practice courts, for room service, for tables in restaurants, for a washing machine at a laundromat. The player gave an example of the kind of foul-up that happened all the time. "You arrive in a city after an all-night flight. You want to get out and practice and adjust to local conditions. So you reserve a court and go there and find there's no net or the lights in the arena aren't on or the door's locked. That used to drive me nuts."

"You have to be adaptable," the woman said. "Anybody who's rigid is going to have trouble."

The fellow confessed that he had been inflexible when he was younger and that had wrecked his marriage.

The woman pointed out that competitive pressures spilled over into private life. "If you're having problems in a relationship, traveling on the tour magnifies them. Successful players tend to be selfish and single-minded, and not many women can stand that. It's like any field where men are workaholics."

This year at Wimbledon, I was pleased to bump into this couple and learn that they had married and were living happily in London.

On the women's tour, any number of players traveled with husbands or boyfriends, and dealt each day with the difficulties this couple had described a decade ago. Very few of them had children, however, a fact that reflected the youth of most players and the problems of combining motherhood with a tennis career.

Carling Bassett Seguso, a Canadian who cracked the top ten in the mid–1980s, was married to American doubles specialist Robert Seguso, and they had two children, ages three years old and three months old. Although she played a bit of mixed doubles with her husband, she described herself as "basically retired. I'm really into my kids. I don't have any help and it's incredibly hard, although worth it. I feel I put in enough time on the tour. I left home at eleven."

Lisa Bonder Kreiss was another player with a child. Once ranked as high as number eight, she was now struggling to stay in the top one hundred and had just filed for divorce. By the end of the summer, she would announce her retirement.

That left Laura Arraya Gildemeister as the only full-time player with a baby. After she reached the quarterfinals—she was the lone unseeded woman at Wimbledon to advance that far—we spent an hour chatting in an empty BBC sound studio. Married to, and coached by, Heinz Gildemeister, a former Chilean Davis Cup star, Laura had been born in Argentina but moved to Peru as a child and now lived in Miami. In 1988, at the age of twenty-four, feeling "I was the eternal number thirty-five on the computer," she and Heinz decided to have a baby. It was a boy, whom they named Heinz Andre.

Tall and trim, with sun-streaked hair and a laughing delivery of even the most serious sentences, Laura said, "When they told me I had to have a cesarean, I thought I would never play again. They cut your stomach muscles, you know, and it was hard to get them back. I felt really uncoordinated. I stopped playing for a year and a half. I nursed for a few months. I knew it was good for the baby."

Because she swam a lot during pregnancy, she never entirely lost her muscle tone. Still, she admitted, "I'm not the kind who goes to the gym. I don't work out that much. I practice three hours a day and run for fifteen minutes and do some sprints. A lot of people say if I practiced more I'd do better, but I'm happy with myself. Coming back is more psychological. I'm a happy person and that helped. It's so much mental. If you feel good, you can do it. Maybe it's different for a man or a top-ten woman, but I thought I could get my old game back.''

And indeed she had. She won two matches in her first tournament and was now ranked in the mid-twenties.

"Actually I'm more relaxed these days," Laura said. "What makes it fun is traveling with my husband and son. After the match I have them around. Otherwise I'd just go to the hotel alone. In Paris, when I lost to Linda Harvey-Wild eleven–nine in the third set, I was really down. But then I saw the baby and my mood changed. I realized there are other things in life except tennis.

"I wouldn't be playing at all if I wasn't married. It's hard to have a life or a relationship on the tour. And I wouldn't do it if I couldn't travel with Heinz and Heinz Andre. At the Grand Slam events with men around it's fun, but the rest of the time the girls are alone. Unless you're in the top twenty, where people treat you nice and take care of you, it's very lonely. You feel like such a little thing in people's minds.

"I worry about Heinz Andre when he's not with me. Then when he is there, sometimes on court I wonder what he's doing or what we'll do on a rainy day. It's hard to concentrate. Of course, it helps to have money. We bring a nanny. That means buying four airline tickets and renting two hotel rooms, but I've been fortunate to win enough." As a quarterfinalist she was assured of $50,000 at Wimbledon. Since having the baby, she had won more than $400,000 in prize money.

Laura pointed out that hotels and airline tickets weren't the only expenses a player faced. "A good coach costs at least a thousand dollars a week, plus airfare, food, and hotel. If you travel with him twenty weeks, that can cost thirty thousand dollars. A hitting partner is less—four or five hundred a week—but some of them don't know any more than you do."

In a sense, being married to her coach was a bargain, but it took its toll in other ways. "It's very hard to have a husband who's your coach. Sometimes I tell him I just don't feel like getting my racquet back, I don't feel like hearing him say it to me again. And sometimes when you're having a bad losing streak, you blame it on the person closest to you. That's when you have to be strong and not be a child.

"What's good between Heinz and me is he played on the tour. A lot of fathers never played in their life and they don't understand that sometimes you just choke. They put so much pressure on the young players. They pushed their daughters since they were twelve years old. But it doesn't just happen. There's only one Gaby or Capriati each generation.

"I'm lucky to have a husband who understands when I win or lose. Sometimes during a match when I'm playing bad and he's there, I say, 'Please leave' and that takes the pressure off. I don't have to look at him like he can help. I can concentrate on the match, not him."

Although she didn't minimize the challenges of being a tennis-playing mother, Laura Gildemeister said, "I'm proud to walk into the lounge with my son. I think for sure some girls envy me because I have a baby. Not too many players have the courage to do that."

○ ○ ○

In her fourth-round match, Steffi Graf boomed her serves, she thumped her returns, she blasted her forehands—and when she kept the ball on the court, she hit winners. But plenty of her shots flew wild, and if her opponent, Amy Frazier of Rochester Hills, Michigan, had been a bit steadier with her ground strokes, Steffi might have been in trouble. Of course, Graf's power was part of why Frazier wasn't steadier. In fifty-two minutes Steffi pounded out a 6–2, 6–1 victory.

Afterward, I spoke with Graf's coach, Pavel Slozil, a small sunburnt Czech who plugged away on the men's tour until the mid–1980s. He and his Davis Cup teammate Tomas Smid had won dozens of doubles titles, overshadowing Slozil's uncanny ability to take singles matches from seemingly more talented players. The consensus was that Pavel could have been in the top twenty if he had ironed out the wrinkles in his backhand. As Rod Frawley, a Wimbledon semifinalist, once told me, Slozil cocked his wrist at an angle that allowed his opponent to read the direction of his backhand, and since Pavel couldn't generate much pop on his shots down the line, he almost always hit crosscourt. Such minute flaws sometimes accounted for the entire difference between number eighteen and number one hundred on the computer.

Slozil's fine flaxen hair had thinned and his face was webbed with crow's-feet. If decades in the sun hadn't been enough to age him prematurely, then working with the Graf family would have done it. As one Virginia Slims employee said, "You have to understand Peter Graf's value system. Steffi means more to him than anything in life. Then comes his dog. Then comes Mrs. Graf. Then comes Pavel Slozil."

"It was a comfortable win," Pavel said of today's match, "but I would like to see Steffi stay low and play slice and be more aggressive. She used to be similar in practice and in games. She played the same in every match, no matter the girl against her. Now she's not concentrating so well and there are differences one day to another." As he needn't have added, "Last year she was not so healthy and the family had problems."

He, too, had had his problems, but he wasn't complaining. "If you work at the top in any business, it's tough, it's hard on the nerves. But all around it's a good and enjoyable job. She's a good kid and this is a good chance for me."

Sober and taciturn, Slozil said his approach to coaching depended on communicating by example. "I try to speak more with my tennis than with my mouth. I watch her opponents and adjust my game." Like every coach, except Carlos Kirmayr, who admitted he couldn't impersonate topspin players, Pavel claimed, "I can imitate all the players, except the left-handers. When I was playing, I didn't have such a good backhand. Now I can hit it better, with slice or coming over it. But we try to make it more interesting for Steffi. If you play the same person every day for thirty weeks a year, you get too used to each other's strokes and tactics. So to mix it up we bring in left-handers, top spinners, two-handed backhand players."

Pavel was married and had a daughter, and he conceded that his nomadic job had an impact on his personal life. "My wife is teaching tennis in Austria. Sometimes I need her and she's not around and that's hard. Sometimes she needs me and I am not there either. But in this we are a typical tennis family. Lately she comes to one or two Grand Slam events, usually Paris. Other times she must take care of our daughter, who is in school now. After Wimbledon we go to Spain for a holiday. I'm looking forward to it."

Yet while he coped with most of the demands of a "typical tennis family,'' there were things that his modest career as a player had not prepared him for. He had never had to worry about the press or public relations. Now with Steffi he found himself trapped in a perpetual maelstrom and had to struggle to keep his head clear.

"Sometimes the German press doesn't have a clue," Pavel said. "They don't realize how hard we're working. They're always making up stories about us. I'm learning better how to deal with it.

"Another hard thing is dealing with the high expectations of the public." As a player he had never felt that the eyes of a nation were fixed on him alone. But Steffi had to bear the weight of her father's demands and the unrealistic hopes of fans all around the world. Even when she won she couldn't please everybody.

"They get bored in Germany when Steffi wins too much. So they look for scandal. She wins millions of dollars and wins the Grand Slam and there are people who say she should change me as her coach." He thrust his hands into the pockets of his faded jeans and focused his pale blue eyes on something far beyond my shoulder. "We are just human beings. I am a tennis coach, but I try to teach Steffi that all happiness, all success, doesn't depend on what happens on court. There are other positive results," Pavel said, "besides tennis results."

O O O

By Tuesday, the weather had cleared and the women's draw clarified along with it. Four Hispanic women—Sabatini, Gildemeister, Fernandez, and Sanchez Vicario—were among the eight quarterfinalists, and except for Sabatini's easy dismissal of Laura Gildemeister, the matches were all dramatic paybacks. Steffi Graf, who had been upset in the previous year's semifinal by Zina Garrison, got an early choke hold this year and asphyxiated Garrison 6–1, 6–3. Mary Joe Fernandez, who had been routed by Arantxa Sanchez Vicario at Roland Garros, revenged that defeat with a 6–2, 7–5 win. And Martina Navratilova, who the week before had frostily observed that the hype wasn't winning Jennifer Capriati any matches, found herself . . . Actually, what befell Martina deserved some explanation.

This Centre Court encounter offered the obvious attraction of any battle of opposites. It was age versus youth, the Kid against the Lege.

(Jenny's shorthand for Legend was misinterpreted by the British press as "the Liege," a feudal term of allegiance.) It was offense versus defense. It was Jenny's mainstream marketability versus Martina's image as the gender-bending Dark Lady of tennis.

Having spent much of her career coping with the original American Cutie Pie, Navratilova now had to compete against Chris Evert's clone, realizing all the while that even when she won she would lose. Despite her nine Wimbledon crowns, her eighteen Grand Slam singles titles and thirty-one doubles titles, Martina commanded far less money from sponsors than this fifteen-year-old phenomenon who in her two seasons on the tour had won one minor tournament in Puerto Rico. While at the age of thirteen, before she had won a match, Jenny had been fawned over by corporate sponsors, Navratilova, arguably the best woman player of all time, was in the insulting position of having endorsement deals only for Yonex racquets, Avia shoes, and Thorlo socks. She didn't even have a clothing contract. That hurt, and Martina wasn't reluctant to say so.

She also wasn't reluctant to roast the adolescent stars who had started to eclipse her. She observed about the mysteriously absent Seles, "Monica is fragile. She's not built as well as other players, so she's handicapped in some ways. And she's defaulted the last couple of years more times than I have in my career."

Concerning Capriati, Martina told *Tennis Week,* "She's not a happy camper. She was burned out last year at Wimbledon. I don't see her enjoying herself as much as she should." How could she when she was doing "all those things for money? I heard she took off three days to shoot a commercial and they had her swimming in a cold pool. I would never do that. The father is going in one direction and the mother in another and Jennifer is stuck in the middle."

Stung by these and similar barbs from critics who accused him of exploiting his daughter, Stefano Capriati had decided to skip the grass-court tournaments leading up to Wimbledon and take Jennifer home to Saddlebrook, Florida, where she trained on artificial grass, concentrating on her footwork and physical conditioning. Now trimmer and more mobile, she had displayed her stamina and emotional resilience in a couple of three-set matches.

Against Navratilova, Jennifer looked undaunted by the occasion. With supreme insouciance she spooned a drop shot over the net to lead 4–3 in the first set. Then benefiting from Martina's double faults, she broke to 5–3. Although Capriati was promptly broken in return, Martina's service motion was a sad, constricted shadow of its former full-bodied puissance. Teeing off like a golfer with her two-handed backhand, Capriati clobbered her returns, taking the set 6–4.

When Navratilova broke to 1–0, then staved off three ad points in Jenny's favor to go up 2–0, it seemed she had assumed the sternly maternal task of curbing this impudent pup of her hubris. It was okay for the kid to kick up her heels and win a set, but Martina didn't want her getting bigger ideas. Four times she had break point to take a commanding 4–1 lead, but four times Capriati clawed back to deuce. When Jennifer held to 2–3, Martina protested bitterly that the ball had been out. She had lost more than a point and a golden opportunity; a cloudburst struck at that moment, canceling play and leaving Navratilova with a precarious grip on the match.

Patrice Dominguez, former French ace and current analyst for *L'Equipe,* felt Martina was finished. If the match had continued, Dominguez thought Navratilova could have played through her nervousness. But now with a night of stewing and fretting ahead of her . . . Dominguez pursed his lips and blew the Gallic equivalent of a raspberry. *"Elle est foutue."*

Dominguez echoed comments that reverberated throughout the press room that evening—remarks that had long haunted Navratilova. For years, tennis insiders had pegged Martina as an extraordinary athlete betrayed by a fragile psyche. As some described it, the situation approached tragic dimensions; she was a larger-than-life hero with a flaw no less fatal than Achilles' heel.

Naturally, Navratilova didn't view herself in these terms. She maintained that although she was occasionally beleaguered by bubbles in the blood during big matches, she was no more nervous than other players. How could anyone call her a choker when she had reached the finals of thirty Grand Slam singles events and won eighteen of them? By comparison, the supposedly unmeltable Ice Maiden, Chris Evert, had lost sixteen out of thirty-four Grand Slam finals.

In Martina's opinion, the problem—if, indeed, there was one—had everything to do with the fact that she wasn't afraid to discuss the deep modulations of her emotions. Far from a flaw, this could be construed as an admirable sign of strength.

It seemed not to have occurred to Martina that a tragic flaw in the truest sense was the outgrowth of a strength. The same qualities of intelligence and honesty that so often carried her to victory could lead to defeat.

As former player and clinical psychologist Julie Anthony explained, the brightest athletes were in danger of "intellectualizing." Instead of acting under pressure, they had a tendency to think. Where a person of more limited intellect might consider one scenario and pursue it with single-minded determination, a player of Martina's genius could visualize the possibility of failure just as clearly as success, and what she could imagine might happen.

A player who couldn't conceive of losing, Julie Anthony said, might win for a while on sheer conviction. But eventually everybody had a bad day, and those who never entertained the idea of defeat had a hard time handling it. That was what had happened to Steffi Graf. Suddenly, her aura of invincibility was shattered, and she didn't know how to regain it. In contrast, players like Billie Jean King, Chris Evert, and Martina had gone through the process of learning that they could lose, then learning how to cope with the panic that that prospect engendered. A great champion could be a great choker at times, but she had the ability to bounce back.

The next day, Martina held to 4–2, then hounded Capriati into a 0–40 disadvantage. One more point and Navratilova would have served for the set. But Jenny refused to fold. She erased all three break points and squeaked through to 3–4.

On Martina's serve, Capriati ripped a forehand to 15–15. Navratilova's next serve was a fault, and she declined to come in behind her second ball. Jennifer made her pay for that moment of timidity. Fifteen–thirty. Again Martina stayed back on her second serve but got to 30–30. After faulting on her first serve again, Martina swooped in behind her second and muffed a forehand volley. Break point to Capriati.

Finally Navratilova put in a first serve but blew an identical forehand volley, losing the game and her lead.

Rushing her returns and pushing her approaches long, Martina fell behind 4–5, and as she served to stay alive in the match, she started to dredge in deep breaths and smiled between points. Billie Jean King believed that smiling relaxed a player, and so her prize part-time pupil wore a rictus-like grin and managed to hold.

At 5–5, Jennifer jumped out to 40–15, then played several loose shots, and suddenly it was Martina's advantage, her eighth break point in ten games. Navratilova pounced on a short ball, rifled it to Capriati's backhand, and rushed the net—only to have her neck nearly wrenched out of its socket as Jennifer blooped a perfect lob. Martina flashed her rictus-like grin and applauded, clapping her hand against her racquet. For the second time she had to serve to stay in the match.

During the changeover, BBC's cameras moved in for a close-up of Martina. Her face was a death mask on which every sign of anguish was indelibly etched. When she forced herself to smile, the result was ghastly. She might have been going to the gallows as she went out to serve.

Capriati could sense this, could see it. She smacked a forehand winner. Love–fifteen. Navratilova double-faulted and screamed, "What?" Love–thirty. Martina reached 15–30, but then Jennifer blasted a service return to 15–40. Double match point. Somehow Martina steadied herself with two service winners but got passed and faced her third match point. She tossed up the ball and hit a fault. She tossed up a second ball and . . . and . . . and pushed it into the net.

As Dennis Van der Meer mentioned in Paris, Navratilova had double-faulted four times in the past year on match point. But none of those calamities could compare with this one. Her dream of a tenth Wimbledon title had been dashed by a fifteen-year-old girl. For the first time in a decade, she hadn't made it to the final.

O O O

By the time she arrived for her press conference, Martina had composed herself and was smiling—a real smile.

"When I didn't get my first serve in," she said, "I was on my heels. That certainly didn't help on my second serve. I was so afraid of her return, I ended up double-faulting, which was a total sin. But that's the way it goes."

"Were you surprised she stayed in so close on your second serve?"

"It was so short, she had to move in so she could get it on the first bounce."

"How much does she seem like Chris?" someone shouted.

"Jennifer hits the ball much harder, but then again it's the equipment and the way the kids are taught today. I think if Chris was brought up today, she'd hit the ball harder as well. But Capriati's bigger, stronger. The ball has more weight on it. She gets free points off her serve, which Chris never got."

"Do you think Gabriela will beat Jennifer?"

"Yes, probably. I don't think Gaby will give her that many targets, the way I did. She's going to make her play more balls."

Speaking of her own plans, Martina wavered between pugnacity and poignancy. "I'm not hanging it up. I still feel that I have some really good tennis in me." But she added, "I just don't know how much of the heart is left."

○ ○ ○

Bouncy, bubbling, Jennifer Capriati had everything left—heart, body, soul, and a slew of giggles. Now that *The National,* John Feinstein's newspaper, had folded, there was no one here to count the "you knows," but Jennifer had plenty of those left, too.

"I was never nervous," she said. "I had nothing to lose. She had everything to lose. I just decided to go for it."

Asked whether she didn't feel a wee bit sorry for Navratilova, Jennifer said no way. "She had her day."

Now it was Capriati's. At fifteen years and ninety-six days, she was the youngest semifinalist in Wimbledon history, and this provoked what passed for serious reflection. As her mother, Denise, contemplated the possibility of Jenny's winning the title, she concluded, "Part of me doesn't want this to happen yet."

In the considered opinion of experts, the danger, as always, was *burnout,* a term that had come to cover every depredation of pro tennis from shin splints to schizophrenia. Tracy Austin, the original Singed Princess of Centre Court, was trotted out by the BBC and asked to describe her sorry experience.

"I was injured," Austin said, "and the WTA was pressuring me on the phone, saying, 'When are you going to come back? When are you going to come back?' "

She had rushed her recovery and ruined her health. But times had changed, she said, and so had the WTA. Austin also emphasized a major difference between Jennifer and herself. "When I first played Wimbledon, I was four feet eleven and weighed eighty-nine pounds." Capriati was already much bigger than that.

What had she concluded from all this? the BBC commentator asked.

"I learned you should listen to your body."

Long past the age where I remembered what teenagers heard from their bodies, I spoke to a highly placed executive on the Kraft General Foods World Tour, who agreed to talk as long as I didn't quote him by name. "I suppose your book will be all about lesbianism," he said.

I assured him it wouldn't, but since he had brought the subject up, I wondered whether Judy Nelson's suit or the gossip about gay girls had any impact on sponsors?

The fellow said no. Fans had digested the news about Martina's bisexuality and still loved her. As for rumors about other girls, they were just that—hearsay. "Lesbianism may have cost Martina some contracts and money," he said, "but it hasn't jeopardized our sponsorship. Unless it was revealed that Steffi, Monica, Gaby, Mary Joe, and Arantxa were all gay, there's no problem for us."

What about the youth of the players? Did he regard it as a factor in the frequency of injuries and emotional troubles?

The fellow waved off the question. He didn't view that as any great difficulty. The thorniest problem on his plate was Monica Seles. "The whole situation has been handled horribly."

"By whom? Monica? Wimbledon? The WTA?"

"Monica. She should have sat down with the press and said, 'I'm sorry. I have such and such an injury and I can't play Wimbledon.' Even if it was a lie, it would stop all this insane speculation."

"Why don't you stop the speculation?" I asked. "Why doesn't the Kraft General Foods World Tour suspend her unless she offers an explanation?"

"Come on, she's a star. Nobody tells her what to do. There's no way of controlling a tennis star and there's no one outside the Seles camp who knows her well enough to know what's on her mind. She calls all the shots. She and her brother, Zoltan. They just don't know much about public relations. Sometimes they're right and what they do works. But this time they're wrong."

Wrong in what sense? Whatever else could be said about her withdrawal, it had "worked" for Monica. By not showing up, by refusing to let her agents deny even the most implausible rumors, she had insured that people would be gossiping about her for months. Like a black hole in space, her absence exerted greater pulling power than the presence of other players.

"Yeah, probably she'll find a way to make money out of this," the man admitted. "That's the thing about stars. Whatever they do, they sell tickets. That's why tournaments will do anything to make a top girl feel welcome—send a limo to the airport, put a car and driver at her disposal, comp her coach, her family, her boyfriend or her girlfriend, arrange promotional fees."

"What do the other players think about that?"

"If they're smart, they'll realize what a Graf or a Seles or a Sabatini means to tennis. They're the ones that make things happen. They generate the media attention and money that pays all the other girls' bills. So they shouldn't object when the stars get preferential treatment—even though," the Kraft General Foods executive added, "it is kind of ironic because all the advantages go to players who really don't need them and the bulk of the money goes to girls who already have millions."

ооо

For the two American women remaining in the draw, the Fourth of July was no celebration. In the first semifinal, Steffi Graf crushed Mary Joe Fernandez 6–2, 6–4. In the second, just as Martina Navratilova had predicted, Gabriela Sabatini forced Jennifer Capriati to hit a lot of balls. Occasionally Gaby rushed the net, but it was her ground strokes that allowed her to take risks. Under pressure, she knew she could always retreat to the baseline and outsteady Jennifer.

At 4–4, Gaby gained the upper hand by chasing Capriati from corner to corner, then gliding in for dink volleys. Leading 5–4, Sabatini survived a double fault and a couple of break points to win the first set 6–4.

The second set was a replica of the first. Gaby zoomed to a 4–1 lead. Capriati rebounded to 3–5, saved three match balls to 4–5, and staved off yet another as Sabatini dived for a backhand volley, missed it, and did a gymnast's roll. But on the fifth match ball, Gaby switched from topspin to a backhand slice that put her into the final against Graf.

Afterward, Capriati conceded, "She was dictating the points, moving me left to right."

When someone asked what separated the top players from the rest of the pack, she stuck up for herself but must have made her English teacher at Palmer Academy wince. "It's not like them top three are dominating. But I guess they're mentally tough."

After she left, Tom Gullikson, her USTA coach, lingered in the interview room talking to reporters. "Jenny has the game to break out of the pack," he said, "and be number one. She's got that competitive spirit. She's really macho."

"What went through your mind yesterday when Jenny hit that lob to save a break point against Martina?"

He laughed. "What went through my mind was, 'Jenny, don't put yourself in such a spot that you have to hit that kind of shot.' "

"How much credit should the USTA take for the success of American players?"

Gullikson was suitably modest. "The players win the matches. Coaches get too much credit and too much blame." But he added, "I think we deserve credit for an assist."

Mention of the USTA prompted a journalist to ask how the Capriatis could justify accepting free coaching.

"Why should the USTA penalize her because she's talented and young and marketable?" Gully snapped. "She's been great for U.S. tennis. Why punish her just because she has endorsement contracts? She still needs a coach."

Fine, then let her pay for one—that appeared to be the press's position.

OOO

On Friday, the field courts were given over to mixed-doubles teams and junior boys and girls. On Court Three, Pam Nelson, the USA's second-ranked junior, played a Korean for the right to advance to the semifinals. A high school student from California, Pam had celebrated her sixteenth birthday this week. A baseball cap held her long straight hair in place, and its bill shaded her freckled cheeks. The shape of her face and body suggested no more than a vague outline of what she might look like as a woman. Everything about her was still half-formed—everything, that is, except her tennis.

On a courtside bench next to me, Scott McCain studied Pam Nelson's every move and whispered to a tan, compact young woman. McCain had competed on the men's tour in the early Eighties. Now he coached at the University of California in Berkeley and helped train Pam. The woman beside him was Patty Fendick, a two-time NCAA champion at Stanford University and currently ranked in the mid-thirties on the Virginia Slims computer.

McCain wanted Patty to take a long look at Pam Nelson, then discuss with him and the Nelson family what Pam should do next. In the accelerated half-life of tennis, the time was drawing near when a decision had to be made. While most girls Pam's age were debating whether to sign up for French or Driver's Ed in the fall, she and her family had to make a choice that would affect the rest of her career. A blunder now could cost a hundred thousand dollars or more and set back her ambitions for years to come.

The question, Scott McCain explained, was whether Pam should turn pro this summer. Or should she stay in school, schedule her practices around her classes, and play just a few tournaments to test herself and sharpen her skills?

McCain, who like Patty Fendick was a college graduate, saw value in "letting a girl have a normal childhood, doing the normal things—going to class, being with friends, going out on dates." As was the case with so many players and coaches, he and Fendick waxed wistfully

Pam in Moscow.

Steffi, her father (above), *her coach* (above right).

The Seles family.

Andrea at home.

Conchita triumphant.

Mary Joe triumphant.

Zina and Willard Jackson.

Arantxa and ex-coach, Juan Nunez.

Martina.

eloquent on the subject. By definition, the tour was not a normal life; everyone agreed on that. Even Jimmy Connors, who heaved himself body and soul into the sport, said he wouldn't want his kids to play pro tennis because "it wasn't a normal life." One had the impression that players, especially the women, viewed their time on the circuit as a kind of purgatory, a period of painful sacrifice during which they satisfied their parents, supported the family, stockpiled cash, and proved themselves worthy of enjoying what other people took for granted—"a normal life."

The underlying issue was seldom addressed. Few people wasted their breath arguing whether the structure of the tour or the schedule of tournaments should be arranged in a more sensible fashion. Even fewer pointed out that just because a kid *could* compete at a pro level didn't mean she *should* do it. The lure of money and the illusion of glamour generally proved irresistible to parents and children alike.

Patty Fendick had been a rare exception. She trained at Nick Bolletieri's academy, began playing pro events as a teenager, and was soon ranked in the top one hundred. "Physically, I was ready for the tour," Patty told me. "Emotionally, I wasn't ready. My mother knew it and said, 'Patty, you don't have to turn pro.' " Instead, she had enrolled at Stanford and felt that that had been the right decision.

Seizing on the distinction Patty made between physical and emotional readiness, McCain said that that cut to the heart of Pam Nelson's dilemma. Whatever her emotional maturity, as a high school sophomore she was already physically capable of competing as the number-one player on a top-flight college tennis team. If she didn't turn pro, what was she supposed to do for the next two years? How could she put her game into a deep freeze and preserve her skills? If she didn't keep working, she risked slipping backward. Yet if she did go on improving, by the time she was in college she wouldn't have any worthwhile competition.

As McCain also stressed, you couldn't exclude financial considerations. Most teenagers playing a sport received free coaching, equipment, clothing, and transportation through their schools or clubs. But in tennis, parents had to pay for almost everything. Scott and Patty estimated that it cost a minimum of twenty thousand dollars a year to train a top junior—and that figure could rise exponentially depending on the coach, the training site, and the player's traveling expenses. Sometimes turning pro wasn't a matter of making money but of saving it. Although it might take more than thirty thousand dollars annually to support a pro on the tour, there was at least the chance of winning a few bucks and breaking even or better.

"Pam's definitely got potential," Patty agreed with Scott. "I saw her six months ago and her game was completely different. But it's a big leap to the pros. She isn't going to get any cheap points like she's getting today. She isn't going to play girls who can't return her serve. And there's the mental part, the grind of being on the tour. Sure, it's great if you're Jennifer Capriati and you're making millions and you can afford to bring along your whole family and your entourage. But otherwise you're alone and lots of weeks you're in a town like Birmingham and all you're doing is trying to cope with the weather, trying to find a practice court, trying to find somebody to hit with. A lot of girls aren't mature enough to deal with what they're going to meet out there."

Part of what Patty had had to deal with almost killed her. The year before at the Lipton International Players Championship in Key Biscayne, Florida, her knee locked during a match, and she forfeited and flew home to California. There she discovered that a blood clot had developed. After four days it moved to her lung and nearly suffocated her. Doctors succeeded in clearing her lung just in time.

Patty named a number of highly ranked juniors who had turned pro early and disappeared. In her opinion, it was absurd how young some girls were when they set out on the circuit, and she questioned whether they had been free to choose for themselves. Given the enormous payoffs involved, she suspected that parents pushed their kids. And who knew what happened to their prize money? What assurance did these teenagers have that there'd be anything left when they retired? What would girls without an education fall back on when they stopped playing?

In the end, Patty Fendick and Scott McCain felt that Pam Nelson should stay in school. "Why not take a little more time," McCain said, "to raise her game to that next level? It's the hardest jump to make."

o o o

As I entered the All England Club the day of the women's final, I saw
an Arab woman with a chador held in place by a Wimbledon headband.
Her outfit seemed less an example of cultural incongruity than a sensible
adaptation to circumstances. After weeks of raw, wet weather, the sun
now shone with such fierceness that people complained about the heat.
The temperature was ninety-five degrees. Although Sabatini had won
their last five meetings, beating Steffi on clay, on indoor carpets, and
on hard courts, Graf led the head-to-head competition twenty matches
to nine and was playing her fourth Wimbledon final. She knew what
she needed to do against Gaby. "I have to attack. I have to go out there
and go for my shots. I have to attack her second serve. On grass it kicks
up, and I have to take advantage of that."

After four raggedly played games, Graf got down to her plan, slicing
a backhand return deep into the corner and bolting to the net. With an
angled volley, she broke to 3–2 and made that advantage stand up for
a 6–4 win. It was the first set Sabatini had dropped at this year's
Wimbledon.

When Steffi started off the second set by breaking Gaby, it looked
as though this might be the sort of summary execution that used to be
Graf's specialty. Thus far she had missed only five first serves. But
then Sabatini got a second ball, chipped it and charged. A moment later,
Graf double-faulted, and the score was one game apiece.

There was another exchange of breaks before Sabatini held to 3–2
and kept applying the pressure. She walloped a deep approach shot,
hurrying Steffi into an error. She whacked a winning return. She hounded
Graf into a wild forehand and barreled in behind a return of serve to
go ahead 4–2. This was the Sabatini that fans had been waiting for—
Gaby unbound, the graceful net-rusher, the fluid volleyer. Why she
hadn't played that way in the first set, even she couldn't say, but she
took control· of the second 6–3.

With each girl determined to take the net before the other had a
chance, the third set unleashed an exciting, if error-filled, fusillade of
shots. Steffi relished playing at a withering pace as long as she was the

one imposing the rhythm, but when Sabatini wouldn't let her get grooved, Graf's percentage of first serves fell and her passing shots might as well have been sprayed from a hose.

While she forced Steffi into mistakes with her bruising returns, Sabatini wasn't serving especially well herself. She simply spun the ball into play, taking everything off it except the Slazenger label. Still, she held to four games all.

Well aware that after every missed first serve Sabatini would come skating in after the second, Graf tried to keep the ball deep, but double-faulted to 15–30. Then at 15–40 she hit a shaky first ball that landed miles long. Nervously tossing up the second ball, she committed another double fault, and Gaby was a game away from the title.

Sabatini's first serve at 5–4 was, in fact, a second serve, a hyp-notically slow spinner that curved over the net, kissed the grass, and bounced high, begging to be buried. Graf smacked it wide. But on the next point, seeing another powder puff float toward her, Graf timed her swing and cracked it for a winner. Fifteen all. She rushed the net for 15–30. Sabatini gave her an easy approach to put away for 15–40, then shanked a backhand into the doubles alley.

Having dropped serve by playing like a pussycat, Gaby turned back into a tigress and scratched her way to a break point. Flustered, Steffi forced herself to go on the offensive, but stroked the ball into the tape. For the second time, Sabatini was serving for the title.

Tennis commentator Mary Carillo has said of Gaby, ''Her second serve is such a duck that when it hits the court, it quacks.'' That was the sound—the quacking death knell—that echoed through the All England Club as Sabatini sailed wounded duck after duck across the net and watched them all fly back in her face. What she needed were a few flat, penetrating first serves. But she continued to spin in her second— and Graf punished her for it.

Still, at 30–30, Gaby had a chance to reach match point. With both girls at the net, Graf dug up a dribbler, flicking the ball at Sabatini shoulder-high. All she had to do was ice it. Instead, she pushed a volley into mid-court without any pace; Steffi ran it down and hit a winner. That brought another break point for Steffi, who converted it with a forehand down the line.

After Sabatini squandered her second chance at the crown, Steffi held to 7–6 and stabbed a finger into the air. One more game and the title was hers.

If ever there was a time for Gaby to get some stick on the ball, it was now. Or she might have stolen a couple of points by swooping in behind her mesmerizingly slow serves. But she stayed back, releasing more disheveled ducks, which Steffi gunned down for an 8–6 win.

The only statistic more remarkable than the match's thirteen service breaks was the fact that neither player had served and volleyed even once. Nobody could remember the last time that had happened in a Wimbledon final.

A decade ago, the press conference room at the All England Club was a cramped cubbyhole at the bottom of a stairwell as steep as a coal chute. One of the smallest on the circuit, it could accommodate no more than a few dozen reporters. Now it had been expanded and could handle more than a hundred. Still, I had to hurry if I hoped to squeeze in.

I wound up sitting beside a lady from the disintegrating Soviet Union who asked if I needed information on Russian players. When I declined with gratitude, she passed me a dog-eared piece on Leila Meskhi. The title, she told me, transliterating the Cyrillic alphabet, was "Georgia on My Mind."

"Fifty dollars," she said.

"Thanks, but I really can't use it."

"Okay, twenty-five dollars."

"No thanks."

"Okay, make an offer. Pay me in pounds if you like."

Graf's entrance cut short the lady's sales pitch. We all fell to copying down Steffi's comments. "The first Wimbledon title is still the best," she said. "But it meant a lot to me to win today, especially coming back twice. Every time she served for the match, I played better. People have been writing me off. To win the match the way I did gives me much pleasure."

This being England, no interview was complete without a question about the royal family. Journalists from other nations groaned as a correspondent—perhaps from Burke's *Peerage*—asked if Steffi had been aware of Princess Diana's presence. And was it true that she had volunteered to coach young Prince William?

Graf answered affirmatively on both counts. Then she said that as thrilling as the match had been and as pleased as she was to win her first Grand Slam title since the 1990 Australian Open, "The tennis today was not of the highest standard."

○ ○ ○

When Sabatini showed up, her scrubbed face smiling, she took polite exception to Steffi's opinion. "I think the tennis was a good quality. She came to net more than she normally does. She returned very well, and I had a bit of bad luck at the end."

Asked about her punchless serving at 5–4 and again at 6–5, Gaby said, "I served the same way the whole match." Indeed she had, and that was the trouble. Still, she declared, "I think I'm satisfied."

○ ○ ○

Andrea Jaeger was working at Wimbledon for HBO. Having dropped off the circuit in 1985, she had played no more than a handful of matches since then, none after 1987. Despite six shoulder operations (she was scheduled for a seventh), she looked happier at twenty-six than she had during her days as a teenage sensation with explosive ground strokes, a foul temper, and a mouthful of braces. Instead of the two waist-length ponytails that had been her trademark, she wore her hair short and curly.

"Gaby's sure taking it well," she told me. "But maybe that's why she lost. She was just happy to be in the final."

Andrea had had experience of defeat in Grand Slam finals. At the age of seventeen, she lost the French Open to Martina Navratilova. The next year she lost the Wimbledon final, again to Martina. But since it was assumed that Jaeger was at the start of a long and illustrious career, these losses weren't viewed as serious setbacks. Tennis writers hailed her as the most gifted athlete to hit the circuit since Navratilova; they claimed she had the best touch of any player since John McEnroe. Her tenacity, her devotion to the sport—she slept in her tennis socks—were said to be without equal. Coached by her father, Roland, a former boxer, bricklayer, and barkeeper, she approached every match with a Spartan's mentality; her motto was win or die.

Before she crashed and burned, she did a bit of both. After turning pro at fourteen, she won 285 matches and $1.5 million, and was number two in the world by the time she was sixteen. But in the process something inside her died. Some say she lost her will. Some say she lost her mind. Some say she simply got sick of having Roland in her face. Whatever the truth—it could have been a combination of all these factors—she was finished before she was twenty.

During a peripatetic interview—we roved from the press conference room to a fax machine to a BBC sound studio to the grounds around the field courts—Andrea attributed all her troubles to injuries. In contrast to her behavior during her last days on the tour, she wasn't belligerent or shelled-in. She responded to every question, never declined to discuss countervailing theories of what caused her to crater, but insisted it boiled down to pain—pain in her legs, in her pelvis, and, above all, in her shoulder.

She was leaving London tomorrow, flying back to the States for that seventh operation. The first six, she said, had dealt "with the symptoms. Maybe this time they can fix it." Meanwhile, she had to get through the flight, and since she suffered allergic reactions to many prescription painkillers, she would have to make do with Advil.

"I didn't start tennis too early," she swore. "I didn't push myself too hard. I didn't burn out or have a mental breakdown. I was hurt. It was just something that happened. I just think my injuries were part of pro sports, and it was really disappointing not to have people focus on that fact. Everybody was more interested in the rumor that a young tennis star had flipped out. But why shouldn't they believe me?"

They didn't believe her because they had witnessed bizarre behavior that hadn't appeared to be injury-related. Even as a junior, Andrea had been eerily self-absorbed and easily annoyed. She taunted less-talented opponents, mugged and made faces during matches, berated linesmen, and once nearly decapitated a bird that had had the temerity to land on a fence on her court. Simultaneously combative and sensitive, she loved to win, yet hated it when players didn't love her for beating them. She especially detested it when they fought back and beat her.

After the 1982 French Open final, she walked off court with Roland chewing at her ear every step of the way to her press conference. Then as her father lurked nearby like a ventriloquist controlling his dummy, Andrea accused Martina Navratilova of beating her with illegal coaching from Renee Richards and Nancy Lieberman. Jaeger claimed they had been in the stands shouting and sending signals. "Mentally-wise, I'm stronger than Martina, and that's how you come back against her. But I can't keep concentration when it's three against one."

Martina replied, "If she's getting this stuff from her father, Mr. Jaeger is a louse."

The consensus was that Andrea had, indeed, gotten this and a lot of other lousy stuff from Roland.

In 1984, *Sports Illustrated* published a story on the Jaegers that read like a script for the WTA's Most Disturbing Home Videos. An anonymous player commented, "Her father is driving her nuts. He never lets up, and she's sick of it." Owen Davidson, who had helped coach Andrea, said, "There are real problems there. I got out when I realized the father wasn't playing with a full deck."

Even Andrea's mother, Ilse, thought Roland had gone off the rails when he kept carping at his daughter for months after her Wimbledon loss to Navratilova. "That's sick," Mrs. Jaeger snapped. "You never give her any credit. Do you know how hard it is to get to a Wimbledon final?"

Naturally, he didn't. Roland was no better than a late-blooming club player, a frustrated hacker who foisted his aspirations off onto his daughter. "I was always his little boy," Andrea complained.

As the pressure of satisfying Roland's expectations began to wear Andrea down, she started strolling through matches like a sleepwalker. At the slightest provocation, she'd tank and head for the shower, offering the lame excuse that she wasn't feeling well. Pressed by journalists to explain what had happened in one sub-par performance, she barked, "Did you miss part of it? I lost." During a spate of lackluster play at the Virginia Slims Championships, she glared at the crowd and demanded, "Why is everybody always watching me?"

Eccentric as her conduct became, Andrea's emotional troubles couldn't be separated from her physical problems. She claimed the WTA

pressured her to play despite her injuries. Others maintained it was
Roland who made her go on when she should have been recuperating.
Don Candy, Pam Shriver's former coach, says of Jaeger, "She played
at times when she had no business being out there. Was it by choice?
Well, I'll be silent on that and let you draw your own conclusion. I
don't believe an injury just comes. If you persist in playing with an
injury, you'll get burned out. Hell, you can burn a horse out if you hit
him with a whip and keep him in one race after another. Well, there
are some good women players who are getting hit with the whip, and
they keep going and burn out."

All Andrea would say about this matter was, "My life in tennis is
something I'd never want to change. Sure, I wouldn't want to be injured.
But I don't regret the tennis. Maybe I was lucky to be forced to quit.
A lot of players would have stopped long ago, but they don't know
what to do afterward."

She lived in Aspen, Colorado, and ran a foundation for children.
She proudly passed out her card. Under the logo, KID'S STUFF FOUN-
DATION, was a globe surrounded by frolicking youngsters. "We give
underprivileged kids an opportunity to learn. I've started a free educational newspaper. Some kids couldn't afford it if it wasn't free."

She was considering the possibility of opening a center where chil-
dren could gather to discuss environmental and cultural issues. Because
Aspen wasn't cost efficient, she said she might locate the center in
Chicago or somewhere in California.

Since she was neither married nor a mother, it seemed surprising
that she was so interested in children. But she explained, "When I was
on the tour, the people I was closest to in age were ball girls and boys.
I always went to hospitals to visit kids. It made a difference to the kids
and it made me feel better. My own health problems let me relate to
those sick kids."

She said she also empathized with underprivileged children because
"I know what it's like to be shunned. When I was little, a lot of kids
felt uncomfortable around me, felt I was a weirdo. So I know it's
important for kids to have self-esteem, and I want to help."

"Do the young girls on the tour ever come to you for advice?"

"I don't think they even know me," she said. "I've never sat down with Monica or Jennifer. Everyone's got a trainer, or they're paranoid about people getting to them. The girls are surrounded now.''

After she quit tennis, Andrea said, ''The biggest adjustment was how I looked at my year. My life used to be divided up by where I was playing. It was always you went to the U.S. Open, then you went back to school. I was never a limo person. But after living in hotels for so many years, I've never learned to make a bed and because I lived on room service, I'm not such a hot cook.''

There had been rumors that Jaeger's troubles stemmed in part from a lesbian relationship that had been forced upon her by an older player, or had been rejected by Andrea, but was still traumatizing. The *Sports Illustrated* profile had tiptoed gingerly around this subject. ''They say I'm involved with a woman,'' Andrea had said. ''I heard I was supposed to be attracted to Wendy [Turnbull]. I'm not gay. I like guys. I just don't date many right now. I get into everything later than other kids.''

She told me she had never felt intimidated by, or attracted to, lesbians on the circuit. In fact, she sheepishly admitted, ''when I was fourteen or fifteen, the other young girls and I used to see lesbians as comical. It really wasn't nice of us. It was like making fun of a racial minority. Our parents might have taken lesbians seriously, but we didn't. I can see how parents would worry, but we just saw it as a joke. Maybe at that age humor is how you cope with the unknown.''

Although she dismissed the notion that players were in jeopardy from lesbians, Andrea felt the locker room was an unhealthy place. Some players loitered there for no better reason than running down other girls, making snide remarks, fueling feuds and petty jealousies. ''It's an American trait to try to take people down a peg. Maybe it's just eagerness to be number one. The Europeans have a different attitude. Americans will do anything to be number one. In the locker room . . . well, maybe it's not good to hang around there if you're a player. You can't trust people in an individual sport like tennis. They have nothing to talk about except each other. I was out the other night and said something nice about Andre Agassi and everybody started ripping him. The number-one player is always going to be a private person.''

Strolling toward an exit from the All England Club, Andrea said she worried about girls on the tour. Because of their isolation, because of the self-protective attitude of women's tennis, young players found themselves in painful situations, yet had nowhere to turn for advice or help. "These people are vulnerable," Andrea said. "They're out there losing every week. You can tell some of them aren't going to make it after tennis. I asked the WTA why they don't start some sort of program to prepare players for later in life. Because some of these girls are really screwed up. Of course, everybody thought I was screwed up, and I wasn't. But I think there should be some kind of career counseling. The WTA will give you the phone number of a psychologist and that's it."

She took a last backward glance at Wimbledon. A few veterans' doubles matches had yet to finish, and this late in the day, with the stands almost abandoned and the light fading, the place had less the look of a high-stakes battleground than of a genteel club—which is what it was for fifty weeks a year.

"The thing people don't realize," Andrea said, "is sports were my whole life. Then somebody says, 'No more.' " It wasn't just that she couldn't play tennis. She couldn't work out, couldn't jog or ride a bike, couldn't even go for a walk without acute discomfort.

"Probably coming back to Wimbledon wasn't the wisest thing for me to do—seeing my friends running, jumping, playing. A friend gave me a racquet and said, 'Come out and hit a ball.' So I took off my shoes and went out in my panty hose and hit one ball just to say I'd done it, I played on grass at Wimbledon again."

I asked if she ever dreamed about tennis and the titles she'd won, the Grand Slams she had played.

Andrea Jaeger shook her head so hard her curly hair whipped her face. "I dream about other sports. I dream about kicking the winning goal in soccer or catching the winning touchdown pass. But I don't dream about tennis. I can't imagine hitting a serve." She shuddered. "It gives me the shivers to think of hitting a serve. So much pain."

The Austrian Ladies Open

Kitsch and Home Cooking

Cradled in a lush valley in the Tyrolean Alps, the town of Kitzbuhel seemed a place where nothing could go seriously wrong. True, there might be minor setbacks, the sort that teach kids the lessons of pluck and luck. But amid these lovely mountains, on the narrow cobblestone streets lined by pastel facades, in the heady air scented with flowers, it was difficult to imagine anything as sordid as a dysfunctional family, a battered child, an abused woman, or two teenage girls crying in misery.

On Monday afternoon at the Austrian Ladies Open—signs for the event were in English—Cristina Salvi of Italy met Monika Kratochvilova of Czechoslovakia in the last round of the qualies. After they split sets 7–5, 5–7, Kratochvilova's mother fetched her a chocolate bar the size of a paving stone, and for the rest of the match, Monika munched the candy during changeovers. It did nothing for her metabolism or her mobility. She lost the third set 6–1, then gaped in disbelief as Salvi, the victor, broke into prolonged weeping.

Kratochvilova maintained her composure until she joined her mother on a bench beneath a swaying stand of linden trees. There, as she was subjected to a nit-picking postmortem, Monika, too, commenced crying. Her mother made no move to console her, just droned on and on in a school-marmish manner. When the Czech girl could stand it no longer, she dashed back onto the court, jogging around it until she had calmed herself. Then she walked with her mother back up into the fairy-tale village.

Kratochvilova went home with $600. Advancing to the first round of the main draw, Salvi was assured of $950 and had a chance to win more. She also had an opportunity to rise a few points in the rankings.

Although it was another way station on the Kraft General Foods World Tour, Kitzbuhel might have been in a different galaxy, so many light-years was it removed from Rome, Paris, and Wimbledon. A Tier IV event, it offered total prize money of $150,000—less than half of what Steffi Graf pocketed for winning Wimbledon. Yet paltry as the money was, the tournament had attracted a strong field. It boasted a top-ten player, Conchita Martinez, and four women whose ranking hovered around twenty—Barbara Paulus, Sandra Cecchini, Judith Wiesner, and Helen Kelesi.

Although there were no men playing in Kitzbuhel this week, there were plenty of them around—coaches, fathers, officials, and agents. In a reversal of the old joke that the only thing wrong with France is that women run the men's room, some people believed the only thing wrong with the women's tour was that it was dominated by men.

By men and by sponsors. The courts in Kitzbuhel were surrounded by a collage of promotional strips, many of them for competing products. While Citroën served as the title sponsor, there were billboards for a local auto dealer who sold Volvos, BMWs, and Ferraris. Ads for Henkell Bier were at cross purposes with those for Kaiser Bier. Tretorn was the official ball, but Penn was plastered on the windscreens.

Despite these discordant commercial claims, the ambiance of the Austrian Ladies Open seemed less mercantile than mellow and bucolic. No more careening cab rides as in Rome, no long Métro trips as in Paris, no crowded commutes in the Wimbledon courtesy van. In Kitzbuhel, I strolled out of my hotel, passed a row of aromatic pastry shops and cafés, crossed the road and entered the Casino-Stadion. Hollow logs overflowing with geraniums bordered the footpaths. Covered bleachers on Center Court and Courts One and Two were constructed of beautiful weathered wood, giving spectators the sense of being cozily enclosed in a chalet.

While the stars traditionally took a break after Wimbledon, many players couldn't afford that luxury. They had gone from grass straight back to slow red clay, trading the cool decorum of England for the volcanic heat and chaos of Palermo. Bettina Fulco, the feisty little

Argentinean, had played there and when I saw her in Kitzbuhel and asked how Sicily had been, she said, "Hot!"

As we stood watching Conchita Martinez practice, I wondered whether any other sport was played under such diverse conditions—indoors and outdoors, in natural light and electrical light, on carpets, on cement, on red clay and Har-Tru, on English grass and Australian grass. After the scorching siroccos of Sicily, where the seaside city of Palermo marinated in 105-degree heat, Bettina had flown here where the temperature was mild, but the air at 2,500 feet was thin enough to throw off a player's strokes.

"I played an Italian in the first round," Fulco said, breaking the silence. "Every other point they were stealing from me. I'm not going there again."

After Bettina's spring and summer of hard-won recovery in the rankings, Palermo had been her first disappointing result and the sort of disorganized mess that players detest—the kind where luggage disappears, phone calls are cut off in midsentence, and practice courts are dry as talcum powder.

"The tournament director did nothing," Bettina said, "except walk around in his shorts. Even the courtesy car drivers couldn't be bothered. They just sat around sunbathing."

It sometimes seemed that opponents were the least of the challenges a player had to overcome. Fans had no idea how hard it was to handle all the distractions and discouragements. Bettina nodded to Conchita Martinez. "In 1988, I reach the round of sixteen at Roland Garros. It's against Conchita and it's like a dream come true. They put us on Center Court. But it's late, around seven o'clock, and there's almost nobody in the stands, and the few there are aren't watching us. Henri Leconte is playing on the next court and people are at the top of the stands watching his match. You understand? They have their backs turned to us. They're clapping, but at the wrong time. You hit a winner and they don't clap. You're in the middle of a point and they're clapping for Leconte. I won but it was a terrible feeling. The next round, the quarterfinals, I play Steffi. Of course, I lose, but at least there are people and they're watching us, and when they clap, we know it's for us."

A short, stocky, dark-haired man joined us. Bettina introduced him as Pablo Villella, her coach. "He's not just my coach," she said. "He's my fiancé." They planned to marry in November.

"Without a coach," she explained, "it's very difficult. Sometimes you don't find a player to warm you up before a match. Sometimes you're not hitting right or you're using the wrong tactic, and you need someone to tell you, someone you trust."

But she conceded that traveling with your coach/boyfriend wasn't idyllic either. "Sometimes it's like too much. You're with each other all the time and can't get any air. It's difficult to separate our love from the game. We talk a lot, so it doesn't get to the point where I get mad when he yells at me about my tennis. He knows I'm very professional and I like to work hard. If I make mistakes in a match, he tells me. He gets mad and I understand.

"He helps me be positive," Bettina said. "He knows when I'm in a bad mood. He knows when it's better to just go shopping. A lot of girls get depressed when they lose and they like to eat then. Like Mercedes Paz, she loses in the first round at Wimbledon and two hours later she's eating and getting big again."

Pablo piped up that "With fathers as coaches it's difficult to have the right distance. Sometimes the father can't give a girl what she needs. He doesn't know enough."

Speaking of fathers, Mary Pierce had won the title in Palermo, Bettina said, and had vaulted from ninety-one to forty on the Virginia Slims computer. It was a heartening breakthrough for the sixteen-year-old American whose short career had been beset by so much aggravation from her father.

Without any transition, Bettina asked if I had heard that in Taranto this past spring Jim Pierce had thrown an equipment bag at Mary, then hit her with his fist. Mary had been so badly hurt she had to withdraw from the Italian Open. Although Fulco hadn't witnessed these events herself, she urged me to speak to Florencia Labat, another Argentinean, who had played Mary Pierce in Taranto.

○ ○ ○

At five feet four and 117 pounds, Federica Bonsignori of Italy gave away ten inches in height and more than fifty pounds to Brenda Schultz of Holland. To refer to this match as a repeat of David versus Goliath was to be reminded that nobody roots for Goliath—not even in this case, where Goliath was a good-natured girl who seemed abashed by her size and strength.

With a serve that whistled along at 110 m.p.h., Schultz would have overpowered the Italian girl on a fast surface, but on clay Bonsignori had time to catch up with the ball, and she scraped through the first set in a tie-break. Then in the second, Brenda turned the tables and won a tie-break herself.

When in the third set Schultz shot out to a 4–2 lead, she looked insuperable. But she began hitting the ball harder and harder and was soon firing bazooka shots that slammed into the fence—without touching the court. Bonsignori recovered to 3–4, was broken to 3–5, then promptly broke back to 4–5. If she could just hold serve, there was every good chance Schultz would crumble.

Bonsignori reached 40–30. One more point would do it. But she slipped back to deuce. Then Schultz got a match ball. Bonsignori saved it with a backhand down the line. Moments later the Dutch girl got another match point and crowded the service line, poised to blister a return. Bonsignori slapped her first serve into the net. She tossed up the second ball, caught it, apologized for the delay, tried to calm herself, but smacked the serve long for a double fault and 7–6, 6–7, 4–6 defeat.

"Che buco di culo!" Federica Bonsignori's anguished cry echoed among the Alps. "What an asshole!"

○ ○ ○

Following a night of hard rain, the weather cleared and the sun baked the courts dry. But soon after play resumed, black clouds flooded over the mountains and into the valley. On Court One, Canada's top-ranked woman, Helen Kelesi, struggled against Noelle Van Lottum, a nineteen-year-old French girl almost as contentious as she. On Court Two, Bettina Fulco couldn't gain a toehold against Florencia Labat. Shellacked 6–0 in the first set, Bettina tried to slow things down and ease her way into the match, but as the sky darkened, the umpire shouted, *"Schnell! Schnell!"* Fast! Fast! He wanted them to finish before the storm struck.

"I can't see the ball!" Van Lottum had to holler to be heard above a roaring wind that stripped leaves from the trees and sent them skidding across the clay. By now it was more like midnight than noon. But when Kelesi objected to a line call and asked the ump, "How much longer are you going to let us play?" Van Lottum lashed at her, "Will you please stop asking? You're asking the same question after every point."

A forlorn Bettina Fulco trotted to the net and kissed her friend Florencia Labat, who had beaten her in straight sets. Then torrents of rain fell and all the players sprinted toward the locker room.

○ ○ ○

On Thursday morning, the rain stopped, but clouds clung to the mountaintops like carded wool, and the humid air threatened another downpour. On a damp court where each shot left a rust-colored streak, Helen Kelesi polished off Noelle Van Lottum. Then she showered and changed into another Ellesse outfit and returned to practice with her father before her second match. Commonly called Hurricane Helen because of her belligerent temperament and howling tantrums, Kelesi was a foulmouthed hellion who argued with linesmen and umpires, shouted at opponents, and screamed obscenities at herself and at her father. At the French Open, in front of hundreds of fans, she had called him an "asshole" and hollered, "I hate you!"

Milan Kelesi was a Czech refugee who had fled during the 1968 revolution. Now he had a daughter who knocked down a quarter of a million dollars a year. A muscular man in his forties, Milan bore a resemblance to a miniature Arnold Schwarzenegger and carried himself with the ease of a natural athlete. But he hadn't taken up tennis until late in life. "It's my third sport," he said. He was better suited to soccer and hockey. A lefty who got little pace on his forehand and hit nothing but sliced backhands, Milan gave a graphic demonstration this week of his modest skills when he lost a practice match 6–3, 6–4 to Sandra Reichel, an Austrian girl ranked 519 in the world. One had to wonder how much he helped Helen by hitting with her.

A source close to the Kelesi family commented that "she and her father have the sort of relationship where they say 'Fuck you' to each other and think nothing of it. Things like that may fire her up and help her tennis, but they've ruined her image and made it really hard to market her.''

As the match started, the name card of an earlier loser lay crumpled under the umpire's chair. Perhaps it was fear of seeing herself discarded in the same callous fashion that prompted Kelesi to mount such ferocious resistance. With her high cheekbones and almond-shaped eyes, she had the looks to be a WTA calendar girl, but it was seldom that anybody saw her smile on court. In the first game against Florencia Labat, she began questioning calls and bristled when the ump misspoke himself in English.

"You said, 'Good,' '' Helen shouted. '' 'Good' doesn't mean 'Out.' ''

After a double fault, she jerked upright and jumped, bringing to life the cliché "hopping mad." There were five straight breaks before Kelesi held for a 4–2 lead and made that advantage stand up until she served for the set at 5–4. It was then that the match deteriorated into something more like psychodrama than sport. While Milan tried to stay loose by stretching in the stands, Helen was broken, fell behind 6–5, and let out a primal scream.

During the changeover, she thrust several cellophane-wrapped racquets at her father. "I need these." He peeled away the cellophane and wound tape around the grips.

Serving to reach a tie-break, Kelesi watched one of Labat's returns rip past her and screamed, "Fucking bitch!" Moments later, Labat banged another winner, and Helen hollered, "Fuck that line!"

"Stay cool," Milan called to her.

But she was boiling, and as Labat got to set point, Helen bellowed at some people passing behind the court, "Please, be quiet back there!" When Labat broke to win 7–5, Kelesi whacked her racquet into the windscreen, then cracked it against a fence post.

Lathered with sweat, she kept cussing and fuming in the second set. She broke to 1–0 and cried out to Milan that she was down to one racquet. She demanded that he rush the others to the stringer. "Tell the guy to do them *now!*"

In her father's absence, she perked up, holding serve, then breaking to 3–0. But the instant Milan returned, she lost two points to 0–30 and whirled on him. "Will you leave? Just leave!" He stayed, and she slipped to 1–3 before it sank in on him that she meant it; she wanted him out of there.

Although he left, it didn't change Kelesi's luck or her language. "Why is she so fucking good?" she wailed as Labat went on cracking forehand winners. Hurricane Helen lost the set and the match, stalked off court, marched straight into the tournament director's office, and growled, "Where do I get my prize money?"

○ ○ ○

Milan Kelesi didn't seem particularly upset by his daughter's defeat or her high dudgeon. When I asked what it was like to coach your own daughter, he said, "In some ways it's easy. In some ways hard. It's easy because you're committed. With someone else you can always quit and go to another player. But when it's family, you're fully committed.

"Then it's hard . . . " He hesitated, weighing his words. "It's hard because you always wonder whether you're doing the right thing. Should it be a little more this, a little more that? It's that way with anything involving your child."

In addition to Helen, he coached two Canadian boys and thought the women's tour was much tougher. "It can always be like a tragedy. If you have a lot of talent and you're winning, this can be a nice life. But when you lose and you have to struggle, it's very hard."

"How hard is it when your daughter screams at you to leave the court?"

Milan shrugged. "You just go. You can't ask why. There's no time for her to tell you a reason. She wins three games in a row while I'm gone and then loses one when I come back and she thinks I bring her bad luck. So I just go. That doesn't change anything, but I go. You have to be professional and detach your feelings.

"A lot of people try coaching their children, but it's tough and it doesn't always work. After a girl is fourteen, it's hard to change her game." He shrugged again. "Maybe it's better if she just has a hitting partner."

○ ○ ○

Florencia Labat and I sat on the grass beside a practice court. A solidly built twenty year old from Buenos Aires, she had dark, straight hair and dark eyes. In ebullient English, she explained that she had turned pro at eighteen, after finishing high school. "My parents wanted me to go to university. But I wanted to try the tour for two or three years. My mother thinks I'm too intelligent to just be playing tennis. But now my parents are happy with my decision."

She was happy, too, when she won. But she admitted, "It's hard to find friends on the tour. A lot of the girls aren't educated or intelligent, and it's hard because they're always talking about tennis."

Then there were matches like today's, which leached a lot of enjoyment from the game. "It's difficult to play Kelesi because of the way she is on the court and out of the court. She's a good player, but I think she wins more matches because of her attitude than her game. A lot of girls go out there angry at her and lose. No one likes her."

When I asked what had happened in Taranto after her match with Mary Pierce, Florencia explained that it had started during the final set. Jim Pierce was shouting at Mary from the stands, and she shouted back. After Labat won and they were coming off court, Jim hurled a bag of balls, hitting his daughter in the leg. Mary didn't slow down, just kept on walking. But her father caught up to her in the parking lot and hit her in the face.

Florencia confessed that she hadn't had a clear view of Jim and Mary in the parking lot. She couldn't say whether Jim had hit her with his fist or slapped her with an open hand. She told me to speak to Petra Thoren, a Finnish player, about that. But Labat felt that what had happened on court had been distressing enough—the shouting, the bag throwing. "I couldn't play with that kind of pressure."

○ ○ ○

Blond, with lively blue eyes, Petra Thoren sat on a bench with her leg extended, an ice pack on her knee. "Tendonitis," she explained before I could ask.

Pretty as she was, she was no delicate bud. Thoren practiced three or four hours a day. "I also lift weights three times a week. I do sprints and jumping exercises to improve my quickness. I throw medicine balls to improve my strength and coordination. I jump rope and jog. Whether you're a man or a woman, I think it looks nice if you have some muscles. Steffi Graf has a very nice muscular body and she makes a good image for the sport. If someone looks too muscular, maybe it's something she can't help."

Petra claimed, "It's a nice feeling on the tour. I think it's great and I like it. It's true it's hard to have good friends. You don't have best friends. But still the atmosphere is good. The better players may be lonely. They don't socialize too much. They don't talk. I think they want to keep a distance. Top players won't practice with you. They don't want to show you their secrets. Even when she was young, Steffi was like that. But Arantxa Sanchez Vicario is very nice and open."

Of course, she said, "if you play badly, it can be tough. I try to think positively, try to play because it's fun. You see people crying after a match, but I've stopped doing that. Tennis isn't *that* serious. Really"—she broke into a big smile—"the worst part about the tour is you have to do a lot of laundry."

Petra came from a tennis-playing family. Her sister had once been the best woman player in Finland. Her father, a bank manager, was ranked in the top five in the over-forty-five division.

"He taught me tennis," Thoren said, "but he was never my coach. A lot of girls have their fathers on the tour and are unhappy. For most of them it doesn't work. I wouldn't want personal things to get involved in the tennis. If my father says I hit the forehand wrong, I might take it that he doesn't like me. But when my coach says it, I can accept it. As a father you're a little disappointed that your daughter loses and you say something that hurts her. I have seen fathers yell terrible things." Then with some agitation she added, "I have seen fathers hit their daughters when they lose."

This led to a discussion of the incident in Taranto, and Thoren confirmed what Bettina Fulco and Florencia Labat had said—that Jim Pierce had swung at his daughter. Petra assumed Mary had been badly hurt. After all, she dropped out of the Italian Open the next week.

Thoren took pains to emphasize that this wasn't an isolated event.

She had seen other girls get hit by fathers and brothers, and she thought it was just as bad when men shouted wounding remarks at their daughters. "These can leave scars just like blows."

But she believed that while some fathers abused their daughters, there were girls who were just as awful to their parents. She cited Helen Kelesi. "She has her father wrapped around her finger. If I was a father and my daughter treated me that way, I'd quit working with her."

O O O

Amid the legions of baseline bangers who wielded their wide-body, space-age racquets like rocket launchers, Sandra Cecchini of Italy was a throwback to an earlier era when the women's game depended on guile and cunning, crafty placement and changing speeds. Sandra dinked, she lobbed, she teased out drop shots. Deceptively fast afoot, equally deceptive with the direction of her backhand, Cecchini had career wins over Chris Evert, Gabriela Sabatini, Natalia Zvereva, and Arantxa Sanchez Vicario.

But it was a style not to everybody's taste. Some fans considered it boring. They preferred to see big hitters. Many players found it frustrating and felt they hadn't been beaten so much as bamboozled.

Anticipating her opponents' shots and blunting their power with touch, Cecchini had already squeezed through a couple of three-set tussles in Kitzbuhel, one of them that morning. Now against Radka Zrubakova of Czechoslovakia, she was in another bruising three-setter and still possessed the nonchalance to strum her racquet strings like a mandolin after saving a match point. But she couldn't save a second, and Zrubakova advanced into the semifinals, where she'd face Conchita Martinez.

Zrubakova had also made the quarterfinals in doubles—and with a surprising partner, Regina Marsikova. Once ranked fifteenth in the world, winner of the Italian, the German, and the Canadian opens, Marsikova had had her career short-circuited in the early Eighties by an automobile accident that resulted in a charge of vehicular manslaughter against her. For three years she was off the tour, confined to a penal institution in Czechoslovakia. By the time she returned to tennis, it was too late to regain her form.

When I asked whether she was making a comeback, Marsikova laughed off the idea and said that Kitzbuhel was so close to Prague she had decided on the spur of the moment to drive down and compete in the qualies. She had been knocked out in the second round, but figured to clear more than a thousand dollars this week, mostly from doubles. That kind of money went a long way in Czechoslovakia, and it explained why so many Eastern Bloc players, some of them so low-ranked as to be marginal, continued to show up at small tournaments and satellite events, often accompanied by a passel of relatives eager to take advantage of the free meals and hotel rooms. In a country where a university professor earned a couple of hundred dollars a month, a tennis player who netted as little as five thousand dollars a year could support an entire family.

Still, Marsikova said this would probably be her last tournament. The game had passed her by. The new racquets, the power, the pace—everything on the women's tour had changed.

What about her own life? I asked. How had it changed?

She chose to talk about the political situation, not her personal affairs. "Everything is so much better in the East. There's no problem about travel and we get vegetables all the time. It's not perfect, but at least there's hope."

At her age, after her experience, Regina believed she had a new perspective on tennis. The key to getting more than money out of the game, she said, was "to enjoy where you are, take advantage of the travel. The trouble is once you lose, you hate the place where you are. Even me, as soon as I lost in the qualies, I didn't care about Kitzbuhel and how beautiful it is. I just wanted to leave. But if you hope to get something out of the tennis life, you have to get over that. You have to learn about the people and the places where you go."

Is that the advice she gave other girls?

Regina Marsikova laughed. "Oh, they all have coaches. Nobody cares what I think."

◗ ◗ ◗

Having beaten Florencia Labat in the quarterfinals, Judith Wiesner of Austria tarried outside the players' lounge, under a cool pavilion of pine trees, waiting for her semifinal against Nicole Jagerman of Holland. On a nearby practice court, Sandra Cecchini and Patricia Tarabini were warming up for their doubles match later that day. Actually, at the moment, they were mostly goofing around. As Cecchini did a comic imitation of Monica Seles's grunt, Tarabini started singing a song in Spanish.

There was something serene about this moment, something to savor, a reminder that tennis was a game, that although money was at stake, these girls were playing, not fighting. In the pressure-stoked cauldron of Wimbledon or the U.S. Open, one lost sight of that fact. But in Kitzbuhel, if one took the trouble to breathe in the sweet scent of pine sap, to listen to the laughter on the practice court, one could recapture a childhood memory of sport as pleasure.

As Wiesner set off toward Center Court, her husband, Heinz, a gray-haired man twenty years her senior, kissed her cheek and patted her behind. Then he let her go ahead while he lit a cigarette and had one last smoke before the match.

A successful sales director for a large insurance firm, Heinz Wiesner was at a stage in his career where he could concentrate on being a tennis husband, an endangered species if ever there was one. Among the top two hundred women, only a handful were married to anyone who wasn't a coach, and as Heinz described his life, one could understand why. For a man, the women's circuit entailed an almost total role reversal. "When Judith says, 'I have breakfast at eight A.M.,' we eat at eight A.M. When she says, 'I practice at nine A.M.,' we practice at nine A.M. When she says at night, 'I will read in the room,' I go and we read in the room. A boy with an ego, maybe he can't do this. But I am old enough"—he was forty-four—"to make the marriage work. I always give. I never wish for anything back. For me it's not difficult. I love Judith."

Although Heinz sounded perfectly acclimated to his role, he admitted, "I hate the travel. I'm afraid of flying. I see a plane and I am sick. I would take a car twenty or thirty hours before I take a plane. In early January I always start thinking, Soon I have to go to Australia. Four times I have gone there. I would never take a plane for myself, only for Judith.

"Staying happy with my wife, for me that's great. If she's happy, I hope she plays ten more years, even twenty. Other people, the fathers, they make so much pressure on the girls and are so unhappy."

Heinz dropped his cigarette and ground it out with his shoe. "I am never angry if Judith loses. It's normal. It has to happen."

o o o

But it didn't happen in the semifinals. Although she didn't look especially athletic, Judith Wiesner had splendid coordination and nimble footwork. She also benefited from the acute stage fright that Nicole Jagerman suffered in the first set.

But in the second, the lanky Dutch girl made a match of it. When serving, Jagerman had a huge windup, like a baseball pitcher with a windmill delivery, and she hit a vicious slice backhand, which she followed to the net for winning volleys. At 3–5, Jagerman hit two drop shots to go up 40–30, but then unwisely tried a third and fell to deuce. Wiesner won the next two points and the match.

The second semifinal, between Conchita Martinez and Radka Zrubakova, was closer, but I saw only the deciding games of the second set, when Martinez hung on to win 7–5, 6–4. The rest of the time I was talking to Juan Nunez, a broad-shouldered Chilean with a thick mustache and a disarming smile. After retiring from the men's tour, he had become the head teaching pro at the Royal Palm Polo Club in Boca Raton, Florida. Though it was a good job, Juan felt "it was frustrating to coach a lady for half an hour once a week and know she'll never get better. I always thought I could do more. I knew I could have more satisfaction. I'll always thank Chris Evert for giving me the opportunity to get into this profession."

Chris had asked him to work with her at twelve tournaments annually. Later Juan coached Arantxa Sanchez Vicario the year she won the French Open. Since then he had trained Andrea Temesvari and Helen Kelesi, and was now under contract to Brenda Schultz and Karin Kschwendt of Holland, and Meredith McGrath of the United States.

"At first," he confessed, "I was skeptical, nervous, even afraid to coach three players. But I found it a bit easier than working with one girl, easier to find a balance. I mean, like it's unusual that two girls will be in a bad mood at the same time. The big thing about girls is their moods. If I'm working with a guy and he's in a mood, I can talk to him man to man, and maybe we raise our voices and we work it out. But if you yell at a girl, she just starts crying and there's no practice that day. With girls," he said, "you first work on the psychological part. Then you begin the technical part. If you push her in a bad mood, you can ruin all your progress. I tell them, 'I want to know when you have your period, because I don't want to push you at the wrong time.' "

At the French Open he had practiced with all three girls simultaneously. "It goes pretty good. I have some drills for two on one. But you have to be careful not to give more to one girl than the others. I don't think you can do this job," Juan said, "if you have a bad temper. Sometimes I just have to let the girl dump her mood on me."

Since he had worked with Helen Kelesi, I asked how much mood dumping he was willing to accept. Juan insisted that their dealings hadn't been anything like the scathing crossfire between Helen and her father.

"She needs someone she can insult and abuse and send off the court," he said. "She's a fighter and she needs to pump herself up. But she couldn't do that with me. She respected me too much. She couldn't scream at me, and that hurt her game, because she really needs that anger to get her going."

Juan agreed with Petra Thoren that "some fathers abuse their daughters and some daughters abuse their fathers. But as painful as it looks to an outsider, the relationship between Milan and Helen may be the only one that works. I once told her, 'I've thought things over. I've watched you and I know just the right coach for you.' Helen said, 'Who?' and I said, 'Milan Kelesi.' He gives her what she needs."

For most father-daughter teams on the tour, he had little but scorn. "Tennis is the only sport where a father puts his daughter into a tennis academy and *he* becomes an expert. You need chemistry between a coach and player," Juan said. "Between a father and daughter, it's not the right chemistry. It's like a husband teaching his wife to drive. It's not a good idea. I see a lot of young players in big trouble. I see their fathers smacking them."

Although he cited Jim Pierce as an example, he named other fathers as well, adding to the list of battered players. What he said reminded me of a comment by Don Candy, who expressed amazement that more girls weren't beaten. "I'm surprised fathers don't go out there with a baseball bat and beat their daughters," Candy told me. "These fathers know nothing about tennis. It's a shame that the person who gets hit isn't in the care of somebody who knows better."

Many women on the tour were, according to Candy, "emotionally all messed up. Some people—fathers and brothers—absolutely destroy the girls."

"What I like about my current situation," Juan Nunez said, "is the parents are staying home." As for fathers who berated or beat their daughters, he lamented, "What can you do? You can't step in and take the girl away from her family. Of course, you could bar the fathers from tennis, but eventually the girl's got to come back home and who's going to protect her then? Maybe the best thing the WTA can do is keep an eye on the problem and talk to the guys and make sure they get counseling."

Juan explained that he arranged his schedule to minimize the difficulties for his marriage. He and his wife "never have more than four weeks' separation, and she knew what she was getting into and she knows how much I love it."

Removing his sunglasses, spinning them by the earpiece, he admitted, though, that he had one recurring problem with his wife. "It's not that she's afraid I'll go off with the girls and be unfaithful. I won't! But she thinks I'm living this glamorous life. I tell her I live in a hotel room and I have to practice six hours a day. I have to warm them up and I have to watch their matches. I have to make arrangements and reservations. In Rome, London, Paris, and Kitzbuhel the only place I get to see is the road from the hotel to the courts. At night you are so tired you don't feel like going out."

While some coaches slept with their players, Juan was emphatically opposed to it. "If I fuck one of the girls, the chemistry is over and you can't coach her anymore. I fuck them just once and it would ruin everything. I give my girls a lot of love and affection, but always with respect and knowledge—their knowledge that it's not going to go any farther. It's important for girls to know you're not in it for sex, you're not coaching them for that."

But he was quick to add that he wasn't a prude who imposed puritanical restrictions. "A lot of coaches don't let their girls have sex during a tournament. I don't have those rules. I'm not against them traveling with boyfriends. They can even have sex the night before a match—as long as they're in bed sleeping by eleven P.M. A lot of girls go to bed early, but they're not sleeping. They're lying there nervous and sweating, thinking about tomorrow." He clenched his fists to show me how tense the girls got. "Whereas if they get a good pop, they'll relax and play a good match the next day." He unflexed his fingers, turning his palms up.

Juan said that much of his job consisted not of teaching players what they didn't know, but of motivating them to do what they already realized was necessary. A lot of girls recognized that they needed to train harder, but they lacked drive and discipline. That was where he, a master of reverse psychology, came in.

"If you go to a girl and say, 'You're too fat,' she'll freak out. You have to have a different attitude. When I'm training them and they start getting muscles in their legs, I stop them and tell them to look at themselves. I get them to like their bodies. That's why girls feel good working with me. I don't use a military approach. I would never accept a fat girl, but I would use a positive approach to change her."

Still, he conceded that a positive approach couldn't solve all problems. Some players needed more than he was in a position to give. "Brenda Schultz," for instance, "has a huge heart. She wants to be liked by people. When she sees a girl is unhappy because she's being beaten, Brenda has a tendency to pull back." At other times, "she uses her power out of fear. She hits the ball five hundred miles an hour because she doesn't want it to come back. When it does come back, it destroys her.

"With her power, Brenda has the potential to be in the top ten. But there's a mental block." Juan said that if she hoped to improve he was going to suggest that she see a sports psychologist. "Sometimes girls are skeptical. They say, 'I'm not crazy.' But it's not a question of being crazy. It's a question of getting control of her nerves, building her confidence. A psychologist will make her believe in herself. He may try hypnotism. You have to get the message to the subconscious mind.

She understands consciously, but you can't be thinking out there on court. During a match you've got to react at a subconscious level. In coaching a girl, you can save a lot of hours by going directly to the subconscious mind.''

Was there anything in his background—anything except his own time on the tour—that had helped him become a better coach?

Juan Nunez smiled. "My father made me understand girls. He made me understand how beautiful they are. I love women. But you don't have to fuck them to love them. I accept them as they are. Sometimes I have this girl on the other side of the net who is moody or acting weird and I try to make a joke, I try to find a way to get her out of it. I snake my way to a solution. I tell you, coaching has helped me with my marriage. Because everybody has his days, and sometimes my wife can be moody or having her period and feeling bad, and I've learned from teaching tennis not to lose my temper, not to say, 'The hell with this.' I stay calm, I tell a joke, and things pass.''

○ ○ ○

On Sunday, during the singles final between Judith Wiesner and Conchita Martinez, Sandra Cecchini waited in the players' lounge for the start of her doubles match. Her partner, Patricia Tarabini, was also there, kibitzing and eating bananas. The lounge had a row of windows overlooking Center Court, and occasionally somebody glanced at the match and called out the score. Eventually Bettina Fulco and her coach/fiancé, Pablo Villella, showed up. Teamed with Nicole Jagerman, Fulco would compete for the doubles title.

Cecchini and Tarabini had reservations on a 6 P.M. flight to England for the Federation Cup. Since the trip from Kitzbuhel to the Munich airport took more than an hour by automobile, they needed to finish their doubles match by 4 P.M.—a daunting task if Martinez and Wiesner went into a third set. Tarabini didn't appear to care one way or another, but Cecchini was on edge.

Pablo Villella was also on edge. Like Heinz Wiesner, he hated airplanes. This evening he and Bettina had to fly to Paris—which was bad enough—then they had to catch an overnight flight to Buenos Aires—which was almost more than Pablo could bear.

Since I shared his fear of flying, I mentioned that I took a tranquilizer on long flights, five milligrams of Valium. On the men's tour in the early Eighties, I had known players who swallowed a pharmacopoeia of pills—Librium, Mogadon, Transine, Equanil, Placidil—every time they set foot on an airplane. But, I said, that was before tennis was an Olympic sport, before there was drug testing.

Cecchini snorted in derision. Sly and witty, a tomboyish redhead, she said there should be more drug tests, and not just at Grand Slam events, where all the players knew about them in advance and could make sure they passed. "I think some people are taking things," she said. "You see some girls, their legs are twice the size of mine. You see their arms. Look at mine." She brandished a firm arm dusted with freckles. "I have muscles. I work out and I'm strong. But you don't see veins. You don't see . . . " She groped for the word in English, then raked the fingers of her free hand over her arm, showing the way that the musculature of body builders was striated.

When I asked why a girl would take drugs, Cecchini said, "To get stronger and faster." She was sure that men players used them, too. So was Pablo Villella.

"But why wouldn't they get caught on the tests?" Bettina Fulco chimed in.

"Because they stop in time," Sandra said, "or they use something to cover the steroid. Look how long it was before Ben Johnson was caught." Some women track stars also depended on performance-enhancing drugs, and after the Berlin Wall fell, growing numbers of Eastern Bloc female athletes had been exposed as steroid users.

When Cecchini named several tennis players—prominent ones—whom she suspected of drug use, Bettina and Pablo disagreed in some cases but shared her suspicions in others. Sandra kept repeating, "Remember how she used to look. Think how she looks now. You don't get that way in a short time by lifting weights."

Given the secrecy surrounding drug testing in tennis, there was no way of proving—or disproving—what she said. The only "fact" to emerge was that some girls felt they were being beaten by players who competed with an illegal advantage.

Steffi Graf later confirmed that she, too, believed some players were using steroids. She called for more frequent and stringent drug testing. In her own experience, the current drug-testing program was too haphazard to be effective. During her eight years on the tour, Graf said, she had been tested just once—at the 1988 Olympics. It struck Steffi as absurd that the winner of ten Grand Slam titles, the longtime number-one player, wouldn't be tested more often.

Responding to Graf's remarks, Chris Evert expressed her doubts that anyone on the circuit was now using performance-enhancing drugs. But she proposed that in the future the semifinalists at every Grand Slam event be required to undergo drug testing.

Days later, Gabriela Sabatini announced that she was taking legal action against a German Federation Cup trainer who had spoken out about steroid abuse and was quoted in the *Welt am Sontag* as saying, "two of the three top-women tennis players resort to doping to enhance their performance." Gaby objected that her name had been linked with doping.

By the time Noelle Van Lottum and Caroline Vis came into the lounge, Judith Wiesner had lost the first set, then bounced back and won the second. At this rate, Cecchini fumed, they'd miss their plane. "Why are you here?" she asked Van Lottum. "Aren't you playing Fed Cup?"

Van Lottum had a mobile, gamine face, pouting one moment, laughing the next as she explained that she had just missed making the French team. Instead, the Federation picked Mary Pierce, the Floridian with a French mother.

This incited a great deal of grumbling about national federations, a never-ending source of grievances in both men's and women's tennis. Bureaucratic politics and sport didn't mix, everybody agreed. Players should prove their worth on court, not in front of a jury of so-called experts who picked their favorites and rejected players who had the wrong coaches or came from the wrong regions.

Pablo believed Bettina should have made the Argentinean team on the basis of her results in Rome and Paris. He felt that the Federation was biased in favor of city girls and shortchanged players from the provinces.

Noelle Van Lottum claimed the French Federation was cutting back on programs for girls in their teens. The assumption was that by that age a player should have turned pro and gone on the tour. If she hadn't shown enough talent by then, the Federation didn't care to keep supporting her.

Van Lottum broke off her complaints about the French Federation and asked me, "Are you the one writing the book about women's tennis?"

"Yes."

"And you did one already about the men?"

When I said I had, the girls asked about the differences I had noticed between the circuits.

Of the dozens I might have mentioned, I pointed to the player party earlier that week. It had been attended by sponsors, journalists, and their wives. Few men came alone and not one was less than middle age. In contrast, all the receptions and cocktail parties I had attended on the men's tour had been thronged by young, attractive, unescorted ladies who had been rounded up and, in some instances, paid to socialize with the players.

"Why don't they do that for us?" Van Lottum wailed. "Why don't they invite fifty or sixty boys to our parties? They invite nothing but old people or nerds with glasses."

This prompted gales of embarrassed laughter as everybody did a double take of my Coke-bottle lenses and white hair.

"We can bring this up at the next WTA meeting," Vis suggested.

"It wouldn't work," Van Lottum said. "We'd still have to wait for the boys to come over and talk to us."

"You could insist that they wear numbers."

"Yes," Van Lottum said. "Then you just say, 'Bring me Number Ten, or send me Number Fifteen.' "

After the laughter and catcalls died down, I asked, "Do you think you intimidate men?"

"Why? How?"

"You make more money and you're better at a sport."

"They're not intimidated," Cecchini said, "if you make money and spend it on them."

"And not all men are intimidated," Bettina Fulco said. "Remember in Rome, that disco party they had for us."

"Of course, *they* weren't intimidated," Cecchini said. "They were Italians." Too agitated to sit still any longer, she stood up and checked on the Martinez–Wiesner match. "Dammit, hurry and finish," she muttered. Then to Tarabini: "Maybe we can go from Munich to Amsterdam. Maybe there's a connection to London."

As Conchita Martinez served for the match, Van Lottum said, "She looks like she doesn't give a shit."

"She always looks that way," Bettina said.

"Maybe that's why she wins," Van Lottum blurted as though she had discovered the solution to a brain-rattling equation. "She doesn't give a shit."

Martinez won the title, then stood by looking listless and absent-minded during the awards ceremony. When Conchita missed her cue to step forward and accept the trophy, Van Lottum said, "She doesn't speak a word of English."

"She speaks only two words of Spanish," Bettina said.

Cecchini was fretting more every minute. All these windy speeches were going to make her late for her plane.

That was another difference between the men's and women's circuits, I said. No man would let a doubles match interfere with his schedule. When they had nothing more urgent to do, male players gave their best effort, but at the slightest provocation, they'd tank. In a final like today's they'd probably reach an agreement to split the prize money. Then they'd dervish through the match in twenty minutes.

Sandra said she had heard that men tanked and sometimes split prize money when there was a great disparity between the winner's and loser's share. But she and the other girls swore they had never seen this happen on the women's tour.

Still, Cecchini decried the fact that at some tournaments the winner got more than twice the loser's share. "That's too big a difference."

"Forget the final," Van Lottum said. "What about the first round? In Palermo you get six hundred and fifty dollars."

"Yes, that's too much," Sandra needled her. "More than you deserve."

Fulco, a first-round loser in Sicily, booed.

"Just kidding," said Sandra. Then she shooed Tarabini, who was still in street clothes, toward the locker room. "Get dressed and let's play."

○ ○ ○

The doubles final was a lot like the previous two hours—full of wicked shots, point-blank volleys, snappy comebacks, lighthearted laughter, and dark fulminations in Spanish, Italian, and Dutch. By the time Cecchini and Tarabini lost a drawn-out first set 7–5, they had as good as missed their plane. Still, they soldiered on, fighting to win the second and force a third set. They saved one match point, then another, and slapped a high five. Although they couldn't save a third, they waited good-naturedly while Bettina Fulco and Nicole Jagerman were awarded their trophies. Then Patricia and Sandra each grabbed a bottle of champagne, shook it to a froth, and chased Megan Bardsley, the WTA assistant to the director of European Operations, around the court, drenching her with spray.

By the time the girls had showered and dressed, it was late evening and the mountain air had cooled. Clothes wet, hair plastered to her head, Megan Bardsley had a towel wrapped shawl-like around her shoulders as she shepherded the players and coaches toward their cars. Cecchini and Tarabini were at last bound for London, although they had no idea by what route they would arrive. Bettina, juggling her luggage and trophy, settled back for the drive to Munich, but her fiancé, Pablo, sat bolt upright as if already on the long harrowing flight home.

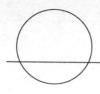

The Forbidden Zone

According to conventional wisdom, male coaches and hitting partners had had a wholesome effect on women's tennis. Players were better conditioned and tactically sounder than in the past, and the circuit was said to be a happier place. Now couples could travel together, and young girls got a chance to mature in a more balanced environment. Supposedly men had also improved the commercial image of the tour, serving as a counterweight to the incessant, exaggerated gossip about predatory lesbians in the locker room.

Yet a number of people expressed misgivings about the situation. They felt that more men meant fewer jobs for female coaches and less input from women officials and executives. This reinforced an antiquated notion that men should be in charge.

Still others saw the arrangement as manipulative and exploitative. "There doesn't have to be sex for a kind of seduction to take place," an American player told me. "When you're sixteen or seventeen, and you have a crush on an older coach, it doesn't take much to get to a girl. The guy will give you a little attention or a hug, or he'll go out to dinner and joke around with you. Maybe he'll rub your back after a tough match. He'll act like he really cares, and pretty soon you're playing your brains out for him. You're running extra laps, doing extra sprints, pumping iron in the gym. You're doing everything you can to keep him happy, to make him like you. But what you're forgetting is that for him it's a business deal. You're paying him and picking up his expenses and here he's got you running yourself ragged to win his approval. It's completely turned upside down, but a girl doesn't realize that until she goes through it a few times—until this coach you thought was so great leaves you because you're losing or leaves you for a higher-ranked girl. That's when you put on your Walkman and put on that old tape of Tina Turner's, 'What's Love Got to Do With It?' A girl's gotta learn she's working to make herself a better player, not to get her coach to love her.''

Although she swore she was too smart to be taken advantage of, the girl named a number of players whose careers had been crippled by a "seduced and abandoned" scenario. In some instances the seduction was literal.

"That's when it's awful," she said, "when you have a crush on your coach and you wind up in bed with him. Some of these guys are married and have kids as old as the players they're coaching. It should be clear right off it can't lead to anything good for the girl. Yet I've known players that stayed with a guy for years and the whole time they should have been out dating. Then the coach drops them for another player and the girl goes through like a divorce grieving process.''

The frequency and effects of sexual contacts between male coaches and female athletes—especially between adolescent girls and older men—are matters of dispute. Since everyone involved has a motive to remain silent, very little statistical evidence exists on the subject. For self-evident reasons coaches aren't likely to confess to behavior that might land them in professional or legal jeopardy. In some jurisdictions, sex with an underage girl is a crime. Almost everywhere it's regarded as a serious breach of ethics.

Helen Lenskyj, a sociologist at the Ontario Institute for Studies in Education, has argued in her article "Unsafe at Home Base" that even when women believe they have been badly abused, they, too, have reasons to remain silent. Like rape victims, they don't relish the prospect of being victimized all over again. "The process of describing an experience of sexual harassment often feels like reliving it," Lenskyj writes, "and that is obviously something that most women want to avoid. In fact, in the chilly climate of sport and physical education, women are perhaps more likely to keep their perceptions private than in other, more supportive contexts.''

As Lenskyj also observes, "Allegations of lesbianism directed at female athletes deter many women from rejecting unwanted sexual attention or complaining about sexual harassment, since they fear that such actions will confirm that they are not sexually interested in men, and hence, lesbian.''

Kathryn Reith of the Women's Sports Foundation in New York City acknowledges that anecdotal information about the sexual abuse of female athletes reaches her group all the time, but it is difficult to get facts and to get anybody, including victims, to discuss the issue.

''Women's sport is so new,'' Reith said, ''and has had to struggle so hard to get where it is, every problem that's brought to its attention is swept under the carpet. Whether it's a question of lesbianism or straight-sex abuse, women in sport are afraid it jeopardizes what they have achieved and so they don't want to deal with it.''

Still, there were those on the tennis tour who didn't shy away from the subject. Early on, at the Italian Open, former player and current Fila executive Marty Mulligan declared it was unethical for a coach to turn a professional relationship into a sexual one. Dennis Van der Meer, who believed most coach/player relationships were now sexual in nature, compared coaches who slept with their players to psychiatrists who had sex with their patients and rationalized this as part of therapy. And Juan Nunez had described how sex destroyed the chemistry that had to exist between a coach and player.

One ITF official wondered whether coaches who had sex with underage players weren't putting themselves and the WTA at legal risk. It was, after all, a litigious age and parents had been known to sue when their daughters were molested by teachers, doctors, and pastors.

Quite often when questions about sexual abuse came up during the course of interviews, the initial response of players, agents, and tour officials was to deny that it was happening. But almost invariably they would acknowledge in the next breath that they were aware of one or two cases, which they considered to be rare exceptions.

For example, Hana Mandlikova said she knew nothing about older male coaches having sex with young players, and she denied that it had happened to her. Yet when asked about a recent case involving a Czech teenager who was rumored to be sleeping with her middle-age coach, Mandlikova conceded, ''That's true. That was very true, yes. Everybody knew that she was in a relationship with him. I think that's sickening. Especially if he's married or something, I think it's terrible.''

"What if he's single?''

"Even that,'' Hana said. "If he's much older, I think that's not right.''

"Is it just the age or is it the coach/athlete relationship?''

"I think it's just not right. I mean, if you're doing a job, you're doing a job, and you're not looking for something else . . . I just don't understand how this can happen, and that's basically all I want to say about it.''

One former Virginia Slims employee insisted that you could never be sure what went on between people in private. Although she admitted seeing a famous coach come out of a teenage player's hotel room at 3 A.M. in his underwear, she disagreed with the proposition that that itself was inappropriate.

It wasn't simply that some people were reluctant to conclude that where there was smoke there was fire. They refused to concede that fires were any real cause for concern. One player, Andrea Leand, wrote an article describing half a dozen cases of sexual harassment or outright abuse, including an anecdote about a coach who walked in on her while she showered. She also told of a player whose coach was sleeping with the girl and her mother. Yet her conclusion was that these were just isolated incidents. When taken together, however, these "rare exceptions'' and "isolated incidents'' added up to a troubling pattern of widespread abuse. Bob Nideffer, a sports psychologist who wound up marrying Ros Fairbanks, a player he was coaching, told Cindy Hahn of *Tennis* magazine that he knew of many coaches who slept with girls on the circuit. "The tour is made for it,'' Nideffer said.

Overall, dozens of sources said they knew of coaches who made suggestive remarks, fondled girls, gave massages that weren't welcomed, and had sex with players when they could get away with it. Some players admitted that it had happened to them. None wanted to be quoted by name, both because of embarrassment and because they feared repercussions from coaches who were still on the tour. But given the obvious pain it caused them to discuss these matters, I had no reason to doubt their honesty or to press them to give up their anonymity.

A South American said, "My father handed me over to a man and sent me out on the circuit when I was sixteen. He told me to do whatever the coach said. So when he said we were staying in the same hotel room, then when he moved over to my bed, I didn't know how to say no."

An Eastern European, a tour veteran ranked in the top twenty, told me, "My coach has always been my lover." She didn't mean that she had always had the same coach—just that whoever coached her became her lover. It was a pattern that had started when she left home as a teenager with a Federation coach who controlled her fate. To lose his approval meant losing her place on the national team, losing her passport, her chance to travel to the West, win foreign currency, and help her family. When he demanded sex, how could she refuse?

I interviewed a coach from her country whose attitude suggested what she and other girls had faced as teenagers. He said of a top-ten player he had trained, "She used to be a great lay. This was back when she was fifteen or sixteen. Then she went off on her own and turned into a lesbian."

As angry and upset as some women were about what had happened to them when they were young, they continued playing tennis. They had either recovered from these early episodes or had settled into a series of damaging relationships. But other women had suffered such ruinous experiences they had to quit the game.

The worst case was a woman who never had a chance to make it onto the tour. While she was a junior, her parents had opened their home to a touring pro who was in town to play a tournament. One night while she was alone in the house, the man broke into her room and tried to rape her. When she resisted, he roughed her up and masturbated on her.

"I never told my parents," she said. "I was ashamed and I was afraid. I knew they'd never believe me, so I didn't try to explain. I didn't explain why I stopped playing either. For years I was a mess."

Although she had given up the game, she continued to follow the career of the man who had assaulted her. After retiring from competition, he had gone on to greater prominence as a Davis Cup captain and coach.

He owned tennis academies, conducted clinics in half a dozen countries, and trained other coaches.

"Every time I watch a tournament on TV," the woman told me, "and they show him up in the stands and say what a successful coach he is, I wonder how he treats the women he trains. I don't believe a man like that changes. It's awful to think there might be others like me who were too embarrassed or scared to tell anybody about him."

O O O

Gregory Briehl, a psychologist in Charlottesville, Virginia, has had more than a passing acquaintance with women's tennis. A former college-level player himself, he taught and coached professionally for eight years. When he was in graduate school, he helped pay his tuition by transporting and installing the portable indoor court used at WTA tournaments. In the course of his travels, he came to know a number of the players and served as a hitting partner. (On the wall in his office is a photograph of him on court with Pam Shriver, Hana Mandlikova, and Betty Stove.) Later, by pure coincidence, he found himself treating a few female tennis players who had suffered emotional problems and dropped off the tour because of sexual abuse by male coaches. In addition to his own patients, Briehl, who is an ordained Lutheran minister as well as a psychologist, said he was aware of at least a dozen other players who had become sexually entangled with their coaches.

Before our interview, he suggested I educate myself on the subject by reading *Sex in the Forbidden Zone: When Men in Power—Therapists, Doctors, Clergy, Teachers and Others—Betray Women's Trust*. Written by Dr. Peter Rutter of the Department of Psychiatry at the University of California Medical School, the book essentially proposes the extension of the medical profession's Hippocratic Oath to all those arenas where men wield authority over women, and where abuse of that authority can bring "terrible, life-shattering consequences to a girl or woman when trust is turned to sexual advantage." Dr. Rutter stresses that a man has a professional responsibility to accept the "expectation that whatever parts of herself the woman entrusts to him (her property, body, mind, or spirit) must be used solely to advance her interests and will not be used to his advantage, sexual or otherwise."

Although Dr. Rutter acknowledges that women can abuse men and other women, "96 percent of sexual exploitation by professionals occurs between a man in power and a woman under his care . . . the male-female power imbalance is reflective of the pattern that exists in the culture at large." And that imbalance, he believes, prevents a woman from giving informed consent when a pastor, psychiatrist, or employer initiates sexual intimacy.

"My position," Dr. Rutter writes, "is that *any sexual behavior by a man in power within what I define as the forbidden zone is inherently exploitative of a woman's trust.* Because he is the keeper of that trust, it is the man's *responsibility, no matter what the level of provocation or apparent consent by the woman,* to assure that sexual behavior does not take place."

O O O

During the course of a three-hour interview, Gregory Briehl took the conclusions of *Sex in the Forbidden Zone* and applied them to coach/player relationships. As he bluntly put it, "Sex abuse is sex abuse." Since many coaches were acting *in loco parentis,* Briehl believed there was no difference between a man who slept with his player and one who did the same with his stepdaughter.

The tennis tour, Briehl explained, was a fertile ground for all sorts of problems. Unlike team sports, which integrated an athlete into a society of his or her peers, tennis tended to isolate a person from school-mates and normal formative experiences. "A kid who really hits the ball is ultimately elevated to a different plane," said Briehl. "She's treated differently by her parents. They put more time and money into the child. She's removed from the mainstream of school, taken out of classes for practice, taken away for days to tournaments." And if she demonstrated exceptional talent, she ended up in the "artificial environment" of a tennis academy or on the pro tour.

"We talk about what divorce does to kids," Briehl said, "but at least they get to stay with one parent. Tennis stars leave both parents and their friends and hometowns. They're removed from a context where they'll be able to develop."

Feeding into this distortion was the influence of agents and tour-

nament directors and the impact of prize money and enormous endorsement contracts. To an outsider this tidal wave of attention and money
might appear to be an enviable bonanza, but to a child, or to a player
arrested at a childlike stage of development, the effects could be as
devastating as those experienced by a disaster victim.

"People come in and assume parental roles," Briehl said. "A tour
official or agent serves as a surrogate parent, a mother hen. Some of
this is well meaning, but some of it is self-serving." He named a trainer,
now no longer on the women's tour, who was often cited as someone
notorious for molesting players.

Experts maintain that sexual abuse exists among all social and eco-
nomic classes, and Briehl pointed out that he had treated women who
had been abused in college, on the satellite circuit, and on the WTA
tour. But he remarked that "the higher the achievement, the more likely
girls are to be abused. A kind of diplomatic immunity applies to people
in the top echelons of tennis. A college would frown on a coach having
sex with a player. But the WTA seems not to notice and to take no
position."

When you cut through the glossy window dressing and discounted
the sport's self-congratulatory rhetoric, Briehl said, "players are com-
modities. If they don't do well, they're forgotten. A commodity is an
object and whenever a person is regarded as an object, the possibility
of sexual abuse is great."

Just how great was difficult to calculate. According to the best
estimates, 25 percent of the general female population have experienced
some form of sexual abuse. In certain professions the rate is known to
be much higher. A 1990 Defense Department study determined that 64
percent of women in the U.S. military have been sexually harassed.

Within what Briehl referred to as "the skewed population" of the
women's tour, he believed the incidence of abuse was quite high. It
wasn't just because the players were isolated, subjected to relentless
pressure, and sent off for months with male coaches. He said you had
to consider the kinds of people they traveled and trained with.

"What type of man wants to be a coach?" Briehl asked. He answered his own question by suggesting that some of them were classic

narcissists, guys with big egos and huge appetites for money and approval.

Then, too, most coaches had been tennis pros themselves and had had the same disorienting early experiences as the girls they worked with. The hope was that this made them more knowledgeable, empathetic, and caring, but there was always the opposite possibility. As Briehl put it, some coaches were "second-generation skewed people." During their playing careers they had been given to understand that they were above the rules and better than other people. Now they were back on the circuit with an adolescent girl, and "they think they're entitled," Briehl said. "That's a dangerous situation. In psychiatry, it's fifty minutes a week. On the tour, coaches and players are together twenty-four hours a day in what can be a sexually charged atmosphere."

While Briehl took pains to protect the confidentiality of his patients, he offered some insights into the price young female players had to pay for the delinquencies of their coaches. One of his patients had been in the top twenty and was sixteen years old when her coach crawled into bed with her. She hadn't invited his advances, yet felt powerless to resist and, at the same time, responsible for what happened. Her instinct was to keep things secret to protect herself and the coach, who was a father figure to her. Although she tried to break off the affair, she found she couldn't. She thought she should have been able to control it, but she couldn't do that either. Having been raised to regard herself as exempt from life's rules, she tried to tell herself the relationship didn't really bother her, yet it did.

Finally, the only way out seemed to be to drop off the tour. When the coach couldn't convince her to change her mind, he told her he didn't care whether she quit—so long as she paid him. They had a contract and if she wanted to leave him, she would have to buy it out. In the end, that was what she had been forced to do.

In Briehl's opinion, his patient wasn't the first or last player who had had to pay off an abusive coach to get rid of him. Nor was she the first or last who was so distraught she decided to quit tennis. "A lot of early dropouts," said Briehl, "are girls who've been abused."

The players he had treated spent lengthy periods in therapy, yet never achieved a complete recovery. They never regained the capacity to trust and never outgrew their tendency to fall into destructive relationships that mimicked the ones they had had with their coaches. Gregory Briehl believed that for those girls and others like them, ''there was trauma just being on the tour. Then the sexual abuse concretized the distortion.''

U.S. Open

Material Girl, Imperial Girl

At the National Tennis Center, early on the first day of the U.S. Open, a crowd gathered at the Reebok booth pawing through what looked to be a pile of charred shoes. Grabbing half a dozen pairs in each hand, Reebok employees seemed eager to clean up the burnt rubbish before more fans arrived.

On closer inspection, I realized I was wrong; the shoes hadn't been scorched black. For reasons best known to some genius at Reebok, they had been designed to resemble footwear excavated from volcanic ash.

David Larson, a Reebok representative, told me, "Since we're the official shoe of the U.S. Open, we wanted to make a statement."

"What's the statement?"

He motioned to the midden heap of black shoes. "Here's something different."

Well, the statement had the virtue of being true. Different they were.

Larson said public response to the Pump Midnight Edition had been heartening. The shoes had "a full pump potential," unlike the old Pump, which inflated only at the toe and tongue. Reebok hoped all its contract players would wear them, at least for a few matches. Larson admitted, however, that approval hadn't been universal. The USTA refused to let ball boys and girls wear black shoes during the U.S. Open.

That veto may have been the first noncontroversial decision anyone associated with pro tennis had made this summer.

○ ○ ○

Twenty-seven days after her disappearance, Monica Seles embarked on her comeback at an exhibition—the Pathmark Tennis Classic in Mahwah, New Jersey—and her pre-match press conference was calculated to rankle tennis purists the world over. Paid more than $250,000 in appearance fees, Seles waved a T-shirt at the cameras like a red cape at a bull. Stenciled on it were ROME, PARIS, WIMBLEDON, MAHWAH—with Wimbledon crossed out. Stopping well short of an apology, she said that shin splints and a stress fracture of the left leg had kept her out of Wimbledon. When asked why she hadn't said that earlier, she cuddled her Yorkshire terrier, Astro, and murmured, "I needed my time alone."

Although she professed not to have realized that she had created such a ruckus, she admitted that both she and brother Zoltan had disguised themselves with wigs whenever they went out. As for the rumor that she had hidden in Donald Trump's Palm Beach mansion during her hegira, she assured the press, "We are just good friends."

"What about Warren Beatty?"

"Who?" she asked.

In a bit of casuistry befitting a medieval scholar, a doctor affiliated with the Pathmark Tennis Classic provided Monica with a document that certified her as fit to play in Mahwah on Friday, Saturday, and Sunday. But on Monday, when she was due in England for the Federation Cup, he advised her to stay off her feet for the good of her health.

Claiming that injury prevented her from competing in the Fed Cup, Seles wanted to participate in the 1992 Olympics. But the International Tennis Federation disqualified her, along with Martina Navratilova and Gabriela Sabatini, who also passed up the Fed Cup.

Monica's next move did little to change the minds of those who suspected that her every decision was undertaken with an eye to main chance. Following in the footsteps of—or should one say, filling the same pants as—Donna Rice, the dish fatal to Gary Hart's presidential ambitions, and Marla Maples, Donald Trump's on-again, off-again squeeze, Seles signed a contract to endorse No Excuses jeans. At the media carnival called to announce the deal, she drew the line when photographers asked her to turn around and let them shoot her behind.

○ ○ ○

Weeks later Monica landed in another imbroglio. Steffi Graf, the number-one seed at the Virginia Slims of Washington, had been forced to withdraw because of a torn tendon in her right shoulder. Tournament officials and WTA executives begged Seles to fill in. On Sunday, the night before the first round, news was released that Monica had agreed.

Hours later Seles announced that there had been a mistake. She had never committed to play the tournament. A WTA official had misinterpreted a message from her mother, Esther, who spoke little English. Mrs. Seles had meant to say that Monica would *not* be playing in Washington.

The initial response of tennis insiders was to blame Monica. In fact, the WTA was at fault, and this resulted in changes in their system of verifying messages. But that was little consolation to the Virginia Slims of Washington, which in addition to lacking a top seed, was assailed on all sides by interest groups that objected to its title sponsor, its location, and its high-handed attitude. Protesters were irate that National Park land was used for a profit-making venture sponsored by a cigarette company. Others objected that government officials had displayed favoritism toward private enterprise, laxly permitting the tournament to proceed without posting a mandatory damage deposit. Meanwhile, black and Hispanic groups complained that they had had trouble reserving park land for ethnic celebrations.

Months later, it surprised nobody when ProServ, which owned the tournament, sold it to Ion Tiriac in exchange for $2 million and the rights to a special event which the agency and the Rumanian entrepreneur would co-promote. Tiriac transferred the tournament to Essen, Germany, and renamed it the Nokia Grand Prix. The special event he had previously run in Essen was switched to Washington and would continue as the WTA's only officially sanctioned exhibition.

With this act of legerdemain a stewing pot of problems disappeared.

True, Washington wouldn't have a tournament with genuine competition, but all people cared about was stars—or so the prevailing theory ran.

O O O

The prevailing theory on the U.S. Open was a more complicated proposition. Many players and much of the press claimed to hate Flushing Meadow, its weather, its facilities, and, above all, its Big Apple attitude which treated aggravation and bickering as spectator sports. One ITF official dubbed the U.S. Open "the orneriest Grand Slam event. It's New York and everybody's hot and irritable, and it's the end of the year and all the players are tired. There are always more fines here."

For years, foreign journalists—that is, anyone not from Manhattan—have filed stories about the Open that read like items from News of the Weird. Even before the tournament moved from decorous Forest Hills to Deco-turfed Flushing Meadow, eerie anecdotes had become part of its folklore. In 1977 someone shot an unsuspecting fan in the leg during an Eddie Dibbs–John McEnroe match. (When did that ever happen at Wimbledon?) In the same year, after the final, the crowd overran the court, and Jimmy Connors vented his frustration in defeat by punching a few spectators. The following year, on a practice court, Connors dropped his shorts and flashed his buttocks in the faces of shocked onlookers. Ilie Nastase, never to be outdone by Jimbo, once changed his shorts on the Grandstand Court at Flushing Meadow. Then never to be outdone by Jane Goodall, Nasty attended a night match accompanied by a chimpanzee.

Unhinged by heat, confused by flora and fauna not found at other tournaments, suffering from acrophobia in a press box perched on the uppermost rim of Louis Armstrong Stadium, reporters aren't entirely to blame for the reputation that has attached itself to the U.S. Open. There *is* chaos and there *is* cacophony. The courts do shimmer like griddles during the day, and at night players have to squint to follow the trajectory of the ball while thousands of yawping fans fling insults and sometimes more substantial items, such as beer cans. In late afternoon there is a smell reminiscent of burnt human flesh, but it's usually just sizzling hamburgers and hot dogs. In 1981, a garbage bin caught fire and play had to be suspended until the smoky stench cleared.

Still, I confess, I like the place. Although it's perfectly charmless and couldn't strike a grace note with anything more subtle than a sledge-hammer, it has no girders or overhanging roofs to obstruct the views. Walkways leading to the field courts are wide enough so that spectators can move from match to match more rapidly than at Roland Garros or the All England Club, and everybody who buys a ticket is assured a seat in the stadium. If genial anarchy distinguishes the Italian Open, if *haute cuisine* and haughtiness are the hallmarks of the French Open, if stodgy hierarchy and proud tradition characterize Wimbledon, then an unabashed democratic impulse is the signature of the U.S. Open. Like New York City itself, the tournament is loud, extroverted, simulta-neously iconoclastic and celebrity-obsessed, yet always saved—just barely—by a sense of self-deprecating humor.

○ ○ ○

During the first week, I roved around the field courts, sampling a smor-gasbord of matches. On Court Six, Sandra Cecchini played Monique Javer in front of a dozen fans and one very large praying mantis. It was poised on a row of abandoned bleachers and got almost as much attention as the match.

On Court Fourteen, Brenda Schultz fought to impose her power game on Akiko Kijimuta of Japan. Sitting with Brenda's coach, Juan Nunez, was Wilt Chamberlain, the seven-foot two-inch ex-basketball star watching the six-foot two-inch Dutch girl who had just won her first WTA tournament a week ago in Schenectady, New York.

Wilt said he preferred the women's game. "There's more to watch. The rallies last longer, so you get to see different strokes. With the men, the ball's moving a hundred miles an hour and you don't get to see much. You hear a man's match. You get to watch tennis with the women."

"Do you have a favorite?" I asked.

"Not really. I like Laura Gildemeister's forehand and Jana Novot-na's backhand slice. I like Capriati's return of serve and Seles's baseline game. I move around and find something to admire in every match."

○ ○ ○

In the third set of her run-in with Elna Reinach, Bettina Fulco was hot-footing it around the court. Her short spiky hair had wilted like the petals of a chrysanthemum and her drenched shirt hung from her shoulders as if from hooks. Between points, she tried to wipe off her sweaty palms, but not a stitch of her clothing was dry.

At other Grand Slam events the final set doesn't end with a tie-break. They play it out until somebody wins by two games. Not so at the U.S. Open, and that had to be a relief to Bettina, whose rubbery legs didn't look like they'd carry her much farther. She held on to win, and Pablo Villella vaulted the fence and embraced his wife-to-be. When they stepped apart, he bore on his shirt a damp imprint of her body.

On the Grandstand Court Jennifer Capriati was dicing and slicing Eva Pfaff of Germany into a fine puree. Separated from the action by a mesh screen, four salad chefs from Racquets Restaurant were doing some dicing and slicing of their own, and while they cut up cabbage for cole slaw, they gazed out through the loosely woven screen at the match.

"You've got a great view," I said.

"Yeah, but you don't want to lose track of what you're doing," said one chef, holding up his bandaged hand.

○ ○ ○

Since the U.S. Open paid men and women equal prize money, that dispute rarely cropped up in press conferences or in private conversation. Still, money was on people's minds, and there were those who felt there was too much moola at Grand Slam events and that, ironically, it had a negative effect on the quality of competition. Because the payoff for first-round losers had quadrupled in the last decade—it was now nearly six thousand dollars—and because Grand Slam events provided various discounts, freebies, and per diem allowances, many marginal players who would previously have skipped the Open were now showing up, sleepwalking their way through matches, collecting their checks and flying home. Although this occurred in both men's and women's events, it didn't matter how many male clay-court specialists paddled their way to an early exit; only the women were harshly judged. Some critics went so far as to suggest that the women's draw should be reduced from 128 players to 98.

○ ○ ○

After routing her first-round opponent, Monica Seles made a valiant attempt to convince the press that it had been a tough struggle, but talk soon turned to the racy tennis outfit she promised to unveil.

"I am definitely going to do one thing. That is for sure. But the clothing, it's tough, you know. People have, you know, traditional clothing. It's very hard to change it. I am trying to bring new things into tennis—the clothing, advance the clothing, the racquets. I think for the fun of it, we should create different outfits just for a few matches so it could be kind of fun for the crowd."

"Could you give us any clue what you have in mind?" a reporter asked.

"I gave like three, four ideas which are very different." Monica galloped off in her Gatling gun fashion, firing words at such speed that the court stenographer, who recorded every press conference, had difficulty keeping up. "I think a few of them [at Fila] were a little bit shocked, but, you know, after I talked to them, they kind of listened to me, said okay, we will try them. You know Italy. They're on vacation a whole month. There was nobody I could talk to. I might be talking to them today. In the second week I think I will love to do something like that."

Infected by Monica's diction, a reporter asked, "Is that kind of like an Agassi kind of thing?"

"It is going to be very different from Nike," she said. "Fila is a different company. It's going to be very sophisticated, but very different, you know. We will have fun with it."

For the rest of the tournament Monica tantalized journalists until they were all salivating like couturier critics eager to catch a glimpse of the fall line. But when I spoke to a highly placed executive at Fila, a fellow I knew from Italy, he was baffled by her comments and said

there was no plan—no chance!—for Monica to wear anything new
during the U.S. Open. He insisted that the outfit she kept describing
didn't exist, not even on the drawing board.

"Monica made a few suggestions," the Fila executive said. "She
wanted some fringe or something on the front of her outfit. Our designers
listened and simply ignored her. I mean, Monica is a great tennis player,
but she has no background in fashion and she has no experience in
marketing. What's the point of putting her in an outfit no one likes or
buys?"

As for letting her play a few matches in a one-of-a-kind outfit just
for the fun of it, the Fila executive dismissed that idea as absurd. "We're
paying her a lot of money and we're doing that to sell a lot of clothes,
not so she can design a dress. Also, there's another thing. It's not nice
to say, but it's true. Monica has a big ass. She doesn't realize how big
it is and how that limits what she can wear."

O O O

Like the link between sport and fashion, the connection between female
athletes and beauty is a mine field of misconceptions. I repeatedly heard
people remark how handsome male players were and how homely many
of the women were. By their nature, such judgments are subjective. But
the skewed perception of female athletes runs far beyond subjectivity
into murky areas involving sexual roles.

Almost everything a male athlete does to make himself a champion
satisfies some conventional expectation and theoretically adds to his
allure. In becoming muscular, powerful, competitive, rich, and successful, a man need have no fear that he's undermining his masculinity
or consigning himself to the fringes of society. Instead, he moves to
the head of the pack, where he has more access to women and more
opportunities to express his sexuality. If he chooses to marry and have
a family, he can combine that with his career. If he prefers to stay single
and sleep around, he may suffer a few awkward bouts of publicity and
pay a bit of child support, but he's unlikely to lose his endorsement
income or his popularity.

For a female athlete, however, almost every decision is freighted
with difficulties that men rarely face. On the tour I was constantly

reminded of the balance that women were forced to strike between their
ambitions and society's expectations, between their determination to be
unique—i.e., number one—and their wish to be "normal," between
their desire to excel and their fear of losing their femininity. All this
was complicated by the fact that while the definition of a handsome
man was infinitely flexible, the ideal of female beauty had a narrow
range. A little extra weight here, not enough there, and a girl was
dismissed as ugly. Just being too tall could put her beyond the pale.

That evening I set off to the WTA's 15th Annual Awards Gala at
the Marriott Marquis. During the day, Clairol, the title sponsor of the
U.S. Open Women's Singles Championship, had been at the hotel doing
cosmetic "makeovers" of players, and the metamorphosis in some
instances was so stupefying that barely pubescent teenagers resembled
vamps, and young women could have passed for *haute couture* models.

In a sense this was the realization of the claim Andrea Temesvari
had made months ago at the French Open. Given the right clothes and
accessories, allowed enough time to get ready, tennis players could look
as lovely as any batch of women you were apt to see at a sorority party
or beauty pageant.

Off court and out of their endorsement duds, they acted like colts
frisking in a field of clover. They didn't stare through each other; they
didn't avoid eye contact with strangers. They laughed; they called out
to friends; they chatted with sponsors, journalists, and guests. Then after
dinner, during the awards ceremony, they spoke with the kind of aplomb
and good humor they seldom displayed in press conferences.

Gigi Fernandez, who along with Jana Novotna won the award for
the year's best doubles team, gave a touching acceptance speech in
which she explained why she relished this trophy. Tennis was a lonely
sport, a selfish one, she said, so it pleased her to excel in an event where
you had a partner and worked together with another girl for a change.

When it was Jana's turn to speak, she shook her head at Gigi's
remarks and said, "I am going to make a little shorter now." That got
a laugh, as did Gigi's reaction. She pretended to stab Jana in the back
with the Baccarat crystal trophy.

Martina Navratilova, nattily attired in a tailored pants suit, also got
a good laugh when she welcomed Nuprin, a new sponsor, as "the official

pain reliever of the WTA. At least once a month we all appreciate your existence.''

Nobody was quite as adept at the podium as Pam Shriver. The newly elected president of the WTA Board of Directors said she had just spoken long distance to Chris Evert and had a message from the past president, who was now in the third trimester of a difficult pregnancy. Chris wanted everybody to know ''she will not be appearing nude à la Demi Moore on the cover of *Vanity Fair* magazine. But she said she'd be willing to appear on the cover of *Inside Women's Tennis* [the official WTA publication], if it would improve circulation—the magazine's and hers.''

The evening ended with more laughter and bonhomie. Then the next day we all went back to work.

○ ○ ○

For American reporters, access to athletes seems an inalienable right, and so it rankled them at most tennis tournaments to be shunted into the role of passive note takers at rigidly controlled press conferences. At Roland Garros and Wimbledon, locker rooms remain off limits, and admission to players' lounges is restricted to short visits. At Flushing Meadow, however, the men's and women's locker rooms were open to the press. (In the case of the women, it was actually an anteroom that was accessible.) And the lounge was often populated with more ink-stained wretches than with players. Along with the other choral figures of the circuit—agents, coaches, and sponsors—we sat at picnic tables, under superfluous umbrellas, eating meals from the buffet, listening to the murmur of half a dozen TV monitors, all of us hashing over the day's events.

''It's an absurd situation,'' one agent bent my ear, ''when hype and the capitulation of the press result in so much publicity and money for so few girls. Some of them have never won anything, some of them are just juniors. Meanwhile, girls in the top twenty, even the top ten, are completely unknown. You don't believe me, go out there''—he flung an arm toward the Stadium Court—''and ask people in the stands. Fewer of them know the name of the number-five girl than know Venus Williams.''

What about Venus Williams? I asked. Why was he so bugged about the poor eleven-year-old black girl whom experts picked as the next Capriati?

"Don't get me wrong and don't use my name," he pleaded. "I don't want to miss out on Venus. I think my agency has a shot at her, we really do. But this is ridiculous. She's only eleven."

"Then why not leave her alone?"

"That's what everybody asks. Like it's agents hustling her and her family, offering these outrageous sums of money. But lemme tell you, we're the ones being hustled. Her father is priming the pump, building a market for his daughter. He's playing the press like a harp. He keeps claiming he wants to protect Venus from exposure, but every time you turn around, she's on TV, she's in *Sports Illustrated,* she's on the front page of *The New York Times.* And nobody, not even the *Times,* asks a single hard question."

"Such as?"

"Who's hustling who? Who's offering all those millions of dollars Richard Williams says people are dangling in front of his daughter? I'll tell you who. Nobody! This is all bullshit. It's not just she's too young. She's black. Okay, it's sad, it's sickening, but face it, tennis doesn't have a great track record with black players. Zina Garrison had to reach the Wimbledon finals before she got a clothing contract. So do you really believe sponsors or agents are falling all over each other to pay millions to a little black girl who's never played anyplace outside of Southern California?"

The agent urged me to call Richard Williams and ask him point-blank for the names of the people who had supposedly offered him money.

Instead, I phoned an old friend, Richard Roth, a correspondent at CBS-TV in Los Angeles. Shortly after *The New York Times* ran its front-page feature on Venus Williams, Roth wanted to do a piece about her for the evening news, and initially her father had been receptive. He allowed CBS to film her practicing on the shabby public courts of Compton, California, and he spoke at some length to Roth.

"We planned careers for our kids before they were born," Mr.

Williams told Roth. "Most parents say, 'I support what my kid wants to do.' But no kid knows what he wants to do. It's up to the parents to decide."

What Mr. Williams had decided was that tennis was his daughter's ticket out of the ghetto.

"He had great discipline," Roth said of Mr. Williams. "A great sense of what's appropriate behavior. There was great affection between father and daughter."

But Roth acknowledged that early on he had a feeling that Richard Williams "was a control freak. But maybe that's appropriate if you're raising a tennis star."

When Roth asked to shoot footage of Venus at home and returning from school, Williams wouldn't permit it. Neither would he let CBS film her in competition at a local tournament. Although the tournament organizer was more than happy to have TV coverage, "Williams didn't want it. He said it would upset other parents."

Roth had a different impression. He thought Williams didn't "want Venus to be seen on national TV in a disadvantageous setting. What if she loses? He was being careful to develop and foster not only a tennis star, but an image and an aura. Presumably that would make her more marketable." Roth pointed out that for all his protests about commercial exploitation, Williams had distributed a booklet about his daughter to potential sponsors.

Shortly thereafter, two attorneys called Roth from Seattle, said they represented Mr. Williams's interests, and inquired about the project CBS planned to do with Venus. Roth told them there was no "project." He simply hoped to shoot a short news feature.

"I was determined to tell her story," Roth said. "They were determined to tell her story themselves." Williams "wouldn't give up his conditions and control." In all his years of reporting, Roth said he had never seen such micromanagement, not even when he covered George Bush's presidential campaign. "I had an impression that if [Williams] said to his daughter to play on hot coals, she'd do it."

When they couldn't reach an agreement about the ground rules, Roth abandoned his piece about Venus Williams. But he wasn't surprised to see her pop up later on the "Today Show." "I assume one of two things. That that was a better venue for the exposure Williams wanted. Or the 'Today Show' was willing to accept the conditions he imposed.

"I thought I was going to be doing a story about talent and innocence," Roth summed things up. "But at eleven years old the innocence was lost."

○ ○ ○

When I telephoned Richard Williams at his home in Compton, California, he asked me to call him right back at another number. Then he explained that he and his family were moving in a few days to Rick Macci's International Tennis Academy at the Grenelefe Resort, not far from Orlando, Florida. Macci, who had coached Jennifer Capriati during the embryonic stage of her career, ran a program that could accommodate up to forty players between the ages of ten and eighteen. The basic charge, waived in the case of gifted girls like Venus, was $2,200 a month for room, board, tennis instruction, and transportation to and from local public schools.

Macci once told *The New York Times* that children at his academy were not "in Florida to work on their suntan. You hate to use the word 'job' in connection with a kid, but if they want to get good, they've got to put in the work."

Yet Richard Williams described Venus's enrollment at Macci's camp as an intellectual opportunity. "We're going to just make sure she going there and stay very clever like she been doing. And we're going to keep pushing her education and get her a great education." Then he said, "Hold on a minute, please." And after a pause, "I'm going to have to cut off this. My attorney . . . uh, is there any way I can talk to you later?"

He suggested I call back in twenty minutes, and when I did so, I asked if in addition to getting a great education in the public schools of Haines City, Florida, Venus would be playing some major junior events. Williams said she wouldn't.

"How many years of seasoning do you feel she needs before she sets out on the tour?" I asked.

"If it was up to me," he said, "she wouldn't be out on that circuit for another nine years. I would like to see her get an education. There's too many kids out there that are nothing but kids and they should be in school.''

He decried the fact that many juniors were manhandled by their fathers and coaches. ''I've seen kids with their wrists broken,'' he said. ''I've seen them getting their behinds kicked, getting choked.

''You kind of wonder,'' Williams mused. ''So many people say you're stupid if you don't do this and you don't do that. You just have to have your own values and your goals and do not detour from it. You see, in tennis, what a lot of people have to realize is money have went up a hundred percent compared to if you look at it ten years ago. But that pressure have gone up twelve thousand percent. There's nothing wrong with having a million dollars. I'm not saying I want to be poor. I'm tired of being poor. But I feel like as long as you have the love of your kids, you couldn't be poor. You have something that's really great. And it's not the kids want a million dollars, the kids just want love. The parents have learned what money can do and what you can have. And I think that when you start prostituting your kid that way, you're not a good parent.''

He said if he kept Venus out on a practice court six or seven hours a day six days a week, ''Sure, I could have a superstar at fourteen. And I'm going to have nothing but a problem at twenty or twenty-two. A lot of people tell me that the younger they are when they go out there, the more money you get. But see, we're not in this for no money. I would rather see her out there when she's twenty years old. By that time she would have had four years of college. There's too many kids out there now not able to talk, they can't speak correctly, they can't make decisions. The agent makes the decisions, the parents are making their decisions, television's making their decisions, newspapers are making their decisions. The kid is just something out there like a piece of meat.''

Richard Williams had spoken of personal values, education, the importance of love, the destructive power of money, and it was impossible to argue with his conclusions. But the fact remained that his daughter was moving across the continent to enroll in a tennis academy, not Andover, not a convent.

I pointed out that there were people who thought he was working the press and waiting for the best deal. Some believed that there had been no concrete offers to date, and he was angling for one.

"You're going to hear all sort of things out there," he replied. "I guess a person has to believe what they read or what they don't read. But there has never ever been a person that has been me, Richard Williams, before, and anyone that know Richard Williams, they'll say Richard is the only guy I've ever known that have turned down this and turned down that. He's really interested in his girls getting an education. I've met a lot of people that's thought that I was waiting to get the best deal in the world, but it's no fake here. We've been offered probably more than any junior. There's never been a junior offered what we've been offered. But offers are not going to make you a better person. Money don't make you better than no one else. It's what type of morals you have. And if you don't have education, you don't have anything. You can have all the money in the world, but you need an education."

Again, no one could quarrel with him about that. Still, I wondered what he had been offered and by whom. When Jennifer Capriati was thirteen she had signed endorsement contracts worth several million dollars. In claiming to have rejected even larger deals, Mr. Williams was saying a mouthful.

"Has Venus signed with an agency?" I asked.

He chuckled. "No, not yet. She's too young."

"Could you say who these people are who have offered these sums of money?"

"No, I, I, I, I couldn't tell you. But yes, we have been made some major offers to sign her up."

"So these are major offers for endorsement contracts, you mean?"

"No. These are anything from investors to management companies. Just name it." But that was precisely what he wouldn't do—name it or them.

"When you say management companies, do you mean the [tennis] agencies themselves?"

"Other kinds of management companies," he said, and let it go without further explanation.

When I returned to the agent who first spoke to me about Venus Williams, he said, "Of course Richard won't name the investors and

management companies. There are none. But at least he's got her at
Rick Macci's. If they had gone to Nick Bolletieri's . . . Well, figure it
out for yourself. IMG owns Nick's chain of academies. They'd have
had the inside track on Venus. Now we still have a shot at signing her
when the time's right. Tennis agents are guilty of lots of things, but
we're not stupid. We're not going to guarantee a little girl millions of
dollars until she's ready to start making money for us.''

◯ ◯ ◯

After Navratilova whipped Patricia Tarabini 6–2, 6–2, a reporter asked
Martina whether she could shut out Judy Nelson's palimony suit during
matches.

   "I don't worry about it,'' Navratilova said. "It's there, but when
I'm on court I don't think, 'Oh my God, what's it costing me now?'
It's going to be there for a while and I've come to terms with that and
I'm just happy because I'm healthy and I'm playing well and it's great
to be in New York.''

   "What's the next step?''

   "There's a hearing in Dallas right after the Open. It's going to be
a beaut.''

   "You say it's going to be a beaut?'' a reporter asked.

   "Yeah, that's a joke,'' she instructed members of the press who
were humor-impaired.

◯ ◯ ◯

Although always loquacious, Monica Seles lacked Martina's willingness
to address every issue from sexual affairs to current affairs. Asked about
the situation in Yugoslavia, she started off by assuring the press, "I
always talk to my grandparents and ask them if they are all great. They
are very safe.'' Then she remembered something. "Well, he died, my
grandfather. So my grandmother is still there.''

   "Where do they live?''

   "They live in the other part.''

   "What part?''

   "I don't want to get into that stuff. I don't really want to get into
politics.''

"What is the name of the city?" someone demanded.

"It's very complicated. You know, it was something and it is now—"

"It's part of Serbia?"

She nodded. "Part of Serbia."

○ ○ ○

On Wednesday, as the press bus rolled into Flushing Meadow, a billboard flashed the time—10:40 A.M.—and the temperature—ninety-four degrees. The heat did little for anyone's mood. While it never took much to nettle Helen Kelesi, the usually good-natured Sara Gomer was also annoyed. She complained to the umpire that Kelesi yelped as she ran for the ball, groaned as she lunged at it, then grunted as she hit it. That was two sound effects too many.

By late afternoon, a pyramid of clouds towered over Court Sixteen. For a few minutes a soothing shower fell. The first scattered drops seemed to hiss as they hit the Deco Turf, delaying a match between Kathy Rinaldi and Gigi Fernandez. But within minutes, the sky cleared, and we were all stewing and steaming again.

Rinaldi's face was blanched with sunblock. Considering how much time they spent outdoors and how often they must have heard warnings about skin cancer, one would have assumed all the girls would wear a sunscreen. But many complained that it clogged their pores and ruined their complexions. They preferred to risk sun damage rather than pimples.

Gigi Fernandez, who hailed from Puerto Rico, appeared to glory in the heat. Her brown arms and legs glistened with perspiration. But a supervisor showed up, inspected the sleeve of Fernandez's shirt, and ruled that she was wearing too many logos. She'd have to cover one of them. Somebody ran to fetch a roll of tape.

"This is ridiculous," Rinaldi said. "Just rip the thing off."

I idly scrawled Kathy's comment in my notebook, doing no more than marking time. A man beside me snapped, "Are you writing an article about this match?"

I said I was doing a book. Noticing a resemblance, I asked if he was Rinaldi's father.

"Yes. I don't want you writing down what we say." Mrs. Rinaldi was with him. "And I don't think you should write what Kathy said about Gigi's patch. That wasn't said to you. It was said to us."

When I pointed out as politely as possible that there wasn't anything even mildly controversial about her comment, he continued to complain that he didn't care to sit here the whole match worrying whether I was copying down his remarks.

I suggested that in that case perhaps he and Mrs. Rinaldi should sit elsewhere. But they stayed put, knotted in sweaty silent anger. Or maybe it was their daughter's play that turned them to stone.

After spurting to a 4–1 lead, Kathy spiraled off into the sort of tailspin she had experienced in Paris. She lost five games in what must have been for her and her parents sick-making succession. At first, the points and games were close, but the farther Rinaldi fell behind, the more she began to beat herself. Plagued by double faults and unforced errors, she tried to recover too quickly, as if hoping to regain the lead with a couple of overpowering strokes.

When the first set went in Gigi's favor, Kathy looked depleted. But her parents bridled with pent-up emotion. No longer able to remain silent, they moved to the far side of the court and spoke animatedly for the rest of the match. They didn't have long to talk. Kathy lost the second set 6–1.

○ ○ ○

Gigi Fernandez's coach, Julie Anthony, retreated to the cool refuge of the players' lounge. In the early Seventies, during the dying days of the Age of Aquarius and the first lively seasons of the Virginia Slims tour, Julie had resembled a flower child who had stumbled dreamily onto the circuit. *New York Times* reporter Grace Lichtenstein described her as looking like "Claire Bloom playing Ophelia. But on court, the sinewy muscles in her tanned arms and legs belied the impression of frailty."

More than just a lovely girl with a long mane of hair, Julie Anthony came closer to being an intellectual than anybody in tennis. "I got interested in yoga because of the parallels between its philosophy and some in psychology, like Gestalt therapy," she told Lichtenstein in

1973. "That's one reason why I'm back in tennis, to try and resolve in my own mind how much control you can exert over your body via your mind."

After getting an undergraduate degree from Stanford, she had alternated stints of pro tennis with stretches of graduate study in clinical psychology. Players and reporters referred to her as Doc long before she finished her Ph.D., and there was general agreement that she could have been highly ranked if she hadn't restricted herself to competing during vacations and summer breaks.

"It was exhausting," she told me. "I would do well at tournaments, but never played enough to get a good ranking. I usually had to qualify. Then in my fifth year of grad school, I reversed things and played nine months of tennis and did three months of course work."

In retrospect, she regarded tennis and education not as antithetical extremes in her life but as points on a continuum. While sport had served as a release from the tensions of school, her studies provided a healthy perspective on the circuit. In principle, a contemporary player could do what she had done—shuttle back and forth between graduate work and tennis—and do it more easily now with the help of wild cards and special exemptions. But she doubted anybody would try.

"I don't see anyone on the tour who's interested in school," Julie said as we sat in a gazebo located incongruously next to a row of buzzing, bonging video machines. Now in her forties, she was still slim and attractive, but had a slight limp from a leg injury. "I played tennis to make enough money to pay for grad school. But of course, I didn't have the temptations of agents telling me to quit high school and go on the tour."

Julie conceded that even if she had had a shot at today's prize money, she would have chosen to complete her education. Still, she didn't care to criticize girls who dropped out. She was in favor of people fulfilling their potential as they saw fit. "I feel it's a privilege to pursue something you do well. If, indeed, you're driving yourself and not being pushed." She pointed out that despite the lip service paid to excellence, despite the claim that tennis taught valuable lessons in life, few players developed outside interests, or bothered to pursue excellence in other areas.

"I think the women gain a little social grace from their experience on the tour, but they don't have time to benefit in other ways. The shame is that they don't get book knowledge. A lot of them shut down and don't even read the newspaper. What they're exposed to they don't soak up. They're so overwhelmed by stimuli, they have to narrow their vision to get some peace. The trouble is, after they retire, how can they open up to the rest of their lives?''

Even now in an era of instant teenage millionaires, Julie preferred to view tennis as a means instead of an end, as a vehicle for personal growth, not a destination. "One of the fun things about coaching Gigi is getting her to understand that what I'm doing has to do with more than tennis.''

In the years after its inception, and especially after Billie Jean King's victory over Bobby Riggs in "The Battle of the Sexes"—that 1973 match still held the record for the largest live audience, 30,472, and highest TV rating of any tennis event in history—the women's tour had been seen as a force for feminine liberation. Players were said to have carved out an identity separate from men and, in the words of their oldest sponsor, come a long way, baby.

Yet while the game had prospered financially and improved technically, there were questions about what else had been achieved. Like a lot of WTA pioneers, Julie Anthony expressed ambivalence. "I see the women's tour as progressive in feminist terms because women can be financially self-sufficient. But there are other ways in which the women's movement has gone backward.''

The tour, Julie said, had always been a small, self-referential universe. "When I went to school, then came back to play tournaments in summer, no one asked where I'd been and what I'd been doing. People in tennis simply can't conceive of a world other than their own.''

Although some viewed those early days nostalgically, Julie believed that the narrow, claustrophobic atmosphere of the circuit had allowed problems to go unchecked. Even in the amateur era and the years of low prize money, there had been fathers who battered their daughters. Julie named examples and said there might have been more "if fathers had been able to afford to travel in my era. In my day they stayed at home after juniors. Today the money allows the fathers to follow their daughters, and that increased the tension and the chances for abuse.''

She hastened to add that troubled families existed in every walk of life and "they aren't any more or less dysfunctional in tennis—except insofar as the money exaggerates everything. If tennis optimizes a family's growth, then it can be beneficial. But if it's all about prize money and rankings, then it can be terribly injurious."

Julie went on to say that she was in favor of girls expressing their sexuality. The problem was that they had so few opportunities. "When tennis players aren't practicing, playing matches, or traveling, they're tired." She facetiously agreed that the average plumber's union probably led more interesting and varied sex lives than players on the circuit.

"The insularity is one of the worst things about the tour," she said. "There's so much paranoia. I came from an era in which we coached one another and helped each other. Now there's no group life. There are independent satellites. The good thing about the money today is it lets players hire a support system. The downside is they don't have friends. Everyone is an enemy. Now that I'm Gigi's coach, I may be seen as in the enemy camp."

The thought that she was anybody's enemy was hurtful given her history in tennis. In addition to playing the circuit, she had been married to Dick Butera, at one time the president of the Hilton Head Island Racquet Club and a prominent backer of Billie Jean King's Team Tennis. She had served as a TV commentator, written books and articles about the game, been on the advisory panel of *Tennis* magazine, and often extended hospitality to players at her home in Aspen, Colorado.

But after Julie and Dick Butera split up and she began traveling with Gigi Fernandez, she said, "people I saw in the past as guests and friends pass me by without any eye contact." She described a scene in the locker room at the Australian Open where she sat icing her knee and counting the number of girls who breezed by. Two out of fifty bothered to speak.

"There's a high level of egotism or opportunism on the circuit. When I was in a position to help them, there was no problem. Now I'm with Gigi and I'm considered toxic. It just seems to me bad manners. I try to make sure I don't adopt their manners."

At that moment, Jennifer Capriati greeted Julie and paid back a few dollars she had borrowed.

"Now, she's a breath of fresh air," she said after Jennifer left. "She always says hello."

Another drastic change since her era was the number of coaches, most of them men. "It's logical to have a male coach," Julie said. "A guy hits harder and if you can get his shots back, you can do it with the girls. It's more expensive for Gigi because I don't hit with her. I had a knee operation and haven't hit in five months." Gigi had hired Peter Moore as her sparring partner.

"I feel a woman coach has more empathy with a woman player," Julie said. "Men might be less understanding because power comes so easy to them. But the crucial thing isn't whether a coach is male or female; it's whether he or she is bright or dumb."

I mentioned that Dennis Van der Meer had noticed an odd phenomenon. Some female coaches were now imitating their male counterparts, shouting, "Come on, move your ass!" or "What's the matter? Are you on the rag?"

"Some people respond to a Marine-type coach," Julie said. "I wouldn't be a good fit with that kind of player. I think whenever a woman adopts a man's way of doing things, it's a mistake."

Carrying a tray of food, Gigi Fernandez joined us at the table in the fragile, latticework shelter. A handsome woman with a zaftig figure, Fernandez had brought a plate of marinated potatoes for her coach, and a salad, three bananas, and some plums for herself. Julie asked her which coaching technique worked better with a woman—the militaristic approach or a more empathetic one.

Gigi smiled and shook her head. She wasn't going to bite on that question—not with her mouth full of salad.

I summarized my conversations with male coaches, all of whom emphasized how different it was to work with a woman. Just before the U.S. Open, Don Candy told me, "When you're dealing with a woman, it's never one plus one equals two. It's always one plus one equals four and three-eighths. They're emotionally far out. Right before a match, they always want to know how they look." He recounted how Pam Shriver once broke into tears before she went on court for fear that her shoes didn't look right.

The hardest thing about coaching a woman, Candy said, was you couldn't threaten her the way you could a boy. "You threaten a boy and he understands. You threaten a girl and it's a heavy scene."

Julie doubted whether threats worked with boys any better than with girls, but Gigi surprised her by saying that she understood what Candy meant. Sure, if a coach bullied her, "a woman might start to cry. Women *are* more sensitive. But sometimes it helps when a coach is tough and won't take any excuses."

Gigi gave a personal example. On the day of a match, she had a tendency, in her words, to "freak out" during practice. Julie sympathized with these pregame jitters. But Peter Moore, Gigi's sparring partner, refused to put up with them. So from now on, she had decided, it would be better if Julie didn't indulge her emotionally. Before a match she preferred to work out alone with Peter in a no-nonsense manner.

"Sometimes it helps to have a coach be tough," Gigi repeated. Then she praised the juicy plums and passed one to her coach.

O O O

By Thursday, Flushing Meadow fried under a Saharan sun. The temperature at court level was 120 degrees. For the first time in its history, the tournament dispatched boys with umbrellas to shade the players during changeovers. Patty Fendick had more trouble with the heat than with her Czech opponent. Her face looked like braised meat. She took a wet towel from an ice chest and yoked it around her neck. Up in the stands, spectators had towels draped over their heads, like bedouins swaddled in keffiyehs.

Mary Pierce was floundering against Lori McNeil, a fine black player who could kill points quickly with her volleys. They split sets, then McNeil bounded to a 5–2 lead in the third. Mary looked finished, looked like someone lost in the desert staggering up an endless dune. But her father never stopped shouting encouragement. Rocking metronomically in his seat, Jim called out, "C'mon, Mar-*ee!*"

Mary broke to 3–5, then held to 4–5. But McNeil had a second chance to serve out the match.

"C'mon, Mar-*ee!*" Jim yelled. "Don't let up."

His daughter did as instructed and broke to even the score at 5–5, and with her father screaming, "Go! Go!" she got to 40–0 on her serve.

But then she was betrayed by her ball toss, a high one that sailed up into the blinding sun. She couldn't put her first serve in. Then she started missing her second. Jim hollered at the linesman, "The ball was in, Goddammit!" But Mary fell to 5–6, and McNeil served for the match a third time.

Jim was screaming louder after each point. So were several thousand spectators. McNeil had contracted Mary's serving maladies; she doublefaulted to send the set into a tie-break. Lori reached double match point, yet couldn't come up with the clincher. When Mary clobbered a backhand winner to knot the score, McNeil had nothing left. Neither did the crowd, which clapped politely, then fled for the shade as Mary Pierce won.

But Jim Pierce still had plenty of adrenaline pumping. He sprinted onto the court and laid into a linesman with a loud barrage of complaints about bad calls. Then he hurried off, and I had to run to catch him in a hallway outside the players' lounge.

Carrying a couple of equipment bags bandolier-style, the straps crisscrossing his round belly, Pierce was lathered up about the match. "Blown away," was how he said he felt. While he agreed that it had been a gutty performance on Mary's part, he griped that she had fallen into this horrible habit of winning the first set, then frittering away the second.

"I know what it is," he raved on. "She's a sixteen-year-old American girl. If she was European or South American or black, she wouldn't be like that. Our kids have so much given to them, they can't concentrate. You take a Russian girl. She comes in out of a blizzard and falls down on her knees and kisses the court, she's so glad to get a chance to play tennis. And she concentrates!"

Steering him out of the pedestrian traffic, I tried to interrupt. But Pierce was mopping his face with a handkerchief and motor-mouthing like Monica Seles. "I wish I had a million dollars. I'm not in this for the money, but if I had a million, I'd take and give it to Jimmy Connors or Guillermo Vilas and say, 'You train Mary. You give her your guts and work ethic.' Hell, she'd pay attention to them. She doesn't want to listen to me, fat and old and fifty-five. She tells me to go to hell. But I don't have the money. It's not like with Capriati, where there's millions and they're flying in coaches after coaches to train her, and they're setting her up with the best doubles partners and she still doesn't know how to volley."

A couple of Frenchmen crowded in to offer their congratulations.

"Mary runs my whole family," Jim said with a laugh. "Sometimes she pushes me and pushes me right up against the wall until my macho says, 'I can't take any more of this.' "

When it became clear I wasn't going to get to speak to him privately, I postponed asking Pierce about Taranto.

O O O

On one of the few spaces at the National Tennis Center not paved with asphalt, on an expanse of grass beneath a clump of sycamore trees, lay a legion of fans who looked as though they had been struck low by heat prostration. Gazing out at them, Juan Avendano might have been reminded of his client, Mary Joe Fernandez. After Wimbledon, while playing a special event in Newport, Rhode Island, she had suffered a severe case of dehydration. She had eaten nothing before the match, Juan said, had lost a lot of fluid in the first set, then had to quit in the second. After that, things took a turn for the worst.

A short, square-set fellow with a flattop haircut, Juan said, "It was like in a movie. I was called into the girls' locker room. Mary Joe was down on the floor and her mother was standing over her. Mary Joe was very scared. Her eyes . . . I saw in her eyes she was scared when they put the oxygen mask over her face. Then they take her out the back way so nobody can see and we go to the hospital in an ambulance."

After a few days on intravenous fluids, Fernandez flew to England for the Federation Cup. From there she moved down to Marbella, Spain, for more exhibitions. But after one match, she had to withdraw. Still not fully recovered from her dehydration, she had been beset by an intestinal disorder. Juan said she had lost "about five kilos," or eleven pounds, and he hunched his shoulders to show how skinny she looked. "We always tell her to eat more, but she doesn't."

Though she was laboring to rebuild her strength, there wasn't time for rest or recuperation. A week after the U.S. Open, she was scheduled to play a tournament in Tokyo. Then she had to return via Europe and participate in Ion Tiriac's special event in Essen, Germany.

"She's not playing so well now, not like Wimbledon when she beat Arantxa. But, well, we're here and she's playing."

○ ○ ○

I wasn't alone in my quest for an interview with Jim Pierce. Camera crews dogged his footsteps. CBS planned to record his comments during Mary's matches with a secret sound boom. ABC shot a feature that would air later that fall. Journalists clamored for quotes, and Jim wasn't reluctant to supply them. Nobody could complain that he wasn't good copy, or that he didn't have a sly sense of humor. Since he had been saddled with the title of Tennis Father From Hell, he played it to the hilt.

"I'm the lead weight around [Mary's] neck," he told *The New York Times*. "To put up with me and everything else, she's got to be like God, mentally. She hasn't gotten a single call in two years because everybody hates me."

Lambasted for letting his daughter drop out of the sixth grade, Jim responded with a ringing denunciation of American education. "High school is some guy scratching his butt, wanting to sell my daughter crack cocaine. I'm trying to get away from that whole mall mentality." Anyway, Mary was taking correspondence courses.

In the spirit of fair play, he didn't spill everything to the *Times*. He told *Newsday*, "As far as the USTA goes, is it too soon to say, 'Go eat your straw hat'? You know what the USTA is good at? Those people are really good at a luncheon with a cocktail in their hands."

To everybody who would listen, Jim touted Mary's talent. "You've only seen the girl. Wait till you see the woman. She's not only going to beat the top five in the world, she's going to dominate them."

I was less interested in whether Mary would beat the top five than whether Jim had beaten her, and I continued to look for an opportunity to ask about Taranto.

○ ○ ○

Notices in the men's and women's locker rooms cautioned players to drink plenty of water before, during, and after matches. They were also urged to eat bananas to replenish the potassium lost through perspiration. Bananas were soon as ubiquitous as Walkmen. Players gobbled them at practice, during changeovers, in courtesy cars, in the lobbies of Manhattan hotels.

A more serious potential health hazard caused concern in some quarters. A highly placed official at the U.S. Open confided to me that people were worried about the sweaty, spit-soaked, and sometimes bloody towels that the ball boys and girls had to handle. What if a player was HIV positive? Could he or she transmit the virus? No matter how remote the possibility, the official felt it would be wise for the tournament to take precautions, either by insisting that players gather up their own used towels or by encouraging ball boys and girls to wear rubber gloves.

Both proposals struck me as improbable. I couldn't see Seles and Sabatini, or Lendl and McEnroe, cleaning up after themselves. And if the USTA frowned on the Reebok Pump Midnight Edition, it was a good bet it wouldn't look favorably on outfitting ball boys and girls like medical-waste technicians.

〇 〇 〇

Out on the field courts I watched two Eastern European girls push themselves to the brink of collapse with punishing baseline rallies. A middle-age man in the bleachers bellowed in a language I didn't understand. It sounded as though he were shouting encouragement, repeating the same word—perhaps "Go!" or "Yes!" or "Good!"

I asked a Czech journalist to translate. He said he'd rather not. "It's not nice what he's saying."

"How bad is it?"

"Very. He's screaming at his daughter, the blond girl."

"Screaming what?"

"Bad things. Because she's losing."

Again I pressed him to translate and he wrote in block letters on his notepad WHORE!

〇 〇 〇

Pale and gaunt, Mary Joe Fernandez arrived at Court Sixteen for her third-round match against Radka Zrubakova. Although Juan Avendano had warned me that she had lost weight, I wasn't prepared for how sickly she looked or how pathetically she played. Perspiration ran in rivulets down her arms and legs, soaking her shirt and even her skirt, leaving puddles on the court. Afterward, she said, "I was sweating so much, I was worried that I was going to slip."

After she lost the first set, she left the court for a few minutes. According to the rules, men are allowed to do this once during a match, but there have been occasions when a player has warned the umpire in advance that he was having intestinal troubles and needed to run to the toilet from time to time. Women are permitted to leave twice for clothing changes and what are euphemistically called "physical necessities."

Mary Joe came back and served to start the second set. Over and over, the game went to deuce. Over and over, Fernandez was victimized by her woeful condition. Breathing with difficulty, moving in obvious pain, she dropped serve, then tried to recover by rushing the net. The idea was right, the execution wrong.

Mary Joe requested an injury time-out, and Kathleen Stroia, the WTA trainer, massaged her legs. Then she wrapped Mary Joe's left leg from the panty line down to the mid-thigh. A fan wolf-whistled, but it was doubtful Fernandez heard him or would have cared if she had. She was sunk too deep in her own misery. She played one game wearing the leg wrap, tore it off, promptly fell behind 2–5, and watched helplessly as Zrubakova served out the match for a shocking 6–1, 6–2 win.

It would have been understandable if Mary Joe had skipped the press conference. But she dutifully endured it and refused to blame the loss on her physical debility. "I just had a flat day." She did admit to being bothered by a strained left hip flexor that prevented her from getting down to low balls.

"I'm going to try to finish in the top five," she said spunkily. "I still have many more tournaments left this year." Which was precisely the problem—too many tournaments, too little time to recover her strength.

ο ο ο

As Jim Pierce and his family headed off to a practice court, I fell into step with him. Although his beefy build and ruff of hair made him appear leonine and menacing, Jim was, as always, affable. "I got ripped by the press again." He was referring to the previous day's articles in *Newsday* and *The New York Times*. "I got my wife mad at me. I got Mary mad at me."

I told him I had a few questions that might make him mad at me. As his family walked on ahead of us, I recounted what I had heard about his behavior in Taranto.

Pierce didn't deny what had happened at the match—that Mary and he had quarreled, that he had heaved a bag of balls at her, and that the two of them had squabbled on the way to the parking lot. But there his version of events diverged from the story told by others.

"Mary spit on me," Jim said, and that had made him mad. "I tried to slap her." He demonstrated with his meaty open palm. "But I caught the corner of her glasses and knocked them off."

Although an onlooker might have concluded that he had struck Mary in the face—which was what he meant to do—and hurt her—which was what he surely would have done if he had connected—Jim swore he missed everything except her glasses.

When I asked whether having her glasses knocked off had injured her—after all, she had withdrawn from the Italian Open—Jim swore he hadn't hurt her and that this scrap wasn't why she dropped out of the next tournament. "I just wanted to get out of Italy. I just didn't want to go up to Rome and pay two hundred and twenty-five dollars a day for the family to stay in a hotel."

Apparently satisfied that he had set my mind at ease, Jim Pierce hurried to catch up with Mary. His wife, Yannick, who had been lugging an equipment bag, left it on the court and climbed into the bleachers to watch her husband and daughter work out. An agent had assured me that whatever else could be said about the Pierces, they were closer than a lot of families on the tour. I didn't know whether to be consoled or disturbed by that thought.

○ ○ ○

That evening there was no break between day matches and the night program. As day ticket holders were herded out of the stadium and 20,491 fans flooded in for the night session, Monica Seles took on the towering Sara Gomer. Since the match scheduled to follow, John McEnroe versus Michael Chang, figured to run on late—in fact, it lasted four and a half hours—tournament officials were eager to get this match over with. Seles happily obliged them, cutting Gomer down to size like someone wielding a chainsaw against a patch of daisies. She tucked the first set away 6–1 in a tidy eighteen minutes.

The second set was closer and not without its stimulating moments for members of the press who followed the match from the video room. As Seles's shirt soaked through with sweat, it became evident that she wasn't wearing a bra. Then a CBS technician with an avid imagination or an interesting camera angle passed the word that Monica wasn't wearing panties either.

Reporters crowded closer to the TV monitor searching for . . . well, for a story. Moments later the CBS source rushed back with an update. Monica did have something on under her dress and it wasn't your standard underpants. More like G-string, he said. But by the end of the match he backtracked and reported that she was, indeed, wearing panties, purple ones.

Seles showed up for her press conference in black jeans, a black leotard top, and a big silver buckle on her belt. Nobody asked about her underwear. Suddenly we all gave a convincing pretense of interest in her tennis.

She snuffled and coughed and dabbed a Kleenex at her nose. "My brother had a cold," she said. "Now he totally gave it to me. I've been coughing up all these things like Becker."

Journalists exchanged startled glances. What things like Becker? Was she saying that when she looked into her Kleenex . . . Forget it! They didn't want to know.

Back in the video room, we watched as the camera zoomed in on John McEnroe, who was wearing a bandeau that looked like something Tatum had bought him at Laura Ashley. Then the monitor showed Monica Seles squeezing into a box seat beside actor Alec Baldwin. His hair greased flat to his skull, his cheeks stubbled with a five-day growth of beard, Baldwin focused on the match. He neither spoke to nor glanced at Monica. Even when a TV commentator crept over to the couple with a mike, Seles was odd girl out—out of the conversation, though not out of the camera's eye.

Although tabloids later suggested a romantic link between Alec Baldwin and Monica Seles, this was a match made not by Cupid, but by WTA and Virginia Slims emissaries who had brought the celebrities together for a photo op under the stands. A movie star with a tennis star—that was the image the women's tour loved to project, the perfect antidote to all the rancid publicity about Martina and Judy. Media flaks urged Monica to go out and sit beside Baldwin. But before she would agree, they had to explain who he was. They reminded her that he was the actor she had seen in that movie about the submarine. *The Hunt for Red October.* Monica remembered and raced to courtside.

ᴑ ᴑ ᴑ

The heat had become so unrelenting it came as a shock when on Saturday a rainstorm dropped the temperature into the low eighties and delayed the start of play for an hour. But as soon as the sun reappeared, the National Tennis Center began to simmer and stew.

Patty Fendick was up a break in the first set on Conchita Martinez. Sweating profusely, Patty had to call for a towel and wipe her hands after each point. As she served for 5–3, something slipped. Perhaps the racquet in her moist palm, perhaps her level of play. Martinez broke to 4–4, then polished off the set 7–5.

Although the umpire instructed spectators to stay in their seats until the changeover, they ignored him. This was New York, and fans did as they liked. They continued to clamber from the creaking, screeching stands. Court Sixteen at Flushing Meadow may be the only one on the tour where the bleachers need to be oiled.

With the score 3–4 and 30–30 in the second set, Patty Fendick committed a double fault, and Conchita Martinez took advantage of the opportunity. When she broke to 5–3, then finished off the match, it highlighted how crucial Fendick's double fault had been. Tennis was a curious game in which individual points and entire games sometimes meant little. A player could actually win more points than an opponent and still lose a match, or win more games—as in a 7–6, 0–6, 7–6 encounter—and come up short. In a tight match, timing and sequence were all-important. Lots of players could pound out winners when the pressure was off, but couldn't buy a point when they needed it.

Tennis was also a game where you couldn't pile up a lead, then let the clock run out, as in basketball or football. Steffi Graf relearned this lesson against Eva Sviglerova. After rolling to a 6–4, 5–0 lead, she waited for Eva to lose the last game. But the Czech girl refused to accommodate her and won five games in a row. In the process, Graf squandered five match points. On the sixth, she killed Sviglerova's comeback but had to be concerned about her wavering powers of concentration.

O O O

As I passed through the International Food Village, an enclave next to the Stadium Court where fans could feast on everything from domestic and imported beers to margaritas, from hamburgers to ham and brie on croissants, I bumped into Gerry Smith, the WTA's Executive Director and CEO. On this sweltering day, he wore a coat and tie and managed to project an aura of cool imperturbability. When I asked for an interview, he cheerfully complied, and we sat at a cluttered lunch table in the shade of a tree.

It would be impossible to exaggerate the extent to which Smith's attitude contrasted with that of most officials on the tour. The usual instinct of tennis authorities is to avoid the press, evade questions, decline to comment on controversial matters, and threaten legal action or physical mayhem when a reporter presses the wrong button. One day at this year's U.S. Open I asked tournament referee Tom Barnes whether Jimmy Connors would be fined for his obscene outbursts at an umpire. Barnes's prompt reply was, "Get out of my office."

"Excuse me? Are you the guy who decides on fines?"

"I'm the guy," said Barnes. "Now get out of my office, or I'll call security."

When I reminded him that I wasn't in his office—I was in a room to which accredited journalists were supposed to have access—he summoned the guards.

In contrast, Gerry Smith was unfailingly polite and personable—

which was not to claim that in discussing difficult issues he always gave a clear answer.

When I asked how the WTA could justify its relationship with Virginia Slims cigarettes, a product that not only generated bad publicity but caused health problems and deaths, Smith repeated what had so often been said by mouthpieces on the women's tour. "There's a strongly linked identity between Virginia Slims and tennis. No sport in the world has had the same sponsor for twenty years. In its formative stages, the women's tour was concentrated in the United States. Thus the relationship between Virginia Slims and tennis grew deeper."

Basically, he was pointing out that women's tennis and Virginia Slims had been in business a long time. Far from an explanation, I said, that restated the problem.

The soul of pleasantness, Smith tried again. "As long as tobacco is a legal product, I think they have a right to participate." He didn't see any great problem now, unlike the year before when Health and Human Services Secretary Louis Sullivan "decided to make an issue and make political hay."

Gerry Smith glanced up at the outside scoreboard on the Stadium Court, where Jimmy Connors was battling Karel Novacek. "Let's get this one over so we can get some women's tennis on."

Taking the cue, I got on with my questions and asked about abusive fathers.

Smith restricted his comments to Jim Pierce, characterizing his behavior as "outrageous. It borders on the point where we may have to tell him he can't have access to the lounge. We may tell tournaments he can't go on the site. I've had some talks with Jim. It's sad. It's bad for Mary. If you watch, you can clearly see she's affected by his behavior. I think he thinks he's good for his daughter, but I doubt it."

Smith broke Pierce's offenses down into two categories. "One, his language in areas he's given access to has a negative impact on parents and players. Two, his behavior has become an issue with umpires, linesmen, and players."

I emphasized that I wasn't talking about Jim Pierce alone, or about rude behavior that offended players and officials. I was talking about child abuse. There were fathers and brothers on the tour who verbally berated and physically battered the girls, cursing them, shaking them, shoving them, hitting them, throwing things at them. While I described what had happened to Mary Pierce in Taranto, I reiterated that this was just one of a number of incidents that had been brought to my attention.

"It's bad," Smith said, "and sad. If I observed something like that at a tennis match, I'd make my feelings known." But minutes after commenting that he might have Jim Pierce banned from the lounge and "tell tournaments he can't go on site," Smith maintained, "I don't have the right to tell tournaments who they can or cannot admit. But we'd certainly make our feelings known. First, though, I'd sit down with Mary and Jim. It'd be interesting to see how she'd play without him and the pressure he puts on her."

Perhaps it was a poor choice of words, but Smith made it sound as if the critical issue wasn't the damage that fathers did to their daughters. It was how they were undermining their performance.

Unprompted by me, Smith brought up Jim Levee, observing that he, too, had been a source of concern and embarrassment. "I don't think his behavior is good for the game. But he hasn't yet had a negative impact on what happens on court. But there have been matches when he's been too vocal in the players' box. There've been complaints from players. And I've spoken to Jim [Levee] and said he's getting near the edge.

"Jim's lawyer wrote and asked me to get involved in his dispute with Peter Graf." But Smith said that since the fracas at the French Open hadn't affected the match, the WTA had no position on the matter.

"When you boil it down," Smith concluded, "Jim Levee has paid some very good money for some good seats at tennis matches. He likes certain players and the game and the glamour. I guess he has a lot of time and money on his hands. I don't think the publicity he craves and gets is good for women's tennis. It's a tough balancing act, though. Some of the girls feel he's been good and they're grateful for his support."

Although Smith declared, "I don't have any intention of forming a relationship with him," and implied that he meant to hold Levee at arm's length, the truth was that Levee was a fixture on the WTA tour, a man who wore a badge that allowed him access to every facility at tournaments. Earlier that week, at the WTA gala, he had made a substantial contribution to the WTA's official charity, the Special Olympics, and had been thanked and introduced from the audience by none other than Gerry Smith.

It seemed hypocritical, not to mention slightly churlish, of the WTA to give Levee VIP treatment and accept his money, then have Smith muse as he did now, "I guess the problem is you don't know what his motivation is."

I asked whether the WTA had a rule, written or otherwise, to protect young girls from sexual exploitation by older people on the circuit.

Smith said there was none that he knew of. "Primarily, that's a parental concern. If things were brought to our attention, however, we'd sit down and deal with it. We want to make this sport as positive, healthy, and competitive as possible."

○ ○ ○

When Connors and Novacek cleared off the Stadium Court, Navratilova came on against Pam Shriver. A swirling wind had sprung up, and airborne trash danced overhead, casting crazy shadows over the court. Once, as Shriver served, a plastic bag fell past her field of vision like a miniature parachute, a sight so unsettling that Pam was still muttering about it after losing 7–5, 6–1. "Between shadows and paper and wind," she said, "it was just weird. It was like the twilight zone."

○ ○ ○

The wind howled all night, and by morning the sky had been scoured to a crystalline clarity. On the bus to the National Tennis Center, we drove down Northern Boulevard past a cityscape that had the aching beauty of an Edward Hopper painting—storefront churches open for services, windows of abandoned buildings winking in an autumnal sun. At Flushing Meadow, the flashing sign said sixty-six degrees—a drop of thirty degrees from yesterday. At a concession booth, waitresses wore hooded parkas; on court, linesmen were in sweaters.

Of today's fourth-round matches, three resulted in straight-set routs. Gigi Fernandez defeated Radka Zrubakova 6–2, 6–2; Jennifer Capriati clobbered Jo Durie 6–1, 6–2; and Monica Seles rolled over

Regina Rajchrtova 6–1, 6–1. Sabatini versus Novotna, a replay of their
collision in Paris, promised to be spellbinding, but it, too, turned into
a straight-setter, and if it revealed anything, it was Novotna's splintery
nerves and Sabatini's lackadaisical play. Gaby hit approach shots that
she failed to follow to the net. She opened the court with her forehand,
then forgot to close it with her backhand. She won 6–4, 7–6, yet convinced no one that she had the form needed to defend her U.S. Open
title.

O O O

On Labor Day, Americans don't work. Neither did the plumbing in the
photographers' locker room. Toilets overflowed and sewage flooded that
room, part of the press conference room, and the temporary quarters of
the International Tennis Federation. ITF supervisor Ken Farrar now
referred to the tournament site as Non-Flushing Meadow.

Perhaps the cloacal odor accounted for the wacky questions during
interviews. The Soviet Union had just survived a military coup and one
reporter urged Natalia Zvereva to speak to the issue that preyed on
everybody's mind—the future of Russian tennis.

"I wanted to ask you, first of all, if you know whether the Soviet
Tennis Federation is still together and functioning?"

"I think it exists. I don't know if it functions," Natalia said. "But
I haven't been talking to the Federation people much. I am on the national
team, but whether they are working or not, I don't know."

Like a renegade from the "McNeil-Lehrer Report," the guy kept
burrowing for nuggets of information. "With the breakup of the Soviet
Union, could there be less funding for tennis?"

"I think in every republic we have a federation and I think there
still exists a funding."

"Some people have said the breakup would be good for current
players. There will be more freedom to travel. But maybe not so good
for development in terms of younger players because there will be less
funding or less focus."

"I really think I am not the one that you would like to talk to,"
Zvereva said. "I can give you some names. You can find those people
and maybe talk. They are really into it."

○ ○ ○

By all accounts, the most popular player at the U.S. Open, the sentimental favorite and by far the dominant media figure was Jimmy Connors. Commentators—not just jock sniffers but editorial writers and deep-think types—heralded his gutty, give-it-all performance as a lesson to young and old alike. The precise nature of that lesson altered with each retelling, but the bottom line seemed to be that years counted less than desire and determination. Regardless of age, any of us could pluck a page out of Jimbo's golden book, heave ourselves headlong into the fray, and win.

In every press conference, players were encouraged to rattle on about how much they admired Jimmy, and men and women both dished out dithyrambic praise. Forgetting Connors's previous incarnation as a crotch-grabbing, finger-stabbing, gutter-mouthed foil for the then sainted Bjorn Borg, everybody agreed that he was a great credit to the game. But privately people on the women's tour whispered that the situation was pathetic and just proved that men's tennis was in such sad shape it had to depend on an over-the-hill player no longer ranked in the top hundred to pump up TV ratings.

Some also suggested that craven sexism kept the press from confronting macho Jimbo with the kinds of questions a woman would be asked. What, for instance, was he doing to his hair? It used to be straight and dark. Now it was fluffy and reddish blond. Did he have it permed? Was he using dye or a henna rinse? Was the new hairdo part of an endorsement deal? Or was he only covering up the gray?

Predictably, Martina Navratilova, going on thirty-five years old, was asked her opinion and she lauded Connors's spirit. But she observed that the real key to his longevity and to hers was being born with a "good body. I mean, that is the basic number one—being healthy." Like Jimmy, she had had just one operation in her entire career and was blessed with a physique that wasn't injury-prone. "That is the extent of it," she stressed, "good genetics."

○ ○ ○

On his thirty-ninth birthday, when Connors played Aaron Krickstein, spectators abandoned other courts and stampeded over to the Stadium.

Even in the players' lounge people huddled around TV monitors cheering as Jimbo clawed his way back from a two-sets-to-one deficit, laughing as he clowned for the cameras and wise-cracked into the CBS sound boom.

But not everybody was amused by Connors's antics and his running commentary on his performance. In fact, quite a few members of the press objected to the whole concept of active players analyzing matches, whether it was as Jimbo was doing here or as he'd done at the French Open and Wimbledon, where he played and also served as an NBC-TV commentator. There used to be a rule against active players occupying dual identities, shifting from participant to pseudo-journalist and back again. But now any number of male and female players were employed by magazines, newspapers, TV networks, and cable channels. Even new WTA president Pam Shriver was a shape changer, and as she gamboled from her role as player to her role as executive to her role as occasional ABC-TV and ESPN commentator, the question was how objective she could be about a player or an issue that concerned the organization she headed. Was her allegiance to her office, or to the fans she was supposed to be informing?

Similar questions had arisen about Andrea Leand, a player who wrote regularly for *Tennis Week*. Her fellow pros felt discomfited by the candor of her inside reports, and some complained that she was depending on her player's badge to gain access to precincts that were off-bounds to journalists. Although Andrea insisted she was careful to keep her dual roles separate, players wondered when she was making small talk and when she was conducting interviews or doing research. Some facetiously suggested that tennis needed a truth-in-packaging rule. Like a leper with a bell, Andrea Leand should wear a press badge, they said, even in the shower.

O O O

Steffi Graf, scheduled to meet Judith Wiesner on the Stadium Court at the conclusion of the Connors–Krickstein match, sat fidgeting in the lounge with her mother and brother. She kept one ear on the conversation and one eye on a TV monitor. When Jimbo won the fourth set and headed into the fifth, Steffi shoved back her chair and crossed to the buffet line, picked up a bagel and some butter, and brought it to the table. Just as she did on court, she moved brusquely and seethed with impatience. Her idea of a relaxing day in the country was a high-speed drive in her Porsche or a helicopter ride, with her at the controls.

She left the bagel half-uneaten, bustled upstairs to the lobby outside the locker room, and stood with her coach, Pavel Slozil. He rubbed her shoulders, then scratched her back. But she had only so much tolerance for this kind of cosseting and stroking. She shrugged off his arm. She was ready to play.

After Conchita Martinez beat Zina Garrison on the Grandstand, Steffi volunteered to play there. When tournament officials vetoed that, she grabbed a racquet and a can of balls and asked Todd Woodbridge, a nineteen-year-old Australian, to have a hit with her. As they strode toward the practice courts, a black boy with a camera tried to snap her photograph. Steffi waved him off and held the racquet in front of her face, like a primitive tribeswoman afraid that a picture would leach away her soul.

Steffi and Woodbridge exchanged ground strokes for ten minutes, then crowded close to the net, smacking volleys at each other so that the ball seemed to bob between them like a gyroscope on an invisible string. A man paused beside me. A moment passed before I realized it was Heinz Wiesner, whose wife had to play Graf. We traded pleasantries, and as he turned to go, I said, "Good luck to Judith."

"Thanks," he said. "But Steffi is too good. It's over."

After all the hype about Connors's never-say-die spirit, Heinz's jovial resignation sounded as discordant as a dentist's drill on a hubcap. I gave him the standard pep talk. Judith's got nothing to lose. Steffi's tight. If Judith stays loose and goes for her shots, she has a chance.

"No, no," Heinz laughed. "Steffi's too good. We're just happy to be here."

As he wandered off, I wondered how many players or coaches or fathers of players could make that claim? Just happy to be here. I suppose it would make a more interesting anecdote if Judith Wiesner had beaten

Graf. She gave it her best before falling 7–5, 6–4. Still, win or lose, maybe Heinz had the right attitude. If you weren't happy to be here, it was absurd to count on victory to make you feel better.

O O O

For the past decade the name of sports psychologist Dr. James Loehr has popped up with increasing frequency in conversations about professional tennis. An expert on burnout, stress management, and the care and grooming of champions, author of ten books and two instructional videos, Director of Sports Science for the USTA, with bases in Florida and in Princeton, New Jersey, he lectured at coaches' conferences, held clinics for parents on the junior circuit, took part in panel discussions, and conducted one-on-one therapy sessions with players. Over the years, he had worked with Tom and Tim Gullikson, Brian Gottfried, Harold Solomon, and Jim Courier. Among the women his most highly publicized clients had been Martina Navratilova and Gabriela Sabatini.

While Arthur Ashe declared that "Dr. James Loehr is the single most important person in tennis today," others expressed misgivings and, on occasion, derision. Some believed that sports psychologists were selling a service for which they themselves had drummed up a dubious need. More serious critics questioned whether Dr. Loehr and his colleagues were truly in the business of "curing" emotionally troubled players. Or were they just interested in keeping them on the tour and protecting the game's image?

Dressed in a purple warm-up suit, tall, lean, and sandy-haired, Dr. Loehr, age forty-eight, looked not unlike one of the circuit's many coaches. He was tan, friendly, and smiling, yet as we sat in the dining room of the Grand Hyatt Hotel in Manhattan, it quickly became apparent that his disarming manner didn't prevent him from speaking his mind as bluntly as anybody in tennis.

He said he had long been involved in sports and it had been a stroke of good fortune when he was able to combine his two primary interests and start the Center for Athletic Excellence in Denver. He had begun by working with a pro football team, a couple of pro hockey teams, and "several great individual athletes." But "in those days," he said, "psychology was associated with problems. Many sports [clients] wouldn't come to see me except in the evening under the cover of darkness.''

This frustrated Loehr. He wanted people to know what he had achieved and what other athletes could hope to accomplish with his help. So he offered to treat Tom Gullikson for a special rate if Tom agreed to "talk about it and help me develop in this specialty area.''

Gullikson accepted the deal, and when he went from his worst year to his best, he credited much of his success to Dr. Loehr. So many other touring pros followed Gullikson to Loehr's office, he had to move to Florida because tennis players didn't like to train at Denver's high altitude.

Loehr noted that there was still some lingering reluctance among players to seek help from a psychologist, even though "the stresses of the tour are unbelievable. They can bring full-grown adults to their knees. In many ways the women's tour is much more difficult. The men form a different bonding with each other. They don't have a feeling of isolation. There's been a prevailing myth among the women that in order to compete you really keep to yourself; you need to just take care of business. You make very few friends along the way and you do that deliberately. The mothers and fathers are very protective and they get caught up in the rivalries and pretty soon you have family feuds. The person who loses in that is the player.'' They had to learn, Loehr said, that there was more to competition "than being cold, ruthless, and distant.''

"A lot of women find the tour extremely lonely,'' he continued. "It's tough on them. They start young. You've got fourteen-, fifteen-, and sixteen-year-old girls walking into the locker room and they feel they don't belong. So they get in and out as fast as they can. As they mature, they increasingly have their own network that's usually quite small. Because there's a constant change of places and so many demands on their time and energy, all they want is isolation.''

To complicate matters for women, there was what Dr. Loehr referred to as "the emotional factor. Things tend to affect them more deeply. It's harder for them to let things just flow away. The guys, at least outwardly, can let a lot of stuff go right through them. Women are more complex.''

There was, Loehr said, an additional factor that made women's tennis more difficult. "There's no other sport, particularly a one-on-one sport, where you have seasoned professionals competing with girls who have just reached their teens. You either have a support system, or it doesn't work. And if that support system blinks, you have a problem. When Steffi's father stumbled, even though she was at a later age, it had a very, very dramatic influence on her performance. I guess that's the message. If you're going to bring somebody into what can be a brutal arena, to protect them against the ravages of the game you'd better have a support system that's balanced and wise, or you'll have real problems."

I asked whether an entourage didn't risk smothering a girl, making it impossible for her to enjoy a normal adolescence.

"The fact is it's not normal," he said. "It's not normal for a teenager to have a bank account of ten million dollars or to be on the cover of *Forbes* magazine. The key is to make the life as normal as possible. We have the stories of Tracy Austin, and we have the stories of Andrea Jaeger, and some of those are very sad stories, not only the psychological impact, but the pounding and wear and tear on the body before it's fully developed. That's what happened to Andrea and Tracy—the first breakdown was the body. It's no fun playing in pain. It's awful. The parents oftentimes aren't aware. Are the kids lazy? Or are they hurt? I think there's a price to be paid. You just go out to the Open and you see the pressure."

He went on to describe stresses "at a level not normal in the psychological development of a teenager. I'm always looking for signals. The element of enjoyment begins to fade. The motivation starts to crumble. Then you see nagging injuries. The body starts to break down. But my experience is that the body and mind tend to break down together. You push the body too far and the psychological part starts to collapse. You see a quickness to anger, a lot of moodiness, problems with appetite, problems with sleeping. They're not as outgoing. They're withdrawn, they tend to get more inhibited. That's a very common occurrence among the women. They retreat into themselves as they lose confidence. You can be exposed to some pretty big time stresses. But the ratio of stress to recovery is the critical factor. That's what has to be monitored among very young players.'' The most important question, he emphasized, was not whether young girls should play on the tour, but how often they were put in pressure-packed situations and how much time they had to heal afterward.

"We've got to focus on what's happening to the person,'' Loehr said. "Even if they have succeeded on the court, if the person emerges from this experience weaker and believing less in herself and [feeling] beat up, then there's nothing that's worth that. We need to continually train parents. What's really on the line? What are we really talking about here? We're not talking about a few bucks. We're talking about people and what's happening to their lives.''

Under the circumstances, did he ever urge parents to reassess whether their daughter belonged on the tour?

"I get very aggressive,'' he said. "I get extremely angry because I feel like I'm the only person that has this perspective, and they need to hear me. Even if it means I'm out, I'm going to give my last word. So many people in this arena have a vested interest. They're interested in seeing the [player] generate money. That's what runs the whole business, that's what runs television, that's what runs the agents. Sometimes if the money's flowing nicely, everybody's happy—except the player.''

I mentioned that I heard girls were being abused or beaten. "Is this something you hear about? Is it a problem that gets brought to your attention?''

"Yeah,'' Loehr said. "I wrote two books about it and I continue to write articles. One of my greatest concerns . . . '' His voice trailed off, then he regathered his thoughts and recounted his recent participation in clinics for parents at junior events. He explained that a parent's role was to provide support, care, and love. "If you're a source of pressure, then you're missing the boat. You're there most importantly when they lose. You try to have empathy with them, you understand what they're going through, and you love them no matter what happens. You protect them psychologically. You make sure the experience is making them stronger, not weaker. That's your role. If you step outside that role, the risks get very high. If you start becoming coach and dictator, and you start orchestrating all the other arenas, then you suddenly find yourself precariously balancing the psyche of your child. It takes a very special parent to walk a lot of different paths and succeed—the coaching path, the manager, the trainer, the psychologist. I have great concern and I don't know any other answer except the parents need to be educated. Once they understand, they get in line very quickly. You have a few pathological parents, and there isn't a great deal you can do. It's just a great tragedy.''

If harmful things were happening between parents and children, why couldn't the WTA or USTA intervene?

''I don't know what can be done. The USTA has done everything it could to help Mary Pierce. But it wasn't able to communicate in a way that was acceptable to Mary and her family.''

''I don't think it's limited to Jim Pierce.'' I mentioned cases of other girls getting slapped around. ''I'm sure this doesn't surprise you.''

''No, no, I've seen this as much or more than anybody,'' Dr. Loehr said. ''I could go on and on about this. And I do. It needs to be addressed. I don't have an answer other than we need to educate [parents] before they get locked up in this crazy system. If they get some help coming in and they're prepared for what they get hit by . . . '' He subsided, then resumed. ''The parents become innocent victims like the kids do. They're just trying to help their kids survive and be successful, and all of a sudden they get caught up in this stuff and they get lost. Parents give up their jobs; they mortgage their homes. Then the kid goes out there and screws around, and the parents go nuts. They totally get blindsided. They have no clue. Capriati looks like something wonderful. It looks like it would be so easy. They're really not prepared emotionally and physically and oftentimes financially for what they're going to hit.''

But he believed that ''if the coaches take a firm position and they really educate the parents, I think we're going to eliminate a good many of these problems. There are always a few kids whose parents are just not capable of handling it and they're going to be abused. No matter whether they play tennis or not, you're going to get some of those.'' Still, he thought a number of potentially abusive parents could benefit from the kind of counseling he and others gave in the mandatory clinics at junior tournaments. ''That's a glimmer of hope for me.''

I asked Loehr whether the subject of sexual intimacy between very young girls and coaches—"guys our age," I specified—arose in his sessions.

"I don't see it being a major, major problem," he started off. Then when it sounded as though he were about to brush off the subject, he changed course. "It happens. Unfortunately, it's more problematic with the women's tour. What we do suffer from is a dearth of male coaches who are available and can travel and have the experience and understand the whole thing." As with players and parents, a lot of coaches, in Dr. Loehr's opinion, weren't trained for life on the circuit. "We need a touring coach school—with ethics and all those things being worked on—to prepare them for the things they're likely to encounter when you're traveling twenty-six weeks a year with a player."

I mentioned that Dennis Van der Meer believed the majority of coach/player relationships were now sexual in nature. Whether his estimate was accurate or not, there were plainly many coaches on the WTA tour, both males and females, who were sexually involved with players. Some of them had ongoing commitments that eventually ended in marriage. Others had transitory affairs. But the ones most likely to lead to emotional problems—

"You have a forty-year-old coach and you have a seventeen-year-old player," Dr. Loehr leaped ahead of me, "and they're traveling together and something happens. The real issue is again the way in which the tour has built-in demands and pressures. If a person isn't prepared and doesn't have a protective mechanism around her, she's going to get hurt. We talk about entourages, well, I believe entourages are very important because they serve as a protection, particularly around young players. I think Jennifer [Capriati] should have a whole army of people around her to protect her because this is a tough business. She needs a lot of bulletproof vests on, because those bullets are flying everywhere."

In the case of players who couldn't afford an entourage, Loehr believed "it boils right back down to the family. The family has to very carefully check into a coach's background and who they are and what they're doing. [They have to] stay closely connected to their kid. They need to travel with the kid to make sure she's okay."

I pointed out that there were families that couldn't afford to hire a coach and fathers who weren't in a position to quit their jobs and follow their daughters. Shouldn't they admit that tennis wasn't the right career for their girls?

"It's very difficult," Loehr said, "after they've spent the last eight or nine years working hard to get to this position where they can give their daughter a chance. That's really tough because they've invested hundreds and thousands of dollars. If people knew what they were getting into before they got started . . . Like, I had one guy who invested fifty-two thousand dollars in his daughter's tennis and he was all over her. He was strangling her. She wanted to quit, and he brought me in to get her motivation back. My response to him was, 'You're the problem and I'm going to ask you to back out in a big-time way.' He just went nuts. He said, ' "I've got receipts for fifty-two thousand dollars, and any time you get fifty-two thousand of my money, you're going to get my undivided attention. Do *not* ask me to back out!' He said, 'My goal was to give my daughter a chance for a scholarship to a great school and I woke up to the reality that I could have sent her for four years to Harvard and paid her way.' He said, 'I'm upset, but I cannot walk away from this. If I'm spending this kind of money, I'm going to be all over her.' "

Dr. Loehr urged me to talk to parents about the cost of producing, not a champion, just a journeyman on the circuit. "It's an unbelievable figure. You cannot justify in any way, shape, or form the investment that you're making in tennis on a financial basis. It's a black hole. I tell parents flat out, 'If you're hoping to see any money, any return whatsoever in terms of finances, you're dead wrong. You'll put in more every year than you did the previous year and you'll wonder where it went.'

"People's hearts tend to be where they put their money and it's difficult for them to walk away dispassionately when their kid tanks a match and they've just spent five thousand dollars of their hard-earned money to go to a tournament. They become total idiots, they become screaming maniacs on the sidelines. There is something about being abusive that works—for a while. You can get kids to do amazing things if you use fear and threats and anger and emotional—most of the times it's emotional, not physical abuse. The kids are fighting for psychological survival. They will fight like they never have before. They will do anything to win. That's why you see these young kids with parents who are totally off the wall doing pretty well. But the problem is the long-term effect. It can be tragic.''

I started to repeat Julie Anthony's observation that girls on the tour lacked opportunities to explore their sexuality, but before I finished, Dr. Loehr picked up the thread and took it further. ''They're lonely,'' he said. ''They have the same needs physically and emotionally as everybody else does. The women's tour comes together with the men's tour rarely, and when it does, it's like they're there and then they're gone. So they don't really develop a normal kind of relationship. They never have the ability to develop mature, stable, consistent human relationships. They don't have the opportunity to work those out in a normal way. So they end up getting hurt oftentimes because those relationships tend to be very shallow and quixotic. Then they begin to distrust, and that whole cycle of isolation and disillusionment begins that you see with a lot of the girls on the tour. It's a very negative cycle. It's a very common cycle. So then they find someone who's stable and it happens to be their coach, and a lot of the girls end up, you know, maybe getting attached to their coaches.''

Other girls became emotionally attached to their fathers and regarded themselves as rescuers of their families. ''Take almost any player's life,'' he said. ''Take Steffi. Most of the players are going through enormous struggles. So many of the young girls that I have worked with are somehow led to believe that although they're not real happy right now, once they break into the top hundred, they'll be okay and the family will come together. Then they think it's not the top hundred, it's the top fifty. Then everything will come together and everything with the family will work out well. Then they get into the top fifty, and it's not the top fifty, it's really the top twenty. It *must* be the top twenty. Then they get into the top twenty and they wake to the reality that that wasn't it either, that the problems are still there. What you're dealing with is the person inside and you've got to enjoy the tour all the way up. You have to find a way of getting your needs met or you end up paying a price that's never worth it. The unhappiness just lingers. Then you have someone at the top who's miserable.''

After we shook hands and said good-bye, one question lingered like the unhappiness that Dr. Loehr had seen in players who pursued their dream—or their parents' dream—without regard for their own needs: Who could listen to James Loehr and ever look at a woman's tennis match the same way again?

O O O

In the quarterfinals, Monica Seles jumped all over Gigi Fernandez, winning the first set 6–1. Though the second set wasn't much closer, at least it lasted longer—thirty-five minutes—and Fernandez fought off two match points before folding 6–2. Then she breezed into the interview room, smiled, and said, ''Hi.''

''She didn't give you much chance to warm up, did she?'' some kibitzer shouted.

Gigi responded with remarkable equanimity, discussing the myriad strengths and measly few flaws in Monica's game. ''She takes the ball early and it's hard to read. She has an unbelievable mind. She's very tenacious. If she improved her physical condition, and could come in and put away a volley, she'd be unbeatable.''

Somebody asked how the other girls regarded Seles, what they said behind her back. It was the kind of question one rarely heard on the men's circuit, but which cropped up often on the women's. Invariably it was asked by a man and seemed to assume that girls, given a chance, were bitchy and backbiting.

''I don't think I want to answer that,'' Gigi replied, but when reporters pressed her, she said, ''I don't think [Seles] is very popular in the locker room, but she never was. But this is not a popularity contest. It's so competitive now and the money's so big, it's hard to have friends. Most of the top players don't hang out. It's difficult to have a friend even if you're number twenty.''

When Seles showed up, reporters hit her with Gigi's quotes.

"I never was a friend of Gigi," Monica retorted, "because she is a very outspoken person. I would say out of the top sixteen players, I am good friends with fifteen."

But her definition of friendship was a lot looser than her ground strokes. Of Steffi Graf, the most Monica would grant was, "We don't hate each other. We have respect. But I'm not going to ask about her personal life, and she's not going to ask about my personal life."

○ ○ ○

That night Gabriela Sabatini wore a white baseball cap. She had worn it all week during day matches to ward off the sun. Why she kept it on after dark was anybody's guess. Maybe to experiment with a new image, the all-American look, à la Patty Fendick and Jim Courier. Or perhaps she didn't want fans to see her face, which, under the cap's bill, registered deepening degrees of distress as Jennifer Capriati knocked off her champion's crown 6–3, 7–6.

Capriati thus became the youngest U.S. Open semifinalist since Andrea Jaeger. After her defeat of Martina at Wimbledon, it was the second time this summer she had dethroned a Grand Slam champ. Still, she couldn't have done it without an assist from Sabatini. Six times Gaby double-faulted; twenty-one times she rushed the net behind poor approach shots and got pounded silly.

This completed a summer that might have delighted a player from whom less had been expected, but Sabatini had set out with such high hopes, she must have been doubly disappointed. Since shellacking Seles at the Italian Open, she hadn't won a tournament. Far from challenging for the top spot, she was now in danger of being overwhelmed by a new wave of teenagers. Where had the confident, creative, carefree Gaby gone?

Steffi Graf offered the best answer to that question when she remarked that every time a woman won a big title, the press claimed she had changed her game and magically gained mental toughness. Then the next time she lost, they accused her of reverting to type. But Steffi said, "I don't think players are changing so much when they win or lose. They are always pretty much the same, and the difference is only a few points here, a few points there. It's more you people change what you write about us.''

O O O

Arantxa Sanchez Vicario loved to run and impose a rhythm that let the rest of her game flow. Because the Spanish girl danced to a fast-paced syncopated beat, Martina Navratilova's strategy was to improvise a slow, discordant melody. But it took time to strike just the wrong note— to start hitting straight at Sanchez Vicario instead of away from her, to vary the spin of her serves and the angle of her volleys. After an early break, Martina drew even at 4–4, but Arantxa had plenty of bounce left and won the first set in a tie-break.

The second set was a replica of the first, only this time Martina gained the early advantage, and Arantxa rebounded to knot the score. Navratilova got another break to 6–5 and served for the set; Arantxa forced her into a tie-break. Although Martina squeaked through, there had to be doubt whether she could hold up in the third. They had been on court more than two hours, and her old knees took a beating on Deco-Turf. But it was Sanchez Vicario, not Navratilova, who wilted. After dropping the deciding set 6–2, Arantxa said, ''The key was the second tie-break. I have a lot of possibilities to win, but I can't finish it.''

O O O

As we cruised into Manhattan in a chauffeur-driven Infiniti sedan, the official car of the U.S. Open, Pam Shriver said her day had gotten off to a rocky start when she stepped out to buy a bagel for breakfast. Her hotel, the Marriott Marquis, was on Times Square, and the streets were swarming with cops. They ordered her to turn back. There was a sniper up in a building firing on pedestrians. Another U.S. Open anecdote for the bedbug file.

Shriver also told how Don Candy, her old coach, used to tease her that ''if they had baseball cards for tennis players, it would take ten Pam Shrivers to trade for one Tracy Austin.'' But Pam had had the last laugh on the Teen Queen whom she once called ''a bitch'' and ''a

fucking asshole'' on court after a match. At least she was still playing.
"Now it would take ten Tracys to get one of me,'' Pam said.

At the Marriott Marquis, we sat in the mezzanine lounge and as I
summarized my interview with Dr. James Loehr, the new WTA president's initial response was one of thoughtful attentiveness. With the
mantle of office draped around her shoulders, she appeared to have
become the woman she and others always claimed she was—Pam "Not
a Tennis Player" Shriver, farsighted and politically adept spokesperson
for the women's tour.

Loehr's emphasis on education struck her as wise and proper. Since
the WTA already had an academy for players, Pam agreed, "It wouldn't
be a bad idea to have a parent and a coach academy. If parents and
coaches understood the tour better, it would be easier all around. There
are a lot of things to learn.''

One thing Dr. Loehr felt it was crucial for coaches to learn, I told
Pam, was ethics. That, in his opinion, would reduce the chances of
young girls getting involved in damaging sexual relationships with older
coaches.

The mantle of office slipped from Shriver's shoulders. The diplomatic demeanor, the politician's unflappable aura, evaporated. She said
she didn't know of any sexual relationships between players and coaches.

Almost at once she recognized the ridiculousness of her statement.
There were so many relationships—straight, gay, May-December, and
June-June—one would have to be blind, deaf, and very dumb not to
notice. Shriver retreated to the position that she didn't know of any
damaging ones.

I explained that in addition to interviewing Dr. Loehr, I had spoken
to a psychologist who had treated several players who had suffered
emotional problems after being sexually abused by coaches. This psychologist knew of twelve other cases where players had become sexually
involved with coaches. Some girls had been so distraught, they had had
to drop off the tour.

Shriver insisted, "I don't know of a single situation where a girl
got involved with a coach and that's what caused her to drop off the
tour or burn out or have psychiatric problems. I think the presence of
men coaches provides a balance on the tour. In the years I've been on

the tour, eating disorders have been a bigger problem, although''—she hurriedly added—''I think on the average college campus it would be the same.

''When you put the whole mix together,'' Pam said, ''I think the tennis world is pretty positive. We have a certain number who are gay, a certain number who have eating problems, but again no more than the average campus.'' The only way the tour didn't resemble a college campus, she contended, was that tennis players didn't drink or do drugs as much as coeds.

I suggested she speak to Dr. Loehr, whose description of the brutal pressures, the verbal and physical abuse from parents, the emotional ravages and sexual misadventures seemed to be at such variance with her vision of the circuit.

Shriver showed little interest in what the USTA's Director of Sports Science had to say. Although Gerry Smith, her fellow member of the WTA Board of Directors, maintained that if information about sexual abuse were brought to the WTA's attention, ''We'd sit down and deal with it,'' the WTA president appeared to dismiss the subject.

''I think it would be great to meet a guy who plays tennis,'' she said, ''and fall in love and be able to travel and train with him. Of course, I guess there is the example of Chris and John. It doesn't always work out.''

When I explained that I wasn't speaking about affairs or marriages involving women her age or Evert's, Shriver replied that university professors sometimes got involved with coeds. Again, the tour was no different from college. But I pointed out that many colleges had rules against faculty members sleeping with their students. And given the age of girls in tennis, the situation was more similar to a high school gym teacher taking sexual advantage of a sophomore.

Shriver said she knew nothing about that. The two subjects of greatest concern to her—she felt they were keys to success—were balance and normalcy. She saw herself as an exemplar of both these qualities, and she believed it had helped her to grow up with two sisters, a mother, and a father in a stable family environment. ''I couldn't imagine dealing with my family being uprooted and moving to Florida, or my father quitting his job and following the tour. My mom came with me in the juniors and that was the rockiest year for their marriage. I don't think it's good for couples to be apart that much." So she had traveled with her coach, Don Candy, and felt he "was a great part of me keeping this balance."

Subsequently, I spoke to a highly placed Virginia Slims employee whose comments could not have contrasted more vividly with Pam Shriver's. Although he allowed that on the women's tour it was often "hard to separate raunchy gossip from fact-based stuff," he agreed with Dr. James Loehr that there should be a program to train coaches, and part of that training, he insisted, should be in ethics. "A lot of coaches and hitting partners step over the line."

After citing several examples, he told me about a European teenager— "a real doll," he described her—who had gotten some good early results and appeared to have that much sought-after combination of talent and good looks that make a player promotable.

"We wanted to work with her," the Virginia Slims employee said. But then it emerged that she was sexually involved with her coach, a man more than thirty years her senior, and that had knocked the public-relations campaign off track. People at Virginia Slims worried that, "If we put her in the spotlight, the story might become more obvious. We didn't want to put her in a position to have her asked by the press about the relationship."

Since Virginia Slims was aware of the affair and felt it was damaging, why didn't it do something besides back away from the player?

"We feel it's the WTA's responsibility to look after this situation. I'm sure they're aware of it. There's too much gossip for the WTA not to be aware. In fact," the fellow added, "they're explicitly aware."

In the WTA's defense, he conceded that it was difficult to intrude into private matters. "Stepping into one of these sexual relationships is like trying to break up a violent domestic argument. You risk having both parties shoot at you."

Then, too, he pointed out that, "Tennis is such a big business, but it's not regulated like other sports. You can't regulate tennis coaches. You can't fine them because it's the players, not the WTA or the USTA or Virginia Slims that pay the coaches."

Still, he didn't deny, or seek to diminish, the extent of the problem.

There was, in his opinion, a "one-to-one ratio between the [numbers of] players who marry coaches and those who have sexual relationships with them" and then break up. While he said he worried about any relationship that confused personal and professional roles, making it impossible to separate a man's sexual motives from his monetary interests, the Virginia Slims employee expressed his deepest concern about adolescent girls who got mixed up with much older coaches.

Even when they weren't sleeping together, there was the potential for trouble. He mentioned a recent case in which a middle-age coach took a sixteen-year-old player out after a match for a few drinks. The girl's parents were furious. Yet the coach kept his job.

o o o

Throughout Steffi Graf's career she had had to contend with injuries, with a chronic sinus condition exacerbated by allergies, with a volatile, demanding father and his lurid legal predicament, and with a German press that considered the most intimate matters fair game for their prurient interest. She had had to endure an adolescence during which newspapers charted her menstrual cycle. Her first puppy love had been subjected to more analysis than the fall of the Berlin Wall—"Germany will not sleep well until it is sure Steffi and Alexander [Mronz] have slept together," declared a tennis magazine—and her relationship with her father was scrutinized as though it were a case study from Kraft-Ebbing. Journalists still gossiped about the way Peter had kissed her on the mouth after a match at the 1988 U.S. Open. A photograph, which might or might not prove whether it was a French kiss, had an asking price of $750.

Yet somehow Steffi had survived and prevailed, and according to the Virginia Slims' arcane ranking system, she was back in the number-one spot. When Graf took the court in the semifinals against Martina Navratilova, it marked the fifteenth meeting between these two champions. They were tied at seven wins apiece, and six of their last seven encounters had come with Grand Slam titles at stake. Martina hadn't beaten Steffi since the 1987 U.S. Open final, but today she made it clear from the start that she meant to punish Steffi's second serve and pick on her backhand.

Steffi's strategy was to stay back and clobber forehand passing shots. But at 5–5, she embarked on one of her rare forays to the net and got burned. A moment later, she came in again and got passed again, giving Martina a break point which she promptly converted.

Leading 6–5, Martina served for the set and seemed to have it in hand when, unaccountably, she let a ball go and watched it land on the line. Unnerved, she lost the next two points and the game, and angrily hurled a ball into the bleachers. That brought a code violation warning from the umpire. Martina managed to regain her grip and took the tie-break 7–2.

In the second set, Graf had trouble with her serve. She couldn't get her first ball in and couldn't get enough depth on the second. Down a break point, she decided to take the net before Martina did, but her shot nicked the tape and fell back on her side.

At 5–3, with Navratilova serving for the match, Graf was at her best. Just as she had at Wimbledon against Sabatini, she summoned up something of her old resolve, that combination of power and indomitable will that had won her ten Grand Slam titles. She reached 0–40, triple break point, wasted all three chances, yet refused to give up. She got a fourth break point, won it, and went on to hold serve and take the second-set tie-break.

In the third set, the advantage slithered back and forth like an eel neither woman could quite grasp. In five of the first six games, neither Graf nor Navratilova held her serve. Then at 5–4 Martina served for the match for the second time.

This was Steffi's signal to dig in her heels. Or rather kick up her heels and bound around the court like an impala. She cracked a service return for break point; Martina responded with an ace. Then it was advantage Graf a second time; still Navratilova wouldn't wither. She served a winner to deuce, coaxed an error from Steffi, then sliced a deceptively slow serve that pulled Graf wide to her backhand. The return fluttered into the net and Martina triumphantly threw her hands in the air.

○ ○ ○

Dressed in a white pullover and salmon-pink sweatpants, her straw-colored hair crackling from the dryer, Steffi Graf was a portrait of wistful melancholy. "My first serve let me down," she said. "She served well. I didn't expect her to be so solid. And I expected a little bit more from me."

When reporters asked Navratilova why Steffi's game had deteriorated, Martina said, "I don't know if it's because she's not playing as well. I think it's more because everybody else is playing better." In the past Graf was "dominating so much that players would go on court wondering how many games they were going to win rather than if they could win the match. Now they think they have a chance."

Martina also believed there were inherent limitations to the baseline game. "You still have to be able to hit the volleys or you won't be able to dominate or be number one. I was watching a girl practice the other day for an hour and she never hit one volley. Her coach didn't either. They just hit from the baseline. Then she lost to Steffi six–love, six–love. I think the key is to learn to volley at the same time as you're learning ground strokes."

"Very few women have ever achieved the number-one ranking," a journalist said. "Do they have anything in common? What does it take?"

"You have to be pretty egotistical to think that you can be the best in the world. It's a big world out there."

O O O

Some women's matches have all the acoustical excitement of a leaky faucet. *Plop-plop. Plop-plop. Plop-plop.* But Jennifer Capriati's collision with Monica Seles resounded like "The Anvil Chorus." The two teenagers hammered every shot, and Seles added to the decibel level with a grunt that became more like a bellow with each game. They seemed determined to disprove Martina's theory and show you could not only dominate without a net game, you could do it without any apparent strategy. Brain-dead tennis—that's what purists called it. Yet what it lacked in finesse, it compensated for with pyrotechnics.

Seles banged the ball, and Jenny banged it back harder. Streams of outright winners alternated with clusters of unforced errors, all flying at the speed of sound. Occasionally Monica lofted a moonball to stay in a point, but as soon as she regained her position, she began pounding her shots again. She broke to 5–3, then served out the set 6–3.

Briskly going about her business in the second set, Monica held for a 3–1 lead as Capriati continued to play each point with hit-or-miss abandon. But suddenly her hits started to exceed her misses, and the points piled up. Jennifer won five games in a row to take the set 6–3.

Like heavyweights, they threw nothing but haymakers in the third set. They weren't just out to win; they wanted to knock one another cold. Each time it looked as if Jennifer had flattened Seles, Monica beat the count. Capriati broke her four times, and four times Monica broke back. Twice Capriati served for the match, nailing 100-m.p.h. first serves. Twice Seles ripped unreturnable returns, evening the score.

If ever there was a match that deserved to go the distance, this was it. They should have kept at it as long as it took for one girl to impose her will on the other. But at the U.S. Open third sets are decided by tie-breaks, and Seles was now in a zone where she saw Capriati's serve as though the ball were the size of a cantaloupe. She swept the tie-break 7–3, and sent Jennifer staggering from the court in tears. Even a hug from New York Mayor David Dinkins couldn't console her.

"That," Bud Collins declared in the interview room, "was a tennis match played by axe murderers." But after almost two hours of bombs-away, blood-on-the-walls combativeness, Capriati blamed the loss on her failure to be more bellicose.

"Tactically, Jennifer, would you do anything different if you had to play it over again?"

"Yeah, I'd win," she said. "I'd try on those service games to really go for it and just be more aggressive."

How? I wondered. Rip up the net post and brain Monica?

"How tough is this loss for you?"

"Well, it's even tougher when you know you could have had the match, and it was just there in your hands and, you know, it slipped away. That is the most"—her voice broke—"that's the toughest part."

"Did you feel it more out there when it was happening, or did it take a while to hit you?"

"Both," said Capriati.

"Which was worse?"

"Now, because, you know, now you are thinking about it. It just happened so fast. Like you shake hands and then you're off the court. And now is when you think about it."

"Will you be rooting for Jimmy Connors and Martina against the teenagers? Or will you stick with your own age group?"

"I'm not going to really cheer for anybody."

O O O

To argue that television—specifically CBS-TV—calls the shots at the U.S. Open is to utter a truism that applies to every pro sport in the United States. When a network pays its millions, it expects to have more than a little say in matters such as scheduling and court assignments. Still, it's worth noting that while the other three Grand Slam events are also dependent on TV revenues, each of them provides a day's rest between the semifinals and the finals, and they showcase the women's championship on Saturday and the men's on Sunday. But at Flushing Meadow, the women play their semifinals on Friday, then the final on Saturday, sandwiched between the men's semifinals. With no fixed starting time, they never know when they'll be called on court and can't reasonably schedule their meals or practices. Worse yet, for Martina Navratilova there was no free day to allow her to recuperate from three consecutive three-set matches.

Competing against a girl half her age, Martina didn't look tired, just a split second late and a tad hesitant. Who wouldn't hesitate with one of Monica's buzzbombs aimed at her belly button? Although she managed—just barely—to hold her serve, she made no headway against Seles's, and the strain started to show. Navratilova saved a set point at 4–5 and labored mightily to reach a tie-break, but then had little except pride left. Monica crunched every service return and won the tie-break 7–1.

Martina started off the second set by dropping serve. In a last spasm of resistance she got three chances to break back and couldn't capitalize. After that, Seles had everything her way, and nothing less than a bulletproof barrier could have protected Martina from Monica's passing shots. Finally Navratilova was reduced to the role of astonished spectator. As Seles smacked yet another ball down the line, Martina joined in the chorus of applause.

The boos began after Monica ran out the match 7–6, 6–1, paraded her trophy in front of a mob of photographers, then grabbed the microphone from Tony Trabert and rattled off thanks to her father and Donald Trump.

At a press conference that lasted almost as long as the match, Martina admitted she had been tired, but added, "I think it was more emotional than physical."

Someone asked if she felt fans would eventually warm to Monica Seles as they had to her.

"I don't know," Navratilova said. "Maybe."

"Do you sense a cruelness toward her from the fans?"

"Well, she hasn't done very much to endear herself to the public. But, you know, her main concern is to be the best player that she can be and to be number one, to win as much as possible and cash in on it while she can. That's what she's doing very well."

O O O

Monica Seles's failure to endear herself to the public may have had less to do with avarice and ambition than Martina imagined. A hoard of contradictions, a whirling centrifuge of precocious sophistication and adolescent insecurity, Monica was a tennis champion who didn't much resemble an athlete; a foreign kid who spoke English a million miles an hour but didn't always understand what she was saying; and a self-proclaimed lover of illusion who had only a superficial grasp of the real world. Small wonder that when all this exotic baggage was transplanted to the fecund soil of Sarasota, Florida, the result was confusion and, at times, comedy.

"How does it feel, Monica?" a journalist shouted.

"Oh, it feels great. It is a big relief off my shoulders."

"After winning three of the four Slams, do you give any thought now about not playing Wimbledon?"

"I think always, whenever I look back to the 'ninety-one season, it may be there. You know, I can't erase it. But as I said, if I were to play Wimbledon, I don't think I could have played the Open. For me the biggest tournament now will be Wimbledon to win, because that is the only one missing from my collection. And that is what I am going to go for the hardest. Then again, I am not going to go for it too much because I always see like what happens to Lendl. I don't want that to happen because a lot of times when you want some tournaments too much, you play half as well as when you take them as any other tournament.''

Before reporters could parse this response, someone said, ''Monica, the crowds here were not really for you the last two matches. You heard some boos as you left the court. I am wondering how that makes you feel?''

''I think one problem, I played Jennifer. I don't know what the word is. Sentimental. I don't know what it means. I don't want to use the wrong word. They wanted [Jennifer] to win because she was so much younger and would have been the youngest. Then against Martina, it was the same thing. Everybody is for Martina because she is older. You know, they will always be for the younger or for the older.''

''Martina said that she thinks you are so focused that all you care about is winning, being number one. You don't care if the crowd likes you.''

''People say how tough mentally I am,'' Monica wailed. ''But they don't realize the backside.''

The what? Journalists exchanged perplexed looks. Whose backside?

''Monica, how are you going to celebrate your—''

''I didn't even finish yet.''

''I am sorry. But what do you care about besides tennis? Does it not matter if the crowd doesn't like you?''

''Wherever I went the crowd loved me,'' Seles insisted. ''They loved me during the championship and also the early rounds.''

After skipping Wimbledon, had she come to Flushing Meadow determined to win the Open?

''No, I was pretty sure I wouldn't. I never played good tennis here. I don't know why I never had much luck here.''

''The hamburgers,'' somebody shouted.

''I really felt more and more comfortable each time with the court,'' Seles said, refusing to pick up on the hamburger cue. ''Because, you

know, the U.S. Open court has a funny way when you look at it. It's
a very funny shape and I think it takes some time to get used to that
shape of the court. I don't know if some other players told you this. I
don't want to really get into it. It just feels very different on one side.''

Suddenly journalists seemed to be feeling very different on one side.
Several got up and left, perhaps to look at the funny-shaped court.

"I don't want to say which side," Monica teased us with the mystery. "It feels like it's not even. A lot of times you get that feeling. So
I think you got to get used to it.''

"When people talk about teenage champions," a reporter broke in,
"they always talk about burnout. What are the things you would like
to do to avoid burnout?''

"I always said, you know, you never know. It is, you know, hard
to say which players burn out. I think everybody is an individual. But
what I always try to say to myself, tennis is a part of your life. It's
definitely a bigger part than anybody else's. I think you should live a
normal life. You should be a seventeen-year-old. You should do whatever you like to do. I don't want tennis to take over my whole life. I
just said to myself, 'It is great what you have done so young. It is
wonderful, but nothing should be greater than being first of all healthy.'
I always say that. And just having a normal life, that is what I try to
do. This is great, but tomorrow is another day.''

○ ○ ○

In the lobby outside the women's locker room, Karolj and Esther Seles
were waiting for their daughter and accepting the homage of various dig-
nitaries, among whom the German sex kitten of the Sixties, Elke Som-
mer, was the most striking in black slacks and a black bustier. When I
offered my congratulations to Karolj, he said, "Not me. I am just father." I pointed to his badge, which identified him as a coach. He
laughed and shook his head. "I know sport. I know little about tennis.''

Yet in the last couple of years he had learned a thing or two about
the tour. "Girls all too young. Monica, Jennifer, Steffi, they start too
early. There should be rule. It's hard, this life. Somebody always there,
always saying, 'Sign this! Do this! Wear this! Meet my friend!' '' As
he barked these commands, Karolj nudged and shoved me, imitating

agents and fans. "And press, one day they say good. Next day, bad. One day, she's nice person. Next day, not nice. I tell Monica, don't read, don't listen. A young girl can't take it. You can't live like that."

If Monica hoped to win Wimbledon, Karolj said, "she need to volley. In practice she can do. In match she becomes chicken. The problem is the physical. She need to be strong, coming all the time to net. They say be aggressive. But there are other ways, not just at net. Look at Martina. She's aggressive at net and loses because Monica is aggressive from back court. Style in sport is part of personality. How do you change a personality? I am cartoonist." He gestured to himself with a beer bottle. "I do drawing and try something new and it's no good. Whether in art or sport, you have personality and style. Monica must change, but within her style."

Jim Levee arrived and gave Karolj and me a high five. Then he slumped against the wall and sagged down onto the carpeted floor. Wearing tennis shoes, tennis shorts, and a T-shirt, Levee looked as though he had gone five sets in the hot sun. His burnished face was thin and drawn; his mustache drooped. He dipped into his shoulder bag and brought out a tennis ball, which he held aloft like a trophy. "I need all the balls I can get. I'm fifty-two and I need balls." His shoulders shook as he laughed at his own joke.

Levee declared he was exhausted. "I've been on the tour seven years, fifteen tournaments a year. Now I've got to start being a little selfish about myself. I'm skipping Australia this year. All this traveling has cost me. It really fouls up my investments. I can't follow my stocks."

He intended to skip Tokyo, too, even though Monica would be playing there. He called out to Esther Seles, who was now speaking with French journalist Judith Elian, "What round did Monica lose in Tokyo last year?"

Like a mother recalling her child's report card, Mrs. Seles had no trouble remembering. "Third round. She had a bye. Then she won a round. Then she lost to Amy Frazier."

"So it's important she does better this year," Levee said. Still, he couldn't make it to Japan, much as he believed "you've got to go to the small events, in the cold and the rain. The girls know who the dilettantes are, the ones who aren't dedicated to the game, guys like Donald Trump who just come to the big glitzy events and try to get publicity.''

A woman walked over and asked Levee where Jill, his fiancée, was, and Jim turned solemn. "I've got some bad news about Jill."

"Now, Jim, don't joke with me," the woman said.

"I'm not joking. Jill's dead."

"Jim, you're sick."

As the woman stalked off, Levee went limp with laughter. People simply didn't have a sense of humor, he said. They couldn't laugh at themselves.

"I'll be at a tournament," he said, "and I'll see the greasiest-looking guy and I'll go over to him with Jill and say, 'Wanna make two thousand bucks?' He'll say, 'Sure.' I'll say, 'Knock her up.' He'll say, 'Glad to.' And Jill will sock my arm and walk off."

At another tournament he and Jill had gone up to a fellow in a dump truck and Jim offered him five thousand dollars to run over Jill. "She didn't speak to me for days. Later she told me, 'You must be nuts asking him to hit me with his truck.' But she's getting better. She's developing a sense of humor."

Monica Seles swept into the lobby wearing a jeans and jacket ensemble by No Excuses, huge candelabra-like earrings, and a gold chain around her waist. Jim Levee leaped to his feet to embrace her, but Monica said, "No. First the women."

She hugged her mother and Judith Elian of *L'Equipe*. Then her father laughed and said, "Now kiss this woman." Monica hugged Levee.

She handed Karolj her U.S. Open championship trophy. He started juggling it, testing its weight. Then he made as if to heave it through a plate-glass window, down into the players' lounge. Monica grabbed his arm, letting out a high-pitched, girlish yelp just as she did during a match when one of her shots went awry. Karolj gave her the trophy and a kiss on the cheek, and they all laughed, especially Jim Levee, who loved a good joke.

Virginia Slims
of Philadelphia

A Week in Philadelphia

The Rittenhouse Hotel offered a serene perspective from which to take stock of women's tennis. In the last several weeks, Larisa Savchenko, a Ukranian, had won the first professional tournament in the history of St. Petersburg, Russia, and Martina Navratilova had registered a couple of new records. Defeating Mary Joe Fernandez in the semifinals of the Fitgar Ladies Indoor in Milan, Italy, she surpassed Chris Evert with 1,310 career singles match wins. The next day Navratilova had a chance to tie Evert's record for tournament titles, but lost to Monica Seles. She got another chance in Filderstadt, Germany, but was upset in the final by German teenager Anke Huber. Then, finally, in Oakland, California, Martina took her 157th title, beating Monica Seles.

Although plagued by shoulder miseries and tendonitis of the wrist, Steffi Graf had won three tournaments this fall and was again challenging Seles for the top spot on the computer. Gabriela Sabatini had played once, in Zurich, Switzerland, where she was stricken with lower-back spasms and lost in the quarterfinals. Jennifer Capriati, preoccupied by her sophomore year at Palmer Academy, hadn't played competitively since the U.S. Open.

Now it was mid-November, and the last golden leaves on Rittenhouse Square were flittering to the ground. The change in seasons quickened everybody's blood, and players, coaches, and agents talked obsessively about the tour's capstone event, next week's Virginia Slims

Championships in New York City. Still, there were other intriguing topics in Philly.

Jennifer Capriati and Tom Gullikson had parted company. The official explanation was that Gullikson wasn't free to travel with Jennifer as often as she needed him. Insiders said it really came down to money. For the right price Gullikson would have made time for Capriati, but the family wasn't willing to meet his demands. The *Washington Post* cited sources who claimed that Stefano Capriati and Jennifer's trainer, Pat Etcheberry, had "engineered Gullikson's departure."

The more stunning news was that Steffi Graf had dropped Pavel Slozil, her coach for the past six years. According to *The New York Times,* when she informed Slozil that they were finished, Steffi was in tears. Her father was at the meeting, but there was no mention that he was crying. Peter Graf's relationship with Slozil was described by the *Times* as "volatile." Graf's agent, Phil de Picciotto, said, "She no longer needs a constant companion. It's not a statement at all about her tennis, but really a reflection of her growing up."

A source close to the Grafs, a person with access to all parties, told me Steffi had soured on Pavel Slozil because she felt he had become too possessive. She was tired of having to check with him whenever she wanted to go out, and she believed he was jealous of everybody she met.

In another coaching change, Juan Nunez had welcomed Natalia Zvereva into his stable of players. In itself, this merited little comment. But because Jim Levee was paying Nunez, people clucked and again wondered what Levee was up to.

All this palaver paled to insignificance, however, compared to the news that the WTA wanted to alter its relationship with its major sponsors, Kraft General Foods and Virginia Slims, and with the Women's International Professional Tennis Council. In a move that many regarded as an attempted coup, Gerry Smith announced that he and members of the WTA board believed it was time for a "long-overdue reorganization" of the tour. In a vague and still evolving scheme to improve the marketing of women's tennis, the players would assume control of their circuit, just as the men had done several years ago. While the number of events would be reduced from twenty-seven to twenty-one, the prize money would increase to $1 million at ten tournaments and $500,000 at eleven others. Top players would be obligated to commit to more tournaments, and in some instances guarantees—the sort of bribery Smith had rejected a few months back—would be paid. The WTA also demanded half the seats on the WIPT Council. Currently they controlled a third of them.

Critics characterized these proposals as a recipe for catastrophe, especially since Gerry Smith wanted to implement them by the start of 1993. The WTA had contracts with Kraft and Virginia Slims that ran through the end of 1994, and neither sponsor showed any intention of stepping aside. Although Smith insisted that this was "a player-driven initiative," only one woman in the top ten, Martina Navratilova, had signed a nonbinding letter of support. Jennifer Capriati had signed, too, but then Stefano notified Smith that his daughter had "reconsidered." Many players complained that they had never been consulted.

Looming large above other caveats and quibbles was an inescapable question: Where was the money supposed to come from? Who would replace the $15 million that Kraft and Virginia Slims currently paid? As one Kraft General Foods official put it to me, "I'm a great supporter of women's tennis. I happen to think it's more interesting than men's tennis. But this isn't an ideal moment for the WTA to imitate the ATP [the men's union]. Spectators simply aren't showing up and the TV ratings are low. If you look, even the men's TV ratings suck."

○ ○ ○

The Virginia Slims of Philadelphia was played in the Civic Center. Normally used for basketball, the court had a blue curtain as a backdrop at one end. At the other end hung a gold curtain, and in front of it an ersatz café had been set up with blue tables, red chairs, and red and white umbrellas.

Infiniti cars and Kodak film, Gatorade and Molson beer, Colonial National Bank and Preferential Securities had pasted up their promotional stickers. Another sponsor, RCA, had a booth in the lobby, and three large-screen televisions showed a videotape of *Ghost*. The tape ran all week, providing a strange soundtrack for matches.

Stacks of Virginia Slims cigarettes were set out each day in the press room, and various versions of the Virginia Slims logo had been plastered hither and yon. There was one at either end of the court, woven into the carpet. In most cases the crouching flapper in high-topped shoes and white middie dress clutched a racquet in her right hand and a cigarette in her left. In other cases, the cigarette had been discreetly replaced by a tennis ball.

Five weeks before Christmas, a tree had been fashioned from balloons and was festooned with tennis balls, each bearing the name of a top-seeded girl. Foil-wrapped boxes under the tree bore the same names. Low-ranked girls were out of favor with Santa.

A single practice court had been installed in a vast, chilly, garagelike space next to the Civic Center. Arantxa Sanchez Vicario was there hitting with her coach, Eduardo Osta, and when a couple of girls came on for their turn, Arantxa wouldn't leave. During the indoor season, practice time is at a premium and it's not uncommon for stars to pull rank. In her heyday, Tracy Austin had a habit of crossing other players off the schedule and substituting her name. A tournament official had to talk reason to Arantxa before she would make way.

Back in the Civic Center, as I watched Larisa Savchenko dissipate a 5–2 third-set lead over Marianne Werdel, Juan Avendano stopped by, and I asked about Mary Joe Fernandez's health.

He assured me she was well, then added, "But with her you never know." All plans to build up her strength had been postponed until December.

By now Savchenko and Werdel were in a tie-break, and Savchenko led 6–2, quadruple match point. Werdel looked stone dead, but with the help of a double fault and a lucky net cord, she evened the score and won 9–7. A smattering of applause, scarcely louder than the soundtrack of *Ghost,* greeted the exhausted players as they trudged off court.

O O O

Attendance improved that evening, and fans were treated to a color guard that paraded on court while the PA system blared a recording of the national anthem. Then a barbershop quartet sang "God Bless America." A flag the size of a circus tent flapped from the overhead rafters. The only thing missing was a twenty-one-gun salute.

Conchita Martinez of Spain and Catarina Lindqvist of Sweden must have thought they were trespassing on some provincial patriotic festival. Maybe that's why they seemed in such a hurry. Martinez made short work of Lindqvist 6–2, 6–4, and spectators might have gone home disappointed if they hadn't caught sight of Monica Seles loping toward the practice court in a pink suede coat with pink fur lining.

"What kind of animal has pink fur?" a fan yelled.

"Thank you," Monica replied and kept on going.

O O O

The prize money in Philadelphia was $350,000, and eight of the top-ten women were vying for it. Since the four top seeds got opening-round byes, fans had to wait until Wednesday to see Seles, Sabatini, Sanchez Vicario, and Capriati. Meanwhile, Natalia Zvereva of Russia played Sabine Appelmans of Belgium.

Appelmans was coming off three weeks of astonishing tennis. Having lost the semifinals in Puerto Rico, she had flown to Phoenix and won the tournament there, then traveled to Nashville and won that title, too. Now she was suffering from too much travel and too little sleep. Dreamy and languid, she looked on in bewilderment when Natalia reached set point and punctuated her advantage by spitting into a court-side flowerpot. Half the crowd chuckled; half murmured in disapproval. Zvereva didn't care. She won 6–4 and soon took the second set 6–2.

Appelmans admitted that she had been "very tired." Still, she was delighted to have received a telegram from King Baudouin of Belgium, praising her performance.

"My parents never played tennis," Appelmans said. "My neighbors had a court, and I started there, then took lessons. That's why I'm left-handed."

"I don't follow," I said.

"I took lessons with a friend who's left-handed. They split us into two groups—right-handers and left-handers. I played left-handed to stay with my friend."

O O O

When no one called Natalia Zvereva for a press conference, Cindy Hahn of *Tennis* magazine and I arranged to talk to her alone. Wearing a white warm-up suit, Natalia curled into a chair like a contortionist, folding her long legs under her.

A year earlier, Hahn had done a profile of Zvereva, dubbing her a "Russian Rebel" and describing her struggle to claim a larger share of her prize money from the national federation. In the end, Natalia's stubbornness prevailed and now all Eastern Bloc players got to keep the bulk of their winnings. But Zvereva had paid a price. As her ranking tumbled from eight to twenty-seven, she acquired a reputation as a quitter, a tank artist. "If I'm not getting paid," Zvereva explained, "I'm not going to work. No way." Now she hoped, with Juan Nunez's help, to climb back into the top ten.

Natalia used to be coached by her father, a physical-education graduate from Minsk.

"He had a difficult time handing the reins to Juan," Natalia admitted. "He wants to go on coaching me. He wants to go everywhere with me. I want him to be happy, but we needed a change. It became very difficult because we're so close, so close, so close."

As she spoke, she combed her fingers through her hair and entwined her supple legs like pipestems. "Say I want to go for a walk in the street. He wants to go with me. I like loneliness. But everywhere I went he wanted to go. He tried really hard. Seventy percent or sixty, he understood. If he would like to go with me sometimes, that would be fine. But I have to be on my own."

Was the decision to change coaches purely personal? Cindy Hahn asked.

Purely personal, Zvereva said. It had nothing to do with tennis. "I just want space. He traveled with me the whole last year."

In fact, he was here in Philadelphia, shuffling around the arena, a small silver-haired man who spoke no English and looked utterly lost. At times, when Zvereva was in the players' gallery watching matches, he sat behind her and stroked her hair, unaware that his smothering attention was driving his daughter away.

○ ○ ○

One of Juan Nunez's other clients, Brenda Schultz, the giant, genial Dutch girl, uncorked a couple of 100-m.p.h. serves that rocked Mary

Joe Fernandez back on her heels and sent reporters scurrying for cover. In Philadelphia, the press sat at one end of the court, but when Brenda served, some journalists skulked off to the sides, and those brave souls who stayed put held on to their notebooks and coffee cups and got ready to duck. She winged one fellow in the shoulder, blasted a Coke can sky high, and swept the first set 6–1.

In the second, Mary Joe appeared to have weathered the worst of the storm and won 6–2. But Brenda got a break in the third and made it stand up by switching tactics. Instead of flailing the ball flat and hard, she started serving an off-speed slice that twisted into Fernandez's body. Even when Mary Joe managed to keep the ball in play, Brenda had an easy volley.

Afterward, José Fernandez kissed and consoled Mary Joe. It was her first opening-round defeat of the year, and it came at an awful moment—just when she needed to get match-tough for the Championships. Nineteen ninety-one had started off with predictions that Mary Joe would at last win a Grand Slam title. Instead, she hadn't won a single tournament, hadn't so much as reached a final.

Nearby, Juan Nunez pressed his hands on either side of Brenda Schultz's smiling face and kissed her forehead. Because she was so tall, he had to tilt her head forward.

With Zvereva and Schultz winning back to back, it had been, he said, "a good day at the office for me." Juan was particularly pleased by Brenda and believed she had achieved a breakthrough the week before in Oakland.

"She played terrible"—she lost in the first round—"but finally admitted something to herself. She admitted she had gone on with tennis because it kept her out of school. She was good at an early age and it got her out of school, so she kept at it, never really asking whether that's what she wanted to do, never asking whether that was the wrong reason to play. Now she's decided she doesn't want to drift along. She wants to commit herself and get into the top ten."

○ ○ ○

That was my goal, too. I wanted to crack the top ten and talk one-on-one to more of the star players. But I wasn't alone in my eagerness to land interviews with the game's luminaries. The Civic Center was thronged with reporters and TV commentators who hoped to have a few words with Seles or Sabatini or Capriati so that they could do lead-ins for the Virginia Slims Championships.

Naturally, the WTA welcomed the coverage. At least it claimed it did, and its media reps, along with those from Kraft General Foods and Virginia Slims, bustled about attempting to pin down players. But the stars, as I learned months ago in my search for Gabriela Sabatini, were flighty, mercurial creatures, and even when they were willing to talk, there was no guarantee that tour officials would let them speak their minds.

On occasion, when I asked for interviews, I was told to put my request in writing, along with a synopsis of the subjects I intended to cover. In other cases, media reps pressed me to clarify for them what I intended to discuss with the stars.

I kept it short and sweet. I said, for instance, that I wanted to talk to Arantxa Sanchez Vicario about growing up with two older brothers who were tennis pros. Four times at the U.S. Open I had arranged a rendezvous with Arantxa. Three times she failed to show up. Once she appeared, said she'd be right back, then two hours later sent word that the interview had been canceled.

In Philadelphia, Arantxa agreed to meet me in the players' lounge, and I arrived moist with anticipation. To my surprise, she showed up and she was alone. I had expected to find her mother, Marisa, at her side, clad in a mink coat and carrying her daughter's pet Yorkie, Roland, in a Louis Vuitton bag, just as she did every day as she sat through her matches and practices.

Curly haired and freckle-faced, speaking English with stress patterns that carried over from Spanish, Arantxa said she had been bothered by a cold. "I couldn't breathe pretty good. I couldn't sleep last night. I try not to think on the court about it."

What accounted for her family's interest in tennis? Had her parents been aficionados?

No, they hadn't taken up the game until Arantxa did. At age four, she said, "I see balls at home and I start. My brothers, they played during the week and on the weekends they skied."

Had it been an advantage or a disadvantage that Emilio and Javier were world-class players? In other families—I mentioned the Austins and the McEnroes—there had been sibling rivalries that had had to be resolved.

"We are very close. No tensions. It helped me that my brothers played. We try to be together."

But how had they reacted when by the age of seventeen she out-ranked them?

"It helped them, my winning the French Open and getting to number five in the world." She didn't specify how it helped them. She just repeated how close they all were. From a coach, she said, she looked for technical help, but when it came to emotional support, she depended on family, primarily her mother. "I'm too young to marry or have a boyfriend, so I have my mom. She comes with me and is a hundred percent with me."

Since she had such a fine family, did she feel sorry for girls who traveled alone or were bullied by their fathers?

She flounced around on the couch and spoke in a rapid-fire manner that could have competed with Monica Seles, yet she never got around to giving an answer that connected with the question. Instead, she fell to talking about her family again. She didn't care to talk about much else. "My father teach me my drop shot. But it depends on who you have most confidence in. I have a great confidence in my father."

How would she characterize her relationship with other players?

"We have a rivalry. We talk ten minutes. That's all."

Did that make the tour a lonely place?

"It's great being in the top five," she said, reminding me of a player on the men's tour who, whenever he was asked how he was, told you his ranking. "Since I start playing I was winning. I won a national championship at thirteen. I was always going up. I miss many things—studying, a career, relationships. But there is compensations. You can learn a lot of things and meet lots of people. Always the King and Queen call me. I'm one of the most popular sports figures in Spain. I'm a great friend of Infante Christina."

How would she cope if she never won another Grand Slam title?

"I have a strong character. I think I can handle whatever happens."

Was there any difference between Arantxa Sanchez Vicario on court and off?

"I always fight on court to the last point. Afterward I am nice and loose."

Nice she may be, but "loose" was the last label to apply to this teenager, who was as tightly wound as a two-dollar clock. When I paused between questions, she asked if I was finished and bounced to her feet before I answered.

"What's the worst thing about the tour?' " I called after her.

"You would like to have holidays." She was halfway to the door. "But if you stop, it's hard to come back."

O O O

By Wednesday, *Ghost* was still showing at the RCA booth, Patrick Swayze was still dead, and Jim Levee had arrived. After Conchita Martinez beat Helena Sukova, Levee nodded to Conchita. "My daughter," he proclaimed proudly. "I first saw her when she was three hundred forty-ninth in the world. I watched her for ten minutes, then wrote her a check for twenty-five thousand dollars right on the spot. She cried. I knew with talent like that she wouldn't stay at three forty-nine. Can you imagine how good she'd be if she had a serve?"

O O O

Carlos Kirmayr and Gabriela Sabatini had also showed up in Philadelphia, each sporting a new look. Carlos had shorn his long, golden locks and wore a week's growth of stubble, like a character on "Miami Vice."

Gaby was leaner, sleeker. Carlos said he didn't know whether she weighed less, but her shape had changed because her diet had. "She's eating less and less meat, and she's drinking no liquids that are carbonated. This," he said sheepishly, "despite the fact that she endorses diet Pepsi. She's becoming more and more conscious of how she looks as a woman."

When she played Natalia Zvereva in an afternoon match, Sabatini seemed to be missing something. Perhaps carbonation. Or maybe the right racquet. The logo on her racquet bag read YAMAHA, yet months after signing a new contract, she was still playing with a Prince—a Prince without a trademark but a Prince nonetheless.

Gaby broke to 4–3, but Zvereva, a right-hander who wears a wristband on her left arm, broke back. Then Gaby broke to 5–4 and—shades of Wimbledon—served for the set, only to drop to 5–5. She broke again and was broken again and screamed some obscure oath in Spanish.

"That's all right, Gaby!" called a maternal voice from the crowd. A lady unfurled an Argentinean flag from the balcony and waved it in encouragement. Zvereva was unimpressed. She spat into a flowerpot before the start of the tie-break, and promptly lost it.

In the second set, Zvereva began to suck Gaby to the net with drop shots, then pass her down the line. Running off four games in succession, she won 6–2, but the effort appeared to exhaust her. She stood huffing at the baseline, looking as though she'd spit if she could just summon more moisture to her mouth. She fell behind 1–3, then 2–4. Now it was Zvereva who got jerked around by drop shot and lob combinations, and it was Gaby who advanced to the next round.

○ ○ ○

That evening, after Seles whipped Marianne Werdel in straight sets, Capriati played Lori McNeil and looked soft and slow. McNeil could—should!—have won the opening set. She blew seven set points, one of them on an overrule by the umpire, then lost the tie-break with a double fault. Although she bounced back to win the second tie-break, she had let Capriati play herself into something approaching her old form. Jennifer ran away with the third set 6–2 and arrived at her press conference wearing a Yale sweatshirt and a pair of wire-rim glasses.

"That's what happens," she said of her spotty game, "when you haven't played a match in a couple of months. I'm just happy to be back out there again."

Yet she didn't sound especially happy, and much of the spontaneity had gone out of her give-and-take with the press. All her responses were curt and monosyllabic. Even as she described how she discovered she needed glasses, she was flat and matter-of-fact. "I always had trouble seeing at night under lights. I said it, but nobody believed it. Then I failed my vision test for a driver's license. Now I can see the other player's face.''

She vowed, however, that no boy would see her face with glasses on. She'd wear contact lenses.

Only when speaking of her disappointing semifinal loss to Seles at the U.S. Open did Jenny betray her feelings. "It affected me a lot. I still haven't put it out of my mind. I still think about it.''

O O O

The Kraft General Foods Media Guide maintained that Manuela Maleeva-Fragniere was five feet eight, but she looked shorter and was slightly built through the upper body. In a crowd of women her age—she was twenty-four—she wouldn't stand out as a world-class athlete, a bronze medal winner for Bulgaria at the 1988 Olympics, a top-ten player with career prize money of more than $2 million. Off court, her expression was solemn. On court, she often appeared to be anguished; her eyes misted over and the flanges of her nostrils reddened. In her book, *Passing Shots,* Pam Shriver mocked all three Maleeva sisters for their melancholy expressions. They reminded her of basset hounds, and she dubbed them Boo, Hoo, and Boo-Hoo.

While this might have amused readers, it struck the Maleeva family, especially mother Yulia, as a cruel caricature typical of American players who, in their opinion, had little culture, education, or sensitivity. Coming from a country with a repressive political regime that regarded their aspirations with suspicion, the Maleevas had had to battle obstacles that western players couldn't comprehend. If, under the circumstances, they didn't wear a happy face, who could blame them?

After she defeated Amy Frazier, Manuela Maleeva-Fragniere met me in the press room, and I asked what it had been like to be one of the rare women coached by her mother.

"I think it was an advantage,'' she said. "A woman wouldn't hit a player or an umpire. That's the nature of a man. My mother is very much into tennis, but she wouldn't beat a player. Many of the players coached by abusing parents have disappeared.'' She cited Andrea Jaeger and Andrea Temesvari as examples.

Her own father, she explained, was "nice and kind.'' Although he had competed on the Bulgarian national basketball team, he became an electronics professor and left the coaching to his wife.

"Our mother was always very hard and strict and ambitious, but she never said you have to play. If we didn't feel well, she didn't make us play. The fathers on the tour are very aggressive and intimidating. My mother is not like that. She was strict with us, but not with others. There were never fights or intimidations."

Still, Manuela didn't candy-coat her tennis apprenticeship. Yulia hadn't beaten her daughters, but she had been a fierce taskmaster and was brutally frank in her appraisal of their talent. She once told *Sports Illustrated* that Manuela, Katrina, and Magdalena "have each fully developed their physical potential. I sometimes wish they were born with more."

"Not many people like criticism," Manuela admitted. "It's natural to take it against yourself. My mother and I have had our moments of anger and arguments. Sometimes with the pressure you can't think clearly. But later you realize she wants the best for you."

When the time came, Yulia, unlike so many parents on the tour, had been willing to step aside as Manuela started training with François Fragniere, who ran the Swiss junior boys team. At the age of twenty, Manuela married her coach. "My mother was happy she could put me into the hands of somebody she trusted—my husband."

It struck Manuela as more than natural—it was positively necessary—to have a close personal connection with a coach. "You must know a coach and he must know you to get good results. We have discussed, my husband and I, whether we should get another, more objective coach. I've told him I don't know whether I could have another coach. I don't think I could trust a person one hundred percent except my mother or my husband. I think it might be better to have a different coach, but my heart isn't there. You have to separate the two things—the tennis and your personal life—or your marriage is in danger. But if you hire a coach who has been with ten other girls, how could you trust him completely? Then he might go on to some other player. I don't want the other girls to know my weaknesses and my difficult times. I can't imagine telling him things, then thinking he might tell another girl."

Her eyes misted, her flaring nostrils reddened at the thought. It was like taking a lover, she said. "You can't do this if you think he'll betray you."

She had seen many young girls on the circuit acting more and more intimate with their coaches. As for what happened behind the hotel doors . . . She shrugged and said, "It is the perfect position for an older man. He knows a lot of things, knows how to take advantage and get to a girl's head." Then she volunteered, without being asked, that "of course it's not just men. You see it a lot with older lesbians who spot a young girl and take up with her. Some stay together only a short time, some stay forever." Manuela was the first and only woman player who maintained that lesbians went after young girls.

"It's such a lonely job. We have no real friends." She mentioned Pam Shriver's book as an example of what made the circuit an icy, forbidding place. Shriver, she said, "is just a sad and frustrated player no longer capable of getting satisfaction from her own game. So she tries to hurt others. This has really hurt me—to be made fun of for showing emotion, for crying after a loss. She made me embarrassed, then she comes up to me and pretends we are the best friends. I have seen Pam breaking racquets in the locker room and showing anger. How is that better? Why is it better to show anger than sadness? That you cannot even cry—not just for losing, but for being lonely—that's what makes the tour hard. The girls make fun and tell your opponent."

She said she would play two more years. Her goal—she conceded it was becoming more like a dream—was to win the French Open, the lone Grand Slam event played on a slow surface hospitable to her style. Then she would retire.

"What then?" I asked.

For the first time she smiled. "Have babies."

O O O

When I asked for an interview with Monica Seles, I was expected to do everything except put down a damage deposit and submit to a polygraph test. In response to a Virginia Slims media rep's cross-examination, I explained that I wanted to talk to Monica about fashion and style. I figured that would be like dangling raw meat in front of a lioness. But Seles resisted the bait. She—or maybe it was the media rep—demanded more information. How long would my questions take? What were they? And what was the rest of my book about?

Days passed and when Monica still hadn't made up her mind, I contacted her agent, Stephanie Tolleson of IMG. Since Seles had a lot of names and faces floating past her scope, I asked Tolleson to remind her client that we had spoken in Rome, at the Hilton Hotel. I hoped Monica would recall that on that occasion I hadn't committed any unpardonable offense against etiquette.

The next day I was informed that Seles had consented to an interview and would meet me in the press room. At the appointed hour she hadn't shown up. The media rep assured me she was coming, but she had a busy schedule and always ran a little late.

Today she ran an hour late—long enough for other reporters to razz me as I sat cooling my heels. Hey, it could be worse, they said, recounting anecdotes about times they had been stood up or left dangling for hours, even days.

When Monica Seles came sloping into the room dressed in a baggy sweat suit, I rushed over to meet her, but I wasn't fast enough. She had a phone at one ear and a finger in the other. The media rep told me to hold on until Seles placed a brief call to Europe. It would just take a minute.

It took fifty minutes. I might have managed to ignore the slow drag of time if a crowd of jeering fellow journalists hadn't been there needling me. "What are you going to ask her, anyway?" "What do you think she's going to tell you?" "Ever consider career counseling?"

At last the media rep delivered Seles, along with an admonition that I had ten minutes. I paid that no mind. Having watched her turn a quick call to Europe into a gab-fest, having listened to Monica motor-mouth her way through many a press conference, I was convinced that once she started talking, it would take a tranquilizer dart to stop her.

Sure enough, as soon as the Virginia Slims minder left us and I asked about her physical-fitness program, it was like lifting the floodgates on the Aswan Dam. Monica behaved as if she had been waiting half her life for precisely this question.

"Jerry Rice and Carl Lewis, they're very strong, but they have lean bodies. That's what I'd like. They're men. I don't know whether that's possible for a woman. I don't want to have big muscles. The ideal body is Madonna—lean. I don't want to have bulk. When you wear an off-the-shoulder dress, you want to look normal. The older you get, the more you want to look like a woman.

"In tennis, I'm always skinny and fragile," she sped up, hunching forward in her chair, tucking her hands between her knees as if to cut wind resistance. "But pounds are coming on easier now. It's hard to say whether I would rather look better or play better. I don't want to have to make that choice. But people are telling me to do weights and get muscles. I'd have surgery," she swore, "if it would make me look like I wanted to look. I can't do it while I'm playing, but maybe later."

"You mentioned Madonna," I said, attempting to force my way into her monologue. "What's your fascination with her? In Paris you said you had just seen *Truth or Dare* and—"

"You can't say what's fake and what's real. I like that—not to know where the line is."

"—and I went to see the movie," I broke back in. "I must say it didn't make Madonna's life seem particularly happy. She admitted she's lonely, bored, isolated by her fame, sexually frustrated, and afraid she'll never find a partner who'll satisfy her."

"I feel like Madonna," Monica jubilantly declared, as though what I had described were a twelve-step program to self-realization. "Like I'm seventeen and I've already met everybody. You can't go out. You just go to the hotel. By the time I'm twenty-six, I'm sure I'll meet as many people as Madonna has. It's awful to feel this way so young."

Given the way she gushed, it didn't sound awful at all. Still, Seles said she was looking forward to retirement and life after tennis. "I'd like to have more time off—to study acting, fashion design, ballet. I like feminine things. In sports, the only other thing I'm interested in is basketball."

"Getting back to Madonna," I blurted, "one thing that came through in her movie was her sexual candor. But women's tennis seems to shy away from that. Do you feel—"

"Madonna is very honest," she jumped ahead of me. "I'm probably the same way. In tennis, you can't be as wild. People aren't as open in tennis as in acting. Men's tennis is more outspoken than women's tennis. People tell us it's bad for our image—you don't want to excite the press. The men are older. They're more outspoken," she repeated. "Maybe later, outside of tennis, I can be that way."

The media rep moseyed in. My time was up. I ignored her. Monica didn't. Although she continued talking, she abruptly changed her tune. "The tour is very free. Whatever you think, you can express. The prize money, it's part of feminine liberation."

When I repeated Manuela Maleeva-Fragniere's comments about coaches, Seles's response was several evasive non sequiturs about her father, "the best coach. He was an athlete and knows the pressure. But it depends. Some fathers don't know much about sports."

What about Zoltan? He had more personal experience at tennis than her father, but there were rumors that he had been rough on Monica during workouts. Did she still practice with her brother?

"Not much anymore. His game can make me crazy. He hits all junk and we both want to win and my father won't choose one over the other. We argue and my father won't make calls for us."

The Virginia Slims minder stood up. Monica stood up, too. I was fifteen minutes over my limit.

O O O

On Friday, Gretchen Magers and Robin White, a couple of doubles specialists, goofed off in the basement beside the practice court. Gretchen had a whiffle ball and Robin a plastic bat, and they took turns belting pop flies toward the heating ducts.

Upstairs, Arantxa Sanchez Vicario ended Brenda Schultz's fling in Philadelphia 6–7, 6–1, 6–3, and Brenda offered a pithy explanation of her defeat. "I got so pissed, I just hit the volleys out. My mind is so strong thinking of an ace, I forget about serving to her forehand."

That evening, by the time Capriati eliminated Maleeva-Fragniere, news had spread that Pavel Slozil had replaced Tom Gullikson as Jennifer's coach. It was Manuela's worst nightmare—a man bouncing from girl to girl, the looming prospect of betrayal, personal secrets flowing to a new client.

Capriati came to her press conference wearing her new glasses and a Penn baseball cap. Asked what she had done in Philadelphia, she said she hadn't been sightseeing yet. But she swore, "I want to see the Liberty Bell, the Declaration of Independence. All that stuff. It's kind of neat that that's what I'm studying now in school."

As for her plans beyond Philadelphia, she said that in January she would play the Australian Open for the first time. Pavel Slozil would commence coaching her there. (She didn't mention that during December she would play exhibitions in Baltimore, Lexington, Charleston, and Sarasota, at fifty thousand dollars a night. Then she would fly to the south of France for a special round-robin event. Usually a star of her prominence got a bye in the first round, but Stefano insisted she play all three nights. She would do so and aggravate an injured leg.)

A reporter asked if she ever talked to the veterans on the tour, ever sought them out for advice.

Capriati cocked her head, as though the notion had never occurred to her. "I guess you could learn stuff from players like Zina and Martina, but no, I don't go to them."

O O O

While Slozil would work with Jennifer on the road, she would continue to train with Tommy Thompson at home in Saddlebrook, Florida. Thompson used to coach Vitas Gerulaitis. He told me he had to interact with Capriati on a more mental and emotional level. "Of course," he said, "some of this may just be her age. She loses concentration really fast. At practice she'll be fine for a while, then her mind wanders."

As for whether it left a girl feeling vulnerable when her coach switched to another player, Thompson said, "It should." He thought Steffi Graf would go into matches against Jennifer feeling at a psychological disadvantage.

Tommy Thompson and I had no sooner parted company than I bumped into John Lloyd in a black leather jacket and a pair of jeans. He was in town to conduct a clinic and had dropped by the Civic Center to watch a few matches. Having trained any number of players, including Chris Evert, Lloyd said, "Coaching women is a twenty-four-hour-a-day job. You feel almost like . . . well, I don't want to say a psychiatrist, but some kind of therapist. You coach a guy, you see him on court, you hit, and that's it. But a lot of the girls want you to be with them off court. They want to have dinner together every night. It's not just coaches pushing the relationship from the professional to the personal. It's the girls.''

In his view, a coach who jumped from one player to another would definitely tell his new girl how to beat the old one. That was his job.

When I discussed the matter with Juan Nunez, he agreed that as a coach got close to a player, he learned deeply intimate things about her, but he drew the line at exploiting this information to give his new client an advantage. ''It's like a doctor or a priest. There are some things you learn in your profession and you just don't use them. I can't speak for others, but that's my ethic.''

O O O

Liz Smylie of Australia lost her first-round singles match and looked as though she might have suffered an injury that made it painful to stretch for low balls. Although she and her partner, Nicole Provis, were still in the doubles, Liz played poorly there, too. For a woman who had won three dozen doubles and mixed-doubles titles, including Wimbledon and the U.S. Open, this was surprising. The defending Virginia Slims doubles champion—in 1990 she took the title with Kathy Jordan—she seemed unlikely to repeat. When I wondered aloud what her trouble was, a fellow journalist informed me that Liz was pregnant. She was four and a half months along.

During a break between the afternoon and evening sessions, Peter Smylie, Liz's husband and coach, sat at one of the café tables and watched his wife hit with Nicole Provis. A slim, friendly fellow with dark hair combed close to his head, Peter explained that this past summer, after Liz won the Wimbledon mixed-doubles crown with John Fitzgerald, his wife and he decided they had put off having kids long enough. Liz would be twenty-nine the following spring and ''if she can't come back, she'll at least feel she retired at a peak. But she's keen to come back, especially in doubles. She's always played better when she's happy, so the hope is she'll be happy with the baby.''

Although Peter was too self-effacing to mention it, much of Liz's happiness, as well as her performance, depended on him. They had met when she was a teenager and he was struggling to rise from the satellite circuit to the main tour. "I won two national junior titles in Australia," he said. "I was a good player, not a great one."

After he fell in love with Liz, he continued playing competitively, but devoted a lot of time to coaching her. "It didn't take us long to realize who had the potential to make a living at tennis," he told me. "Instead of each of us putting fifty percent into the game, we decided to put a hundred percent into her game."

Her results confirmed the wisdom of that decision. A week after their wedding in 1984, she reached the final of a tournament in Brisbane. By the end of the year she was number thirty-six in the world.

Initially, they didn't intend to travel together. The plan was for Peter to hold down a full-time teaching position and for Liz to make month-long forays, then return to their home base at Hilton Head, South Carolina.

"I had a job at Rod Laver's place," Peter said. "I loved it, but Liz wanted me with her. It didn't work out for her. She'd go off for three or four weeks, but by the end she'd always get lonely and lose early in singles and skip the doubles and come back. So I left Laver's and we started traveling again. It was hard for me. I mean, coming from a male chauvinist country like Australia, my mates from the men's tour gave me a hard time. They said, 'That's what I should do—marry a woman who plays. It looks like easy work.' "

Before their marriage, he and Liz had entered a few mixed-doubles events. They won the title at Beckenham, and one year at the French Open "we had a big crowd watching us because we were fighting on court." Peter laughed at the memory. "I'd say, 'Come on, hold serve,' and she'd say, 'If you crossed more, maybe I could.' "

But then Liz paired up with John Fitzgerald and won the U.S. Open mixed-doubles title and, Peter said, "that was the end of us playing together." It was also pretty much the end of Peter Smylie's existence in the public eye.

When you married a woman player, "the wife is in the limelight," he explained. "Everything revolves around her. If you're not an easy-going person, you can have a lot of conflict. Our only conflict is over how to play tennis. I like her to get to the net more in singles and use the volleying skill she has from doubles. But she's afraid to come in as much as she should, and it does really frustrate me.''

In the beginning, Peter had been the only man on the women's circuit. Now there were dozens. ''What I hate is guys who say, 'Women's tennis sucks.' Then you turn around and see them out there coaching.''

He also decried the favoritism and fawning that poisoned any possibility of harmonious dealings among players. ''You know who's winning by the way people treat the girls. You learn who your friends are. The girls would get along great if it weren't for the agents, parents, and coaches. The players want to be together. The time they like best is when they put on the show at Eastbourne [the week before Wimbledon]. But they're in a business where it's you or her. We all like to think we're one big happy family, but we're not.''

So he focused on his own family and on ''helping Liz get the best results possible. Four or five years ago some of the other girls asked if I'd work with them. Liz said, 'Why would you help my opposition?' I said, 'Sometimes I don't get the kind of response from you that gives me satisfaction.' She said she'd try harder.

''We went through a rough period. Liz just wasn't listening. There was talk of finding another coach. But I know her game best and it makes no sense to hire somebody for a thousand dollars a week or more to tell her what I already tell her.''

The key, Peter recognized, was to know when it was better to say nothing at all. Their life was, in his words, a perpetual roller-coaster ride, and sometimes Liz wanted him near her and ''sometimes she tells me to leave the court. This year during a match at Wimbledon she said, 'Go!' and you just have to slink off and hide.''

Like every married couple, they had their differences, and these could be exacerbated by the grind of the tour if they didn't allow each other lots of leeway. ''She likes to handle losses on her own,'' Peter said. ''The way I'd handle them, I'd go have a few beers and dinner and say, 'I'll do better next time.' But Liz has always looked at it as a personal failure. She'll punish herself. She won't go out to dinner. I can't get her over that.''

Much as he might voice quiet reservations and acknowledge that

"I'm looking forward to the time when I can do some things for myself," he derived deep pleasure from what Liz had accomplished and was proud that they were closer than most couples. "The main thing is we don't want to be apart"—and if that meant reversing traditional roles and deferring to her career, then Peter Smylie was willing to do it.

By the time Peter finished talking, Liz had showered and joined us at the table. She wore a pair of slacks and a pumpkin-colored blazer that couldn't have been a better expression of her personality. Bright and extroverted, she was an attractive woman with the broad smile and glistening teeth of a model in a toothpaste ad. She had gained only five pounds during pregnancy and hadn't had a single day of sickness. "Chris Evert sends messages that it's not fair." Chris had just given birth to a baby boy after a difficult pregnancy and a long labor that ended in a cesarian section.

"Up till now—four and a half months—I've played and practiced as normal. In singles I can't cover the court, but in doubles I'm all right for another week."

The prospect of interrupting her career to have a baby didn't daunt her. "Laura Gildemeister proved something," Liz said. "You can come back. The baby had a calming influence on her. If I hadn't been a tennis player, I'd have had children a long time ago. Combining tennis and kids will hopefully open up another aspect of our lives. I'll have plenty of babysitters on the tour. A lot of these girls are frustrated mums."

After Peter excused himself to make a phone call, Liz said she shared Manuela Maleeva-Fragniere's sentiments. She'd be suspicious of a coach who had hopped from player to player. "Some girls only feel comfortable with a coach who loves them. I can understand that. I'm definitely a better and more complete player because of Peter. He knows the game. He knows the feeling of being down thirty–forty and having to serve a second serve."

And of course he knew her. In seven years of marriage they had "never spent more than a month apart. We're together every day. If I sometimes tell him to leave the court, he realizes it's a heat-of-the-moment thing. Peter is number one in my life. We're both aiming for the same goal—to win!"

While that might be their mutual goal, Liz was candid enough to

concede that for a man there was something painfully awkward about
the fact that his wife was out on court, in the spotlight, winning matches
and prize money. "His role is more difficult. I know what I have to
do, what my role is. But for a husband traveling with a player, there
are no rules. We had to make it up as we went along."

She was also honest enough to admit that there had probably been
times when she took Peter for granted and resisted the notion that they
were an unusual couple. When she stopped and thought about it, she
supposed it must strike outsiders as extraordinary that two people led
such a nomadic existence in which the woman's physical condition was
of paramount importance, not because of her nurturing or childbearing
ability, but because of her athletic talent and money-making potential.

"My parents always say we live an abnormal life. But in tennis the
abnormal is normal," Liz Smylie said.

O O O

On Saturday, the first semifinal, Seles versus Sanchez Vicario, was a
replay of the French Open final. But this match took place on a fast
carpet, not clay, and even a retriever as indefatigable as Arantxa couldn't
keep up with Seles's blistering pace. Every time Arantxa reached around
to the small of her back, plucked a ball from its plastic holder, and
patty-caked one of her 60-m.p.h. second serves, Monica walloped it
for a winner. In half an hour, Sanchez Vicario found herself on the
short end of a 6–1 score.

The second set was marginally closer. Arantxa finally broke Monica's serve, but she had little luck holding her own and lost 6–2.

Waiting to be called on court for the second semifinal, Jennifer
Capriati stood in a hallway in front of a full-length mirror fussing with
her hair. A few fans stopped by and she posed for a photograph. She
looked loose. Having beaten Gabriela Sabatini at the U.S. Open, she
was confident she could do it again.

Back near the temporary WTA offices, Gabriela Sabatini planted
her feet wide apart and performed a series of stretching exercises. As
she wagged her head back and forth on the sturdy column of her neck,
her limbs radiated tensile strength. It was one of the few times I had

seen her off court when she wasn't smiling. She had put on her game face—a glowering expression in which petulance and anxiety competed.

Her agent, Dick Dell, came in and wished her good luck. Then Carlos Kirmayr spoke to her in a low, intense voice, squeezing her shoulder as he gave last-moment instructions.

"She's really ready," Carlos told me, "really strong."

In the opening game, it didn't look as though she'd need to be strong. Jennifer handed her a passel of free points and a quick break. But then nothing went right for Sabatini. Throughout her career she had had the ability to dominate baseline exchanges; tonight the longer the rallies lasted, the stronger Capriati looked. It didn't help that Gaby's serve seldom exceeded 80 m.p.h., whereas Jennifer's was consistently close to 100 m.p.h.

After Capriati won, she said the key to beating Gaby was "to take charge of the points from the start."

What was the key to beating Seles tomorrow?

"Just play my game."

O O O

On Sunday, fans at the Civic Center had to wade through a picket line of protesters who chanted, "Tennis yes, smoking no!" Several protesters wore death's head masks and swung papier-mâché scythes. Others carried placards: SMOKING IS THE WRONG WAY, BABY; SMOKING IS A DOUBLE FAULT; SMOKING KILLS 146,000 WOMEN A YEAR; PHILIP MORRIS IS A DRUG PUSHER.

Deft as Virginia Slims was at damage control and as often as players repeated that loyalty to their sponsor didn't mean they personally endorsed cigarettes, journalists speculated that Gerry Smith's proposed reorganization of the tour might have been prompted by a desire to escape the Virginia Slims stigma. No executive liked being put in the position of defending the indefensible, and regardless of what Smith or anybody else said, the perception remained that women's tennis approved of smoking.

Even as Capriati and Seles took the court, reporters were fulminating in the press row right behind Monica. "What's the message the public comes away with?'' one man demanded. ''Lots of kids love tennis. What do they conclude? That tennis is a healthy sport? Or that cigarettes are all right?''

Neither Seles nor Capriati gave any evidence of being distracted by such questions. Instead, they picked up where they had left off at the U.S. Open and treated the crowd to another high-velocity rendition of ''The Anvil Chorus''. There were no arabesque shot patterns and long rallies. At most, Capriati might fool Monica by going down the line instead of crosscourt, or Seles might hit behind Jennifer rather than into the open court. The rest of the time they simply drilled the ball.

When Seles streaked to a 4–1 advantage, Jennifer came steaming back. She evened the score at 4–4, edged ahead to 5–4, but faltered as she served to get into a tie-break.

After Seles took the first set 7–5 and held serve to open the second, Capriati suffered a letdown. She blew a 40–15 lead and was infuriated when the umpire overruled and awarded a point to Monica. A moment later she demanded an overrule in her favor but didn't get it. With Seles serving at 2–0, a close call went Jennifer's way and she sarcastically cried out, ''Oh, very good.'' She scrapped to stay in the match, but Monica was a murderous front runner and never gave her a chance or another game. The set ended 6–1. The match had lasted only an hour and nine minutes.

Jennifer fled the court, raced up a tunnel and around a corner, where her father hugged her. Once her tears had dried, she straggled back to accept her runner-up prize.

Stefano accompanied his daughter to her press conference. I was behind them and noticed that she had a slight limp. ''What should I say?'' Jennifer asked her father.

''Just say it's a little pain,'' he whispered.

As soon as we were all seated, someone asked about her leg.

''I have a little pain.'' She delivered the line in a deadpan voice. ''I felt it in practice.''

''Why'd you run off court at the end?''

''I had to go to the bathroom.''

Some hack decided there had been enough hardball questions. ''Jennifer, America seems to have a love affair with you. You're always the favorite.''

She waited for him to make his point. But this valentine was his point. Once that sank in, Capriati said, ''There are a lot of good girls out there.''

○ ○ ○

Among them, Monica Seles was the best, but when asked what set her apart from her competitors, she confessed, ''It's hard for me to say what the difference is. I'm in the match. I'm not thinking much.''

''Are you afraid 1991 will best be remembered as the year you skipped Wimbledon?''

''I hope not. It's like Magic Johnson. I hope people aren't just going to remember his AIDS.''

No Seles press conference would be complete without a question about the antipathetic emotions she sparked in other players. Monica dealt with the subject as brusquely as she would with a short second serve. ''When you start at fourteen and are beating a girl every time, of course she's not going to like you.'' Then she concluded with an observation well worthy of ending anyone's week in Philadelphia. ''I definitely have some friends who are not my friends.''

Virginia Slims Championships

Do You Believe in Magic?

Professional tennis has no off-season, no real start or finish. Like the ancient symbol of eternity, it resembles a snake eating its own tail. Although the schedule of the Kraft General Foods World Tour suggests a linear progression, the circuit moves in cycles, and while the top women showed up at Madison Square Garden in the third week of November for what was billed as the Championships, a season-ending exclamation point like the World Series or the Super Bowl, the fact was that for players this was just a whistle-stop on the endless tour. They would go on to participate in exhibitions throughout December, then fly to the Southern Hemisphere for a series of special events and tournaments leading up to the Australian Open in mid-January.

Still, the Championships offered a sizable chunk of cash—$3 million—and a treasure trove of publicity. This was one of the few major events where the women didn't share the spotlight with the men and where the semifinals and finals were broadcast on network TV, not cable. The tournament attracted a full contingent of writers from England, and a smattering of journalists from as far away as Asia and South America.

Tennis was one small part of the competition taking place this week, and the $3 million purse was little more than loose change compared to the jackpot at stake in the game going on behind the scenes. Gerry Smith and the WTA Board of Directors (or was it only a few members of the Executive Committee?) continued to make plans (or were they just making noise?) to break away from Kraft and Virginia Slims and organize their own tour. The media guide listed a daily calendar of meetings involving an alphabet soup of tennis potentates. The WTA and WIPTC, the ITF and USTA held formal proceedings, while dozens of agents, tournament directors, Kraft Foods executives, and Virginia Slims officials gathered in secret conclaves. For public consumption, all sides presented a confident face. But while Gerry Smith and WTA president Pam Shriver kept swearing they were serious, representatives from Kraft and Virginia Slims retorted that they had to be kidding.

Despite Smith's continuing claims that the WTA's push for autonomy was a "player-driven initiative," no player would speak about it for the record. Few would talk even off the record. If the power-grab had any support, it was keeping a curious silence at what appeared to be a crucial juncture.

Monica Seles boldly stated her nonposition. "I'm not going to talk about it for three weeks because I'm concentrating on tennis. And I don't want to have distractions now. When the Championships finish I want to hear the story." Translation: Wake me when it's over.

With all the women, except Shriver, wavering on the sidelines, Gerry Smith began to look very lonely and very much on the spot.

○ ○ ○

In Monday evening's opening match, Steffi Graf steamrollered Conchita Martinez 6–0, 6–3, then excused the Spanish girl's pitiful performance by saying she thought Conchita had gotten tired. Since the rout hadn't lasted an hour, this didn't speak well for Martinez's conditioning.

Some shameless shill called out, "There are no easy matches here, are there?"

Steffi agreed. "I expected a good match and I think we had a good match."

"Is it strange not having Pavel [Slozil] around?"

"I think I am long enough in the business to know what to do, and it is just more or less always a routine. Obviously I'm doing okay."

OOO

After beating Lori McNeil 6–4, 7–5, Martina Navratilova fumbled for a word to describe her play, then settled on "pedestrian."

"Are all athletes as nervous as you?" a reporter asked.

The question touched a raw spot and bordered on insult, but Martina responded politely, pointing out that everybody was nervous. It was just that "I am willing to talk about it. Believe me, I think it gets worse when you get older because you realize you don't have much time left, and everything becomes much more intense and concentrated and meaningful."

Since she had played excellent tennis for the rest of the summer, someone wondered whether the loss at Wimbledon hadn't actually helped her.

Martina chuckled. "No. That sort of thing doesn't help."

OOO

On Tuesday, two singles matches were influenced by injuries. Helena Sukova flattened Mary Joe Fernandez 6–2 and kept the second set close by combining her heavy serve with a sequence of fluffy-light drop shots. Moving as if she might be hurt again, Mary Joe mishandled many of the drops. Those she managed to keep in play, Sukova lofted over her head with lobs. But in a tie-break, with the score knotted four points apiece, Fernandez got a boost when Sukova was called for a foot fault on her second serve. Fernandez won the second set and was tied two games all in the third when Helena pulled up lame. She had strained the hamstring in her left leg and retired in tears.

Afterward, Sukova explained that she had cried "in disappointment, not so much pain. I felt I had the match in the second set. I was two points from the match."

Asked to assess Fernandez's prospects for the future, Helena said, "Right now I'm thinking more of my future. I'm sorry. I thought I should have won the match. I can't really talk about Mary Joe."

OOO

With her acrobatic volleying, Zina Garrison figured to give Arantxa Sanchez Vicario fits on a fast indoor carpet, and when she won the first set 6–4, she seemed a good bet to advance to the second round. The difference in prize money was a tidy $12,000. First-round losers went home with $14,000; quarterfinalists got $26,000 and a chance to win far more. But suddenly Zina, who usually shimmies as she receives serve and jitterbugs after every ball, couldn't budge. Arantxa piled up passing shot after passing shot and ripped through the next two sets.

Zina hobbled into the interview room with ice packs on both ankles. For the past week she had been suffering from inflamed Achilles tendons. "I think she's very beatable," Zina said of Sanchez Vicario. "I think she's just riding on what she did this summer."

○ ○ ○

If Arantxa was riding on last summer's results, then Gabriela Sabatini was skating on thin ice. Her most recent tournament win had come seven months before in Rome, and her breakthrough at the 1990 U.S. Open was now ancient history. Yet during her match against Katrina Maleeva, when footage of her first and only Grand Slam title flashed on a video screen above the court, the crowd exploded with applause. New Yorkers, like fans the world over, loved Gaby. That must have given her a lift, and she needed it to recover in a second-set tie-break and win the match.

○ ○ ○

Each evening, after clearing off the dinner plates, waiters laid out snacks for the press, and that night I sat in the dining room eating popcorn and drinking beer with an Australian whose playing days were long behind him and who now concentrated some of his enormous energy on coaching. He didn't care to be named, but like everybody else at the Virginia Slims Championships, he had his opinions about the past week's changes.

"I think Slozil's all wrong for Capriati. Jennifer's one hundred percent American and outgoing. Pavel is Eastern European and reserved. That kind of personality difference is a recipe for trouble."

He couldn't understand why the Capriatis hadn't kept Tom Gullikson, but it didn't surprise him. "A lot of coaches get good results with a girl, then the girl drops him. Look at Arantxa. She won the French Open with Juan Nunez, then switched and hasn't won an important title since.''

The trouble, he claimed, was that players, or more likely, their fathers, didn't care to pay the money a top-flight coach had a right to expect. At the start, a fellow might work for a thousand dollars a week, but once he proved his worth, once his player started winning titles and big money, it was reasonable to ask for a decent share—three thousand or four thousand a week, or a flat fee plus a percentage of the prize money. If a girl was knocking down more than a million a year, the coach wasn't out of bounds when he demanded a six-figure deal.

He said Heinz Gunthardt, a former Swiss Davis Cup star, had the inside track to become Steffi Graf's new coach. Another mistake in his opinion. ''Okay, he was excellent at doubles and knows the net. But since she's so emotionally fragile these days, the last thing she needs is a person like Heinz, who was always pretty jumpy and nervous himself.''

The story often told about Gunthardt went back to his playing days when, at a tournament in Canada, he ran around the locker room before a match complaining that he couldn't find his shoes. How could he play without shoes? At that point another player glanced at Heinz's feet. Heinz looked down, too. Together they discovered what had happened to his shoes. He was wearing them.

The Australian suggested that Dennis Ralston was the right coach for Graf. ''Look what he did with Chris Evert.'' But then he mused, ''Probably a lot of coaches wouldn't work with Steffi because of her father.''

Although Seles wasn't known to be in the market for a coach, he said he would match Monica with his Australian mate Neale Fraser. ''He's a lefty and he had a helluva serve. I don't care if it cost her five hundred thousand dollars''—he was digging for the last kernels of popcorn and washing them down with beer—''it'd be worth it. Fraser could give Seles a complete game. He'd improve her serve and volley and her smash. If she doesn't get a complete game, mark my words, the other girls will learn to beat her just like they learned to beat Steffi.''

O O O

On Wednesday, the *New York Post* published an interview with Martina Navratilova that relegated the Virginia Slims Championships to the back burner and brought sexual politics front and center. Little more than two weeks before, Magic Johnson had announced that he'd tested positive for the HIV virus. Because of Magic's immense popularity, his boyish charm, and bankable image, America embraced the black basketball player as it had no other carrier of the AIDS virus. The media praised Johnson's courage for speaking out and maintained that he would make an excellent ambassador, a man who could carry a message to areas that had previously been ignored. He could reach the ghetto, the young, and all those heterosexuals who foolishly assumed they were invulnerable.

After Magic appeared on "The Arsenio Hall Show" and was interviewed in *Sports Illustrated,* insisting that he was straight and had contracted the deadly virus from one of the numerous women he had "accommodated"—his word—the public stayed behind him. President George Bush appointed Johnson to the National Commission on AIDS, and various sponsors, including Pepsi and Converse All Star Basketball Shoes, planned to feature Magic in public-service announcements about safe sex.

It was in this context that Dave Hanson of the *New York Post* asked Martina Navratilova what she thought the reaction would be if she tested HIV positive.

"Like if I had the AIDS virus," Navratilova said, people wouldn't be so understanding. "They'd say I'm gay—I had it coming. That's why they're accepting it with [Johnson], because supposedly he got it through heterosexual contact."

While she expressed sympathy for Magic and agreed that his situation was a tragedy which might lead to a cure, Martina observed, "If it happened to a heterosexual woman who had been with a hundred or two hundred men, they'd call her a whore and a slut and the corporations would drop her like a lead balloon. And she'd never get a job in her life. It's a very big-time double standard."

She knew whereof she spoke and pointed out that she had been largely shunned by sponsors. While Capriati, Seles, and Sabatini were paid millions to endorse cosmetics and clothes, she didn't "have one damn endorsement outside of racquets and shoes."

Navratilova went on: "What I don't understand is like Magic says he was trying to accommodate these women. That is just terrible. Just think about the word. He's preaching the wrong message. He's saying it's okay to be promiscuous as long as you use a condom. That's not good.

"It's sad. What does it say for you? Ayn Rand says in her writing, you are who you sleep with. Who you surround yourself with, your friends and your lovers. What does it say for these men who hop in bed with a woman every five minutes? It's sad that these women throw themselves in bed, but that doesn't mean he should do that. Be a gentleman. Have some self-respect."

O O O

That evening, before, during, and after matches, the press room rumbled with debates about Martina Navratilova. Some people argued that whatever the validity of her comments, she was exploiting Magic's calamity. Others felt that she was the last person who should criticize anybody for promiscuity or sexual misconduct after her highly publicized series of affairs. Judy Nelson's palimony suit was still pending. Navratilova had proposed a settlement of approximately $1 million in cash and property, but she demanded that Nelson promise not to write a book about their relationship. When Nelson refused to accept that condition, the agreement stalled, and the case looked likely to be resolved in court.

But most members of the tribal village of tennis responded favorably to Navratilova's remarks. *USA Today* quoted Pam Shriver as saying it was "terrific. She did it in true Martina style—open and honest."

Mary Carillo, once a player, now a TV commentator, said, "Martina has always had to suffer the effects of her sexuality. I don't think anything she said wasn't right on the money."

Chris Evert's reaction was more muted: "I had mixed feelings about what she said, but she's right."

Evert's "mixed feelings" prompted some journalistic snickering, none of which, of course, ever made it into print. Throughout her career, Chris had been the Teflon Princess of Pro Tennis; no sordid stories ever stuck to her. While Navratilova had had to endure incessant speculation and bad press about her sex life, Chris had enjoyed a free ride. Evert had traveled the world for eight years as a single girl, then for six years as a married woman, part of which time she was estranged from John Lloyd. She had traveled as a divorcée and finally as a remarried woman. Her name had been linked with a rock star, an actor, a TV commentator, and President Ford's son, Jack. Yet she was always described in the press as "dating," not having sex; she was "involved" with men, never sleeping with them. When Navratilova took up with a mother of two, the headlines screamed of "sex orgies"; when Evert, before her divorce was final, took up with Andy Mill, a man still married to his first wife, they were said to be "having a relationship."

Privately, reporters pointed out the irony in the current flap. Navratilova was at low risk for AIDS, and yet she had felt compelled to speak out about the double standard. Meanwhile, Chris Evert, one of the tour's truly liberated heterosexuals, managed to express no more than "mixed feelings."

Many reporters regarded Chris as a phony, a woman wildly different from her image. Yet they seldom acknowledged their complicity in the creation of that illusion. It wasn't Evert's responsibility to publicize her faults; it wasn't her role to present a more realistic picture of the way a wealthy, successful, and attractive woman athlete lived her life. That was the press's job, and it was their failure—their own phoniness—that had helped cast Martina into such an unflattering light by depicting her longtime rival in a false light.

O O O

While waiting for Seles to play Julie Halard of France, I spotted Monica's brother, Zoltan. It was hard to miss him. His platinum hair glowed like a fluorescent bulb, and while his clothes might have provided camouflage in a Soho gallery, he cut an exotic figure at a tennis tournament. He wore a pair of baggy black pants pegged at the ankles, black sandals with white socks, and a fuzzy black sweater over a white T-shirt.

A former top-ranked junior in Yugoslavia, Zoltan had once reached the quarterfinals of the European Championships, where he lost to Emilio Sanchez. Now he devoted himself almost exclusively to his sister's business interests. He had worked with, and for, her since 1986 when he was discharged from military service and moved with Monica to Nick Bolletieri's Tennis Academy in Bradenton, Florida. For six months, they lived alone in a two-bedroom condo, the twenty-one-year-old brother serving as surrogate parent for his twelve-year-old sister. After Karolj and Esther arrived, Zoltan and Monica had to share a bedroom until she was fifteen.

He told me Monica was beginning to make many of her own decisions. This was in line with the family's wishes; they wanted her to understand business so she wouldn't be taken advantage of. Still, Zoltan said, a player needed help wading through the welter of offers and invitations. She had to keep her head clear for tennis.

"There's no off-season," he emphasized, "and that's damaging to the sport and the players. It might have psychological effects on young players like Monica and Jennifer. You always have to prove yourself. There's no psychological rest, and you're never playing at home. There's no home-court advantage. Because of the competitiveness, you can flip out. Tennis often results in professional and ego deformation."

Although his English had the same faint traces of an accent as Monica's, his vocabulary was more sophisticated, his delivery professorial. Hers were the intonations of an American teenager; Zoltan sounded like a European intellectual. "Tennis is very orthodox," he groused. "It resists creativity and change. I am not jealous of Monica, but sometimes I wish I could pursue some of my own interests in fashion and creativity and movies. But I have obligations to the family. With the competition as it is today, it's hard to rest." He stressed that this competition existed between family and family, agent and agent, as well as player and player.

"You become closed off in your own world." He cupped his hands over his eyes. "Some of the players are very paranoid. You go into the locker room and people look at each other with suspicion."

While many families felt that a coach served the purpose of protecting a girl on the tour, Zoltan didn't agree. "Some coaches manipulate the players and make them emotionally dependent. Then the coach asks for unreasonable money, and they break up and the player is upset. It's like being in love. It's a comparable relationship. Of course, some of them are lovers. A lot of coaches take advantage and try to make themselves important in a player's life, not just in her tennis. We've already been through one relationship like that.''

Although he mentioned the man's name, Zoltan insisted it was off the record. He accused the fellow, a hitting partner, of attempting to inveigle his way into Monica's favor. The man had been an object of rumors during Wimbledon when Seles was said to be pregnant.

A few fans in Madison Square Garden recognized Zoltan and asked for his autograph. Although he obliged them, he muttered after they left, ''It's scary when someone comes strong on you. You always wonder what the motives are. People react differently when you become a celebrity. When you give money to charity, they say it's for PR. When you don't give, they say you are a shit. Still, you have to keep trying. Monica wants to get more and more involved in charity. But it's hard to go through life thinking everybody wants something from you.''

Could he imagine meeting somebody who didn't want anything and instead had something to offer Monica?

''You mean business?'' Zoltan said.

''No, something personal.''

''I cannot imagine.''

Although the Seles family had long since left Bolletieri's and moved from the two-bedroom condo into a house befitting Monica's income, Zoltan remarked that their real ''home is now airplanes and hotels. My father becomes so exhausted flying back from Japan or Australia, he goes to bed for two or three days.'' Once Monica's career ended, ''I think my mother and father would like to go back to Europe. Their friends and their roots are there. Monica and I have adapted quite well to America.

''The important thing we're doing is trying to plan for Monica's future. So many star athletes retire and don't know what to do. They become depressed. They do drugs. We want her to be happy. It will be hard for her to meet a man who's not intimidated and who's interested in her for herself, not her money or her fame.''

Meanwhile, every day on the circuit was a new lesson and sometimes another mistake. About this year's Wimbledon, Zoltan said, "We learned a lot. We learned if you don't speak, other people will fill up the silence with speculation. Monica felt she said all she was obliged to say. She was hurt and disappointed not to play. She could have won the Grand Slam. She was very disappointed. She couldn't say more about her injury because she didn't know any more. None of us thought that people, that reporters, would speculate like they did. I mean, to say she was pregnant, that could cause real damage to a young girl.''

O O O

By now Monica had mauled Julie Halard in the first set and was shutting her out in the second. While Seles went on grunting and walloping the ball, the French girl giggled. She won just six points in the second set and the match lasted only thirty-four minutes. When you get blitzed that badly, it's either laugh or cry, and Halard chose the former.

Though far from a competitive masterpiece, the match was a landmark. By advancing to the next round, Seles ensured that she would break Martina Navratilova's record for prize money in a single year. Monica had already earned $2,183,758 and would collect $224,000 more if she won the Championships.

In her press conference, she said she hadn't realized she set a new record. "I don't look for those things."

"Do you count your money?"

"No. It doesn't matter if you win the tournament, if you get the money, the bonus-pool points, the ranking points. Just go out there and play tennis the best you can and everything else is a bonus. That is how you have to look at it, if you want to stay here for a long time."

"Do you have any mixed feelings about playing in a tennis tournament named after a cigarette brand?"

"No. I mean, we play the whole year around and the tournament is based on—"

The reporter interrupted. "Some people think that it is like advertising for the cigarette companies. What do you think?"

"We went over this so many times," Seles snapped. "Virginia Slims doesn't make me smoke. They don't ask me to smoke. I am just playing. I'm just doing my job."

O O O

Still bothered by a strained right thigh, Jennifer Capriati had no end of trouble with Nathalie Tauziat, the titian-haired Frenchwoman with a nice volley, but no dependable route to the net. Since neither her serve nor her approach shots had much sting, she had to wait for a short ball from Capriati. They split sets, stayed even in the third, then played a tie-break that was a microcosm of the match. When Jennifer lengthened her ground strokes, pinning Tauziat to the baseline, the French player couldn't keep up. Capriati applied the *coup de grace* with a 105-m.p.h. serve, the fastest of the night.

Afterward Jennifer said she won because "I really didn't want to let the crowd down."

When Tauziat was asked whether the partisan spectators had bothered her, she pursed her lips. "I don't want to talk about that." The loss, she said, came down to one thing. "She play better the tie-break than me."

O O O

Recently I had received a tip that a USTA coach had been fired for sexually harassing some girls he was training. When I called the USTA to confirm the story, a source there agreed to talk, but only if I offered an absolute guarantee of anonymity. This didn't surprise me. Plenty of people in tennis prefer to remain anonymous. The circuit and its support system are in a constant process of permutation, and this week's enemy might become next week's friend; this year's rival might be next year's colleague or boss. But the source's high level of anxiety seemed extraordinary. Only later would I learn that it was well founded.

The USTA employee acknowledged that there had been some anecdotal information about a coach and his inappropriate language and touching. But since there had been no formal complaint or official finding, it would be inaccurate to state that the coach had been fired for sexual harassment. As the USTA employee preferred to put it, there had been allegations. Period. The man in question had resigned and accepted a coaching position outside the USTA. Period. Full stop.

Yet after this punctilious refusal to grant any cause and effect, the

USTA employee agreed that there was ample reason for the grumbling about sexual harassment. There were so many male coaches working with girls, there were bound to be incidents. "Parents are absolutely paranoid about the possibility of lesbians coming on to their daughters," the source said. "They don't want these young girls exposed to that life-style. So they travel with them or send them off on the tour with male coaches."

"And the irony," I said, "is these coaches, some of them, hit on the girls."

"The parents would rather that happen. They'd prefer that to their daughters having a lesbian experience. Even if it's an older man or a married man, they figure that's better than a lesbian."

The source proceeded to say that concern about lesbians had limited the opportunities open to female coaches. Just think of the excellent female players of the Sixties and Seventies who were now retired and available to coach. Yet few had jobs. Even straight women coaches feared that people would stigmatize them as gay. It all came back to a basic ambivalence about women and sport. Some people automatically regarded any female athlete as suspect. With some shame the USTA employee admitted sharing that suspicion on occasion.

○ ○ ○

That evening, the Navratilova–Sanchez Vicario match was no more than a prologue to Martina's press conference. Journalists and TV talking heads from all over the country had congregated to ask follow-up questions about Magic Johnson, AIDS, and women athletes. The bulletin board in the media center was papered with articles presenting pros and cons of the issue. *USA Today* quoted George Lois, chairman of an ad agency, who observed that if Navratilova contracted AIDS, "she'd not only be dropped from advertising, she'd be burned at the stake."

A market survey indicated that Chris Evert, who hadn't played competitively in more than two years, was still number one in popularity among tennis celebrities. Martina ranked number twenty-seven.

Although Navratilova received a rousing welcome from the crowd, she looked tense and brittle, and lost 6–1 in eighteen embarrassing minutes. But gradually she got her nerves and her shots under control, and started to pressure Arantxa with sliced returns of serve. She took the second set 6–4, then ran away with the third 6–2.

Reporters, photographers, and camera crews packed the press room and jostled for places down front. When Arantxa Sanchez Vicario showed up first, there was an audible sigh of disappointment. "Cut away from her," a TV commentator called to her cameraman.

Normally a great media favorite, the Spanish pepper pot was treated as an inconvenience tonight. After a few perfunctory questions and answers—"Maybe she play more intelligent than me on the big points"—Arantxa departed and Martina arrived carrying her dog, K.D., short for Killer Dog. Fine blond hair framed the sculpted planes of her face. Without makeup, her features had the pale, smooth-grained character of a pine carving.

When Tommy Bonk of the *Los Angeles Times* started to ask about the reaction she had gotten to her remarks about Magic, Martina cut him short. "Let me get into that in a minute. Just do all the tennis first, then we can talk about that."

"At the end of the first set," someone said, "you held up a white towel as if to say, '[I] surrender.' "

"I had to laugh," she admitted. "I mean, I was getting blown off the court, and it was either get really pissed off or make light of it."

After she had discussed her ball toss, her service percentage, and the importance of balancing power with placement, a reporter said, "Half-and-half question, Martina. All the stuff that has been going on in the last couple of days, did that have any bearing on your attitude any time tonight?"

"No, not at all. I was just playing my match. I was astonished by the response. I am sure I could have said that President Bush is a closet cross-dresser and I wouldn't have got this much response."

"A closet what?"

"A closet cross-dresser." The room erupted with laughter. "He isn't," Martina hastened to add. "I don't know if he is. Oh God, I am in trouble now."

Someone asked whether she had received any negative reaction.

"So far most of it has been very positive, at least from what I have heard. A lot of people have been thinking those thoughts, but have not been stupid enough or brave enough to say them. A lot of people are thinking that, but they are not being interviewed. You know, I certainly didn't mean my comments to be in any way negative toward Magic. Because selfishly I wish that he hadn't gotten it so I could watch him play basketball. He was one of my heroes as a basketball player. But I felt that I needed to say what I felt.''

While underscoring her sympathy for Magic, she insisted on certain distinctions. ''Nobody deserves AIDS. Nobody deserves to get cancer, but you can prevent AIDS a whole lot better than you can prevent cancer. But I think the message should be 'Don't be promiscuous.' I think we should promote loving, caring relationships, monogamous relationships, with people that really mean something to you. And then, when you do make love, take precautions. Not only for AIDS, but preventing pregnancies that you don't want. There are plenty of them out there. I mean, there is this horror story about this woman having an abortion in her eighth month. You know, that kind of stuff could all be prevented. And people just need to be a little more careful. But again, the problem lies a lot deeper in society than just wearing a condom. Some of these people don't care whether they are living or dying, so they are certainly not going to care about getting pregnant.''

A current of electricity close to giddiness sizzled through the room. This was the sort of scene many of us daydream about—the moment when we drop the formulaic responses of our mundane identities and speak the unvarnished truth to an audience that actually listens. For people who covered the WTA tour, it was proof that a story could involve more than scores and hype. Despite its often unrealistic idea of itself and its choreographed image, women's tennis related to, and was in its way shaped by, the same forces that affected everyone's life. Love, sex, pregnancy, abortion, disease, and death—these were themes all human beings had to grapple with, and as Martina admirably demonstrated, an athlete could address them without running the danger that the circuit would self-destruct or fans would stay away or the press would attack.

''I am not judging anybody,'' Navratilova said. ''I don't want people to judge me, I am certainly not going to judge them. I am not perfect. I have done plenty of things that I could be embarrassed about, that I wish I hadn't done." She mentioned a fan who accused her of being thoughtless and surly when she asked for an autograph. "The only thing I owe anybody is to be good out there when I play my match and give it one hundred percent. But at the same time you can't be rude to people, you can't be doing drugs on the side, even if it doesn't affect your performance. You can't be drinking and driving. I mean we are role models. I wish I hadn't been that rude to the lady. We can all do better, I think, and the male athletes can certainly do better in their sexual habits." But, she added, "the double standard is there and it makes me mad as hell."

"What about the double standard within your own profession?" I asked. "I called the USTA today to talk to them about the increasing frequency of male coaches on the tour. And the official I spoke to attributed this to parental fear of lesbians."

Navratilova rolled her eyes toward the ceiling. "Oh please, USTA, wake up and smell the coffee. My God!"

"When I said then, were they not afraid that these male coaches might get involved with the girls, the response was the parents would prefer that than the other."

Martina laughed. So did the rest of the room.

"What is your reaction to a double standard within your own profession?" I repeated.

"I think it is not even a double standard as much as it is people living in the Dark Ages. I mean, what do they think, that gay women attack every young girl that they see? That is the problem with the whole stigma of gay people, that all they think about is sex—which is not at all the case, just like heterosexuals don't just think about sex all the time. We are all the same, and the labels that are put on and the images that people have of gays attacking people in elevators and doing this kind of crazy stuff, it just amazes me. And if that is really what is happening with the USTA, I guess I am out of a job."

○ ○ ○

Martina Navratilova's press conference was so long, reporters didn't get back to the court until Jana Novotna and Steffi Graf had split sets, and Novotna had stunned the crowd, not to mention Steffi, by taking a commanding lead in the third. Even as Jana's advantage lengthened to 5–1, her history of blowing matches should have encouraged Graf to hang on and hope. The old stubborn, fiercely proud Steffi would never have given up. But this wasn't the same player.

Graf lost the deciding set 6–1, and within minutes we were back in the interview room, no longer exhilarated by a player who dared speak her mind, but confronted by a young woman who seemed not to know her mind.

"Now that you are at the end of the year," a journalist said, "where you have lost your number-one status, where your results, by your standards, have not been that good, do you think you have to reassess your game and make some changes?"

"Well, I think most importantly, I think I have to look a little bit differently at tennis." The words sounded reasonable, even sanguine, but her eyes roved the room as though searching for an escape hatch. "I have to just be a little looser. I haven't been really able to do it. Even I knew that I had to, but I take everything a little bit too serious right now. I think I have to just enjoy it a little bit more. Definitely, I mean I have to make some small changes in my game."

"Steffi, can you remember the last time somebody so dominated you in a third set?"

"I don't want to look back." But she had no sooner spoken than she did look back. "I don't know. No, I don't think so."

"Is there any way you are actually going to make it a bit more enjoyable? Take it less seriously? Are there any practical steps you can take?"

"I think it is more in my head. That is why I think it is necessary for me to take a few weeks off right now, to get really my mind on other things, and get all those things straightened out which are not straightened out, and try again."

"Where are you going to go to—Germany or Florida?"

"No, much further away."

"Where?"

"No answer to that one," said Steffi in a distant voice as though she were already on her way there—wherever it might be.

○ ○ ○

Mary Joe Fernandez had lost to Monica Seles five times this year and she didn't want to make it six. So she mixed it up; she rushed the net and volleyed; she dropped one hand from the racquet and hit a backhand slice. Still, Seles served at 5–3, survived a break point, and won the first set.

As usual, Mary Joe suffered an injury. A trainer rushed out and stretched her shoulder. Even in the processed air of Madison Square Garden, she perspired heavily and had to run off and change her skirt as well as her shirt. She labored mightily and cleverly to come back, canceling three break points in the third game of the second set, only to drop serve on a double fault.

After Seles won 6–3, 6–2, Mary Joe said that against Monica, "you're fighting for every single point. Nobody's going to beat her banging the ball. She bangs the ball better than anybody."

○ ○ ○

It was difficult to believe Monica could out-slug anybody the way she slouched into her press conference sucking on a chunk of hard candy. She wore black No Excuses jeans and a black turtleneck sweater.

"What flavor is it?" someone shouted.

"Cherry. This is the best tournament because in the locker room they have all these different kinds of candies. It's dangerous. Once in a while I haven't had dinner and I am very hungry."

Her slurping and lip smacking were audible as she sucked the candy and said she was tired. "I am going to bed early tonight. I am not going to the [Michael Bolton] concert."

"How many times have you been, Monica?"

"Twice. But half and half. I didn't see the show even once the full time."

As always, Seles argued that it had been a tough match, in doubt until the last point. Which prompted a reporter to wisecrack, "If she was so good and you were not quite as good as you would like, why was the score three and two?"

It was all a matter, she said, of a break here and a lucky shot there. "I had to really work some great points."

"The other day you said you don't think about all the money you make, but do you think about it when you spend the money? Like when you go shopping, do you think about how much things cost?"

"Not really. But I don't go into expensive stores. The money goes very fast there. I usually go to the same stores I went before. You know, the casual stores. But when I want to go window-shop, I go to designer clothes. But I look at the tags there and when you see a five-thousand-dollar tag for a coat, I say good-bye. They are pretty pushy, a lot of times. Like I buy a lot of clothes, so a lot of stores that I go into, the salespeople like are all around because they think I am going to spend so much money. They can't wait for me to come to their store to see their stuff because somebody told them that if you get Monica in the store, you will have a sure sale."

"When you look at the price, do you say this is a first-round win?"

"Yeah, I do. It's embarrassing but I do."

"Last year you got lost in Bloomingdale's. Have you had any adventures this year?"

"No, I didn't have time this week to go there yet. As soon as I got back from Philadelphia, I was tired. I am just resting this week. Tell you truth, I have done my shopping this year in Milan."

"What did you spend in Milan?"

"We stayed there three extra days. I really spent some—bought some clothes, winter clothes. A lot of times when you charge it, when you give your credit card, you don't realize, especially in Italian money, how much it is. When I got home and I see the total, I said, 'Monica, you really done it.' I was not too happy with myself. I told myself, 'For a month and a half, nothing.' I have three more weeks to go."

"What was the total?"

"Whoa!" was all Monica would say.

"What do you prefer buying?"

"I have so much black stuff that it is unbelievable. I personally have seven black turtlenecks. I only buy black. My mom is always mad and she always says, 'Why do you wear black? I never see you wear any colors.' And it's the truth, but I just feel the most comfortable in black.''

"Except on court?''

"Yeah, well, that's not my choice.''

"Was this the first time you've worn shorts?''

"Oh no, I have been wearing them since Milan because Fila—the new line was coming out. They said they can't make skirts because I have grown. The skirts were just too short. I felt I am not going to go out there in that short of a skirt. They told me, wear the shorts.''

"Mary Joe was the crowd's favorite. This is happening a lot to you.''

"Everybody likes the underdog. And you know, it is a strange feeling, because I mean I feel personally I am the underdog also. Inside I never feel number one. I always feel I am still upcoming.''

O O O

Jennifer Capriati felt that she, too, was up and coming. She had whipped Gabriela Sabatini three times in a row, and after dusting her off so cavalierly in Philadelphia, she went into her quarterfinal brimming with confidence. But tonight Gaby took her to the woodshed and administered some disciplinary action—a 6–1 licking in the first set.

In the second, Jenny started off in a hurry. That was part of her problem; she liked to play fast. But after Capriati went up 2–0, Gaby became more deliberate, taking her time between points, patiently setting up shots, waiting for the right opportunity to rush the net. She regained Jenny's early break and got one of her own for a 6–4 win and a place in the semifinals.

O O O

By Friday, the WTA's attempt to take control of the women's tour appeared to be ending with an embarrassed whimper. After brash talk about redefining its relationship with Kraft and Virginia Slims and finding other sponsors willing to fund ten $1 million tournaments, Gerry Smith scrambled for a face-saving formula and seized on a classic bureaucratic ploy. In simultaneous press releases, the Women's Tennis

Association and the Women's International Professional Tennis Council announced the formation of "a Working Group to evaluate the existing tour format and to explore opportunities for the growth of women's tennis in the future."

The WIPTC announcement stressed "its support of the five-year Kraft General Foods World Tour sponsorship agreement, which continues until the end of 1994." WTA president Pam Shriver pledged that "In the pursuit of our goals, the WTA never intended to break any existing agreements. . . . WTA has always demonstrated loyalty and a unique commitment toward its sponsors. We look forward to working with our sponsors, Kraft General Foods and Virginia Slims, as we seek ways to unify the marketing strategies for women's tennis."

One longtime tournament director and irreverent observer of the game's Machiavellian business machinations told me, "Gerry Smith not only put his foot in his mouth. He put in every appendage. He totally misread the situation. Philip Morris [which owned Kraft General Foods and Virginia Slims] has the greatest PR people in the world. They have to. They're selling death. If they can do that, they can certainly handle Gerry Smith."

But another tournament director, this one a European, wasn't convinced that the matter had been laid to rest, and on Saturday, as he gave me a ride in his chauffeur-driven limo to Madison Square Garden, he argued that the WTA still planned to break away from the present tour structure. "It won't happen until the current contracts run out, but it's going to happen. The only thing I wonder is why Gerry tried to force the issue now."

To him it was all the same whether the WTA, the WIPTC, or the ITF controlled the circuit. He was a businessman and recognized that his profits depended on delivering a product that customers would buy. Like any entrepreneur in the entertainment industry, he had to book performers who were bankable, and in tennis, that meant stars. Which, in turn, meant he had to offer some form of inducement. Despite the WTA's denials that women players accepted guarantees, this tournament director claimed to know differently.

"For some tournaments," he said, "that's the only way of surviving. Of course, I don't pay the guarantee myself. The sponsors do. I go to them and say, 'Do you want this player?' If they do, I tell them what we must pay. Sometimes they ask the girl to put a patch on her sleeve or to speak for a product.

"The top girls know what they're worth and they get it. Take the tournament in Leipzig. It's an event created for Steffi Graf. When she or Anke Huber play, people come out and watch. This year on Friday there were five thousand spectators for Anke Huber's match against Jana Novotna. For that evening's match—Katrina Maleeva against Barbara Paulus—there were two hundred people."

Huber and Paulus both lost and both received the same prize money. But when one girl attracted twenty-five times as many paying customers, it wasn't logical, the tournament director said, to claim that they were worth the same money.

○ ○ ○

Monica Seles was on court practicing with her current hitting partner, Sven Groenevelol. Karolj hovered in the background, and a maintenance man knelt in the foreground. The man was stapling and taping the carpet at Groenevelol's end of the court. But the tall Swede danced around the guy, nimbly retrieving Monica's shots.

After the Seles camp cleared off and the maintenance man finished, Martina Navratilova dissected Jana Novotna as deftly as a scientist laying bare the inner workings of a simpler organism. Winner of five previous Virginia Slims Championships, Martina gave evidence of having the stuff to claim a sixth title.

A pleasing marriage of ballet and ballistics, the first set went to Navratilova. But as is so often the case when a player starts off at high pitch, Martina soon had problems. Having lost just three points on serve in the first set and none as she streaked to a 3–0 lead in the second, she suddenly couldn't keep the ball in play. Jana broke her, then held to 2–3, and from there on the match was a farrago of double faults, fumbled volleys, false hopes, and lost opportunities. After five straight service breaks, Martina eked out the set 6–4 and was into the final.

○ ○ ○

While Monica Seles had had to content herself with going to Michael Bolton's concert, Gabriela Sabatini had been going out with the man himself. Perhaps Seles regarded this as a personal affront. Maybe it was a case of hell having no fury like a teenage tennis star scorned by a rock singer. There had to be some explanation for what Monica did to Gaby. As Sabatini staggered off court after a mere forty-seven minutes, victim of a 6–1, 6–1 mugging, she must have felt as if she'd gone through a threshing machine.

Did you lose your confidence? a reporter asked Gaby.

"I didn't have time to lose my confidence."

Was it Monica's pace or her power or her consistency that was the problem?

"Everything."

By Saturday night the days had dwindled down, as had the hopes and illusions of all the pretenders to the throne. Steffi, Jana, Arantxa, Mary Joe, Jennifer, and Gaby—all gone and by their fans and agents grieved. I spotted Mary Joe Fernandez leaving the Garden with her father. "Are you going to spend all your time between now and the Australian Open lifting weights?" I asked.

She giggled. "Oh yes. I'm going to get big and burly."

O O O

A replay of the U.S. Open final, the Navratilova–Seles match once again boiled down to a single question: How often could Monica pass Martina? Everybody in Madison Square Garden, everybody in the national TV audience, knew Navratilova would rush the net. Yet although it was said that she couldn't win unless she went on the offensive, the trouble was, once she got where she was going, she had to play defense; she had to stand up to Seles's passing shots like a human shock absorber.

In the opening set, she served so well that Monica couldn't unleash her laserlike ground strokes. Punctuating each game with an ace, Martina reached 4–4 and eased ahead 40–15 on her serve. But with two brilliant returns, Seles brought the score to deuce, then got a break point.

As Martina started her service toss, a flashbulb went off at the far end of the court. She caught the ball and struggled to compose herself. Finally she served, swooped to the net, and cracked a decent volley, only to have Seles chase it down and pass her. Navratilova had played a nearly perfect set, a nearly perfect point—and it wasn't enough. Monica served out the set 6–4.

In the second, the players stayed on serve to 3–3. Then the advantage swung to Seles, who had two chances to break. When Martina came up with a couple of aces, Monica complained about the calls and was upset when the ump wouldn't overrule. She dropped her own serve and Navratilova hung on for 6–3.

In the third, Monica turned up the volume. Grunting as she clobbered the ball, she bounded to a 3–0 lead and didn't blink when Martina twice came back to tie the score. Seles kept on swinging knockout punches and just when it looked as if the set was headed for a tie-break, she landed a haymaker for a demoralizing 7–5 win.

The fourth set was a formality, as Martina discovered you could dash into a cannon's mouth only so many times before you became shell-shocked. "The mental part comes into it," she said afterward. "I had a little let down and she jumped all over me. I hit good serves, exactly where I wanted it, and she just nailed it."

Result—six games to Seles, goose egg for Navratilova.

For Monica, it was a fitting end to a year in which she had taken three Grand Slam titles. With $250,000 for winning the Virginia Slims Championships and $550,000 in bonuses, she brought her official 1991 earnings to $2,457,758. That didn't include the millions she had made on endorsements and exhibition matches.

Martina paid proper tribute to Monica the tennis player. "She puts more pressure on you from the baseline than anyone I've ever played against. Because she hits it on both sides, you never rest. With Monica, you don't really have an opening. You can't relax for one second. She is very mentally tough, and the points don't last long."

But about Seles the person, she had reservations. "She walks to a different drummer. She's not your run-of-the-mill human being. But I guess that's part of why she's number one. The number-one player in the world isn't an average human being."

〇 〇 〇

Still, Seles gave a pretty convincing imitation of an average goofy, giggling teenager. Sniffling from a cold, she showed up for her interview in black jeans and a black turtleneck, and although no one asked about the outfit, she said, "Third day in a row."

What excited her most was that she had won a new Jaguar XJ–5, compliments of Kraft General Foods. It was, she said, her first car. "I'm not going to let anybody else drive it. I'm not going to let my brother take it from me."

Giggling more by the minute, she said she wanted the Jag to be black, her favorite color. "Black convertible top, black interior, black everything!" The thought of it broke Monica Seles up. "Like a funeral car," she screeched with laughter.

The rest of us broke up, too—broke into laughter, then broke to file stories, then broke away from the circuit until next time.

o o o

A couple of weeks after the Virginia Slims Championships, I received a long-distance call from my USTA source. This anxious soul spoke from a pay phone for fear of using an office phone and leaving a record of the link between us. It seemed that my press conference questions to Martina Navratilova had prompted a USTA inquiry.

No, it wasn't an inquiry into the double standard. The USTA didn't attempt to determine whether parents had any reason to be worried that lesbians might molest their daughters. It didn't bother to ask whether male coaches were sexually harassing or abusing girls. The inquiry was aimed exclusively at tracking down the person who had spoken to me.

"I've never felt paranoid around here until this," the source said. "But now I really do. I'm afraid I'll lose my job." The USTA employee had every intention of denying that we had spoken and wanted reassurance that my guarantee of anonymity wouldn't be violated.

I repeated my promise, then confirmed with the source every point of our previous conversation. Finally, I asked who was conducting the inquiry.

"Marshall Happer."

This was no low-level inquiry. M. Marshall Happer is the Executive Director of the United States Tennis Association. In his previous position as Administrator of the Men's International Professional Tennis Council, Happer had taken sharp exception to what I had written in *Short Circuit*.

After the warning from my USTA source, it didn't surprise me to receive a letter from Happer, informing me that "all relevant employees of the USTA" denied speaking to me. "The suggestions" in my questions to Martina Navratilova, Happer insisted, "have never been authorized or made by the USTA." Since he knew I was now writing a book about the women's tour, Happer warned me not to "attribute any of the suggestions in your questions to Martina . . . as statements, positions or anything relating to the USTA."

It also didn't surprise me that Happer hadn't expressed the slightest interest in the substance of what the USTA employee had said or in anything I had learned on the tour.

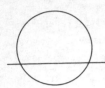

Epilogue

In the category of business as usual, Monica Seles won the Australian Open, the first major event of the 1992 season, for her fifth Grand Slam title. Monica beat Mary Joe Fernandez in the final.

Although Mary Joe again fell short of winning a Grand Slam, she played aggressively throughout the tournament. Rushing the net and volleying far more than in the past, she shocked Gabriela Sabatini—and perhaps herself—with a straight-set triumph in the semis. Yet one thing about Fernandez remained the same, and that was her habit of changing coaches the way some girls change T-shirts. Now she was working with Harold Solomon, the half-pint clay-court player who had clobbered her in a practice match last spring in Paris.

Yet another thing on the women's tour remained the same. Steffi Graf switched coaches and was training with Heinz Gunthardt, but was still beset by a puzzling succession of physical maladies. On the long flight to Australia, she came down with the flu and arrived in Perth with her ears so blocked up she couldn't maintain her equilibrium. Once she recovered from that, she contracted a severe case of measles and had to withdraw from the Australian Open and hurry back to Germany for medical treatment.

In early February, Martina Navratilova won the Virginia Slims of Chicago for her 158th title, breaking Chris Evert's record of 157. *Tennis Week* pointed out that Martina had won more titles than the other nine women in the top ten combined.

What Navratilova hadn't managed to achieve, however, was a resolution of her legal problems with former lover Judy Nelson. That took yet another month of wrangling. Finally, on Friday, March 13, it was announced that the suit had been settled. Nelson would receive a house in Aspen, Colorado, valued at $1.3 million. What's more, Nelson retained the right to do a book about her relationship with Martina. "This book I would have written if Martina and I were together still," Judy told reporters. "I think she'll love it."

More on the subject of love—Bettina Fulco had married Pablo Villella and the honeymooners were back on the tour. Kathy Rinaldi, Shaun Stafford, Marianne Werdel, and Nicole Provis announced that they, too, would soon marry.

Liz and Peter Smylie had a daughter whom they named Laura Elizabeth. Meanwhile, Anne Minter, following Liz's example, played until her fifth month of pregnancy. A twenty-nine-year-old from Melbourne, Minter had married her coach, Graeme Harris, three years ago.

In a recent poll, male players had voted Steffi Graf the girl with the best figure on the tour. Perhaps in an effort to verify the accuracy of that selection, a photographer hired a helicopter and flew over Graf's house in Boca Raton, Florida. He spotted Steffi sunbathing in the nude next to the pool and snapped off a roll of film. "He only got my back," Steffi said. "Otherwise I would be crazy."

In her interview at Wimbledon in 1991, Andrea Jaeger seemed to have completed the transition to life off the tour and made peace with the injuries that ended her career. But in 1992, it was revealed that Jaeger had filed a $6 million suit against the International Management Group, claiming, it was reported in *The New York Times*, that IMG had "provided improper advice regarding [the] purchase of disability insurance." She also charged that "she suffered a career-ending injury in eighty-four but was urged to continue playing because IMG collects twenty-five percent in commissions."

IMG's position, as articulated by Bob Kain, was that the agency had advised Jaeger about comprehensive disability insurance coverage, but she chose to take out a policy that limited her indemnity to a total of $60,000. Far from urging her to continue playing despite her injuries, the agency maintained that it had helped Andrea quit tennis. Kain told

The New York Times, "Her father was the one who encouraged her to play. Now we're probably going to have to file a suit against him even though we don't think he did anything so wrong."

Meanwhile, Jennifer Capriati, currently the youngest player in the top ten, was the talk of the tour. But for the first time the talk wasn't about her boundless potential, her astronomical endorsement income, or her youthful exuberance. Suddenly both tennis insiders and tabloid writers wondered what had gone wrong with the fifteen-year-old phenomenon. It wasn't simply that she wasn't winning titles. She seemed professionally and personally miserable.

After a straight-set defeat to Gabriela Sabatini in the quarterfinals of the Australian Open, Jennifer acted shaken and inconsolable at her press conference. Then she flew to Tokyo, where in the Pan Pacific Open she suffered one of the worst and earliest losses of her career. After Magdalena Maleeva, only sixteen herself, beat Capriati 6–1, 6–2, Jennifer was heard screaming at her father, complaining about her schedule. One tabloid reported that she shouted, "You're destroying my life!"

Capriati dropped off the tour for five weeks, but when she came back at the Lipton International Championships in Florida, she seemed sullen and easily distracted, as if she would rather be anyplace than on a tennis court. After winning an error-ridden, second-round match, she said in a televised interview with Mary Carillo that she would like to spend more time with her school friends and less time on the tour. She admitted that there were moments when she felt like quitting altogether. Although she reached the semifinals by whipping Monica Seles, Jennifer continued to look miserable and to answer every question with brusque monosyllables. *Sports Illustrated* described her as "a chunky, acned vessel of hormones, a kid so lost in a fog of adolescent alienation that she couldn't string together more than a few guttural sounds for conversation."

While normal adolescent growing pains are enough to unhinge any teenager, Jennifer's problems were magnified by the fact that everything occurred in public, in front of millions of fans and a press corps that was often obtuse, when not downright rude. Then, too, her situation was complicated by a witch's brew of financial considerations. As Cindy Hahn of *Tennis* magazine pointed out, every young girl worries about her complexion, but in Capriati's case an embarrassing attack of acne caused something close to a corporate crisis. An official at Oil of Olay confided that Capriati's endorsement of the skin cream "hasn't worked out like we'd hoped."

There was another thing in Jennifer's life that wasn't working out. She and her new coach, Pavel Slozil, hadn't hit it off. Or perhaps it would be more accurate to say that Slozil and Stefano Capriati didn't hit it off. Whatever the truth of the matter, the Capriatis dropped Slozil. Jennifer said, "The chemistry just wasn't there. There wasn't the communication and that's it."

By the time the Capriati entourage arrived in Rome for the Italian Open, it was in complete disarray. Asked whether she would have come there if her contract with Diadora hadn't obliged her to, Jennifer conceded, "I really don't know." Playing lethargically, she lost in the third round to Amanda Coetzer, then had to endure a press conference where an Italian reporter asked her point blank if she had been beaten because she was too fat. That sent Jennifer reeling off to the locker room in tears.

By the time the tour reached Paris for the French Open, Pavel Slozil had gone on record with his version of the break with the Capriati family. He criticized Stefano as unprofessional and boorishly inconsiderate, and said that Jennifer lacked motivation and discipline. Unlike Steffi Graf, who was so eager to practice that Pavel had to force her off the court, Slozil said he could seldom convince Jennifer to work for any concentrated period of time. Pavel ended by announcing that he was fed up with women players and their families. If he ever coached again, he swore it would be a man.

Aside from the whispers about her personal woes, Jennifer Capriati made little impact at Roland Garros. Once again the tournament belonged to Monica Seles, who showed up with a new hairstyle and a new color, dark brown. Although she blamed the color on a beautician's mistake, Monica played for the rest of the summer as a brunette and seemed to be having just as much fun as she had as a blond. She thumped Capriati in the quarterfinals 6–2, 6–2, came back from a break in the third set to take the semis from Sabatini, then collided with Steffi Graf in an epic final that lasted two hours and forty-three minutes. Having squandered four match points in the third set, Seles struggled for another hour before prevailing 6–2, 3–6, 10–8 for her third straight French Open title.

Although bitterly disappointed, Graf took heart that she had come so close and that she had nearly matched Monica's mental toughness. This gave her a boost as Wimbledon began, and she sailed serenely through the fortnight while other competitors were beset by difficulties. Seles in particular was plagued by the Beastie Boys from the tabloids who insisted on rehashing rumors about her absence the previous year. Then one enterprising soul brought what he called a "Gruntometer" onto Centre Court and recorded what he claimed were grunts that equaled the decibel level of a freight train. With so many reporters complaining about the noise, it wasn't long before players started to object. During the quarterfinals, Nathalie Tauziat of France, a combative redhead, asked the umpire to issue a code warning against Seles for her disruptive grunting. Then in the semifinals, Martina Navratilova, who had never complained in the past about Monica, decided she could no longer abide the racket. She asked the umpire to tell Seles to quiet down.

When Monica survived the challenge, advancing to her first Wimbledon final, Steffi Graf admitted that she herself might lodge a complaint if Seles grunted during their match. Like a number of other players, Graf protested that Monica's grunt was distracting enough when she was walloping the ball with all her might, but it was even worse when she bellowed as though about to blast a crosscourt drive, then dinked a shot that barely cleared the net. In that case, the grunt was a decoy, not a genuine groan of exertion.

To everybody's surprise, Monica played the final as if she had been struck dumb. Not once did she unleash her patented two-syllable roar and perhaps as a consequence, not once did she unload her ground strokes with the kind of authority and accuracy that fans had come to expect. In a match marred by repeated rain delays and marked by clusters of clean winners from Graf, Seles was trounced 6–2, 6–1—her first loss in a Grand Slam final.

After Wimbledon the normal path of the circuit wends its way back to the United States for a series of hardcourt tournaments leading up to the U.S. Open. But in 1992, many players stayed in Europe to prepare for the Olympics in Barcelona. With Seles, Navratilova, and Sabatini ineligible because of their refusal to play the 1991 Federation Cup, Steffi Graf was the odds on favorite to repeat as a gold medalist. Arantxa Sanchez Vicario was given an outside chance because she was playing in her home town.

Few experts would have bet on Jennifer Capriati, not after her mediocre results and emotional funk of the past spring. But she came to Barcelona about twenty pounds lighter, having worked out in Florida with the Spanish great, Manuel Santana. She moved into the Olympic village, out from under the thumb of her parents, her agents, and hordes of corporate sponsors, and there, in the company of other world-class athletes, many no older than she, Capriati took on the mantle of "Queen of the Cafeteria." As she told *Sports Illustrated*, "You just look for an open seat and sit down, and right away it's great."

Right away her tennis was great too, and for the first time in months she played with the sort of verve and confidence she had shown three years ago as a thirteen-year-old. In the semifinals, she squeezed past Sanchez Vicario, undaunted by a partisan crowd that included King Juan Carlos I and Queen Sofia. Then she confronted the only top player she had never beaten, the defending Olympic champion, Steffi Graf. After they split sets, Jennifer kept it close in the third, pinning Graf deep in the court with high bouncing forehands and an occasional one-hand slice backhand. Capriati got a break to 5–4, then showing no trace of shaky morale or wavering concentration, she served out the match and won the gold medal.

In doubles, Mary Joe Fernandez teamed up with Gigi Fernandez to take their share of the gold. This win helped Mary Joe compensate for a disappointing spring and summer. After finishing as runner-up to Seles at the Australian Open, she had seemed poised as she had so often in the past to break through and win a big title. But then she was upset early at the French Open and Wimbledon, limped through a few tournaments with injuries, and came into the U.S. Open playing so poorly that she sought the counsel of sports psychologist Jim Loehr.

A number of other women might have been wise to follow her example. Martina Navratilova, for instance, had enjoyed a fine run this summer, knocking off Seles to win a tournament in Los Angeles. But at Flushing Meadow she seemed not so much physically exhausted as psychically drained. In the first round, she struggled to survive a three-set match against Shaun Stafford and complained afterward that she had found Stafford's constant smile irritating. Then against seventeen-year-old Magdalena Maleeva, Navratilova was distracted by a spectator who had the temerity to read a newspaper during the match. With a drop-dead look, she coolly said, "Would you mind reading that later, please?" But this did nothing to settle her jangled psyche or to save Martina from the ignominy of a second-round defeat, her quickest exit from the U.S. Open since 1976.

When Jimmy Connors, the only player at Flushing Meadow older than Martina, also cratered in the second round, it called into question the marketability of Jimmy and Martina's much hyped match scheduled for late September. What had been billed as "The Battle of the Champions" began to look suspiciously like a meeting of mangy toothless old lions. Utterly lacking the intensity and significance of Billie Jean King's 1973 match against Bobby Riggs, this $500,000 winner-take-all, pseudo-event promised little more than one last large pay day for the two competitors. Although Connors would have only one serve and Navratilova would get to play half of Connors' doubles alleys, the odds makers in Las Vegas, site of the match, installed Jimmy as a 4–1 favorite.

Buoyed by a summer-long high that had lasted since the Olympics, Jennifer Capriati had convinced some people she was a legitimate threat to take the U.S. Open title. Instead, she took the pipe and went down the tubes against Patricia Hy, a refugee from Cambodia who had fled to Hong Kong, then to Canada, where for the last few years she had been coached by her boyfriend. After her loss, Jennifer stoically, if euphemistically, remarked, "Stuff happens." Once out of the camera's eye, she broke into tears.

There were no tears from Gabriela Sabatini, at least none in public, and no real effort to account for what had happened to her in 1992. While she once again enjoyed a fine clay-court season in spring, she had fallen short at the French Open and Wimbledon, barely played all summer because of tendonitis in her left knee, then lost in the quarter-finals to Mary Joe Fernandez.

Monica Seles's silent collapse at Wimbledon set the tone for the rest of her summer. Still struggling to regain her confidence and struggling just as hard to restrain her grunting, she went down to mute defeat in two more tournaments and came into the U.S. Open suffering from a head cold and a sore throat. She overwhelmed Fernandez in the semifinals and, at last giving full throat to her exuberant grunt, ground Sanchez Vicario into the dust for her second consecutive U.S. Open title. Seles thus became only the third woman—Navratilova and Evert were the others—to win the U.S. Open without dropping a set.

As the ear-deadening, mind-numbing drumroll continued to beat for the Battle of the Champions between Jimmy Connors and Martina Navratilova, critics declared that this vaudeville extravaganza would surely set tennis back a decade or two. But those of a more cynical frame of mind insisted that the match didn't so much suggest the game's early barnstorming days. To the contrary, it struck them as a lurid foreshadowing of the future when more and more tennis would amount to little except one-shot special events and greedily conceived celebrity circuits like the senior tour that Connors wanted to start.

With an infallible eye for casting, someone assembled a team of commentators who were assured of keeping the pay-per-view audience awake by the simple expedient of making people's skin crawl. Grinning smarmily, Barry Tompkins kept insisting that the evening had the "atmosphere of a heavyweight championship," a claim that seemed all the more absurd the longer the preliminary event lasted. Sugar Ray Leonard and Dick Van Patten played what was billed as a celebrity doubles match against Cathy Lee Crosby and some obscure TV ingenue who looked like she had spent ten hours putting on makeup and ten minutes acquainting herself with a tennis racquet.

Bobby Riggs, sounding like a terribly sick man, coughed up an occasional bit of chauvinist bile. But his heart didn't really seem to be in it.

Betsy Nagelson was on hand, one might assume, to offer a female perspective. She was, after all, a tour veteran as well as an experienced tennis announcer. But there was always the countervailing possibility that her husband, Mark McCormack, had muscled her into the booth with strict instructions to protect the interests of the IMG agency by saying nothing remotely controversial.

As for Joe Namath's appearance on the bill, there can be only one explanation. Ann-Margret must have been otherwise engaged. So Broadway Joe, immaculately man-tanned, his eyes masked by tinted glasses, agreed to substitute and toss a coin to determine who would serve first.

By the time a hair-tree in a tuxedo trundled out to midcourt, introduced Connors as "the greatest male player in tennis history" and Navratilova as "the greatest woman athlete of the twentieth century," then roared, "Let's get ready to ruuuuumble," one might be forgiven for concluding that it was time to turn off the TV. But the tennis, once it finally started, wasn't entirely without fascination.

The first surprise was how seriously Connors focused on the match. He didn't clown and kibitz, didn't play to the spectators, or do a running commentary on his own performance. He played tennis—or, at least, tried to.

That was the other shock. Jimbo looked pathetically ill-conditioned, even if grimly determined. Martina had observed that the key to the match was not letting Jimmy take a minute between points. "He's not in shape," she said bluntly.

Indeed, he did appear to be short of breath. But that may have been due to something even more amazing than his physical frailty—he was nervous. The man who had always claimed not to be afraid of anything looked to be overwhelmed by the magnitude of the moment as well as by the sharpness of Martina's ground strokes. Navratilova broke him in the very first game and held to 2–0.

But then Jimbo's jitters vanished, and Martina seemed to be abashed by the fact that Connors was doing little more than keeping the ball in play. She had her chances, yet reacted as if she suspected that Connors was trying to sucker her into a more aggressive game. Double-faulting, she lost her advantage and slipped to 3–3, stayed even with Jimmy from the baseline, but then again had trouble with her serve. At 5–6, ad to Connors, Martina double-faulted to hand him the set, prompting Billie Jean King, her sometime coach, to remark to an interviewer, "Jimmy isn't winning it. Martina is losing it."

Although no more elegant or artistic than the first set, the second set was at least looser. Both players went for a few winners, and sometimes their exchanges were genuinely entertaining. Still, Martina piled up a slew of unforced errors. Jimmy, as Bobby Riggs remarked, wasn't playing great tennis, yet he was in control of the match. After Connors won 6–2, Riggs conceded, "I was surprised that Martina could play him this close."

Afterward, Jimmy left open the possibility that there would be similar matches in his future. Who would pay to watch them was a question not asked. Pocketing $500,000 in prize money, on top of a reported $500,000 guarantee, Jimmy dismissed all criticism that this was burlesque by observing that, "Tennis purity is long gone."

Martina tried to pass the whole thing off as a learning experience. Education, it seemed, was everybody's second prize. But she also came away with a reported $500,000 guarantee and a heartfelt sense of relief. "I guess I'm glad it's over," she said.

O O O

The year ended in dramatic fashion—not with the Virginia Slims Championships but with a discovery concerning Jim Pierce, the loud, obstreperous father of twelfth-ranked Mary, the fellow whom ESPN commentator Mary Carillo called one of "the most dangerous men in tennis" when he punched out two fans at the French Open. For years tour insiders had wondered whether Pierce's antics were simply a crude sort of gamesmanship intended to egg Mary on and intimidate her opponents. Or was Pierce as unstable and menacing as he appeared to be in his darker moments when he upbraided umpires and linesmen, barked at other players, and mercilessly berated his daughter?

Journalist Cindy Hahn went a long way toward answering this question when she decided to do what tennis authorities should have done long ago. She did some serious digging into Jim Pierce's past and discovered that the truth about this unfortunate fellow was more frightening than anyone could have imagined.

Born in Greensboro, North Carolina, the man whom the tennis community knew as Jim Pierce was actually Bobby Glenn Pearce. An eighth-grade dropout who had had repeated run-ins with juvenile authorities, he had joined the Marine Corps at eighteen, but was given a bad conduct discharge little more than a year later. Returning to his hometown, Bobby Glenn was convicted of forgery and ordered to serve an eighteen- to twenty-four-month sentence in a work-release program. But after a week he took off for New York City, and his family didn't hear from him again until he was shot and seriously wounded in the course of being arrested for armed robbery. After recovering at St. Clare's Hospital, he was convicted and did time at the Tombs in lower Manhattan, at Sing Sing, and at Clinton Prison. On several occasions he showed what were, according to legal documents, "schizophrenic and paranoid tendencies" and was committed to Bellevue for observation.

After finishing his sentence in New York, he was extradited to North Carolina to do time there for forgery and escape. During this period, he again experienced emotional problems. According to court records, Bobby Glenn Pearce was, in the the words of the North Carolina Prison Department's medical director, "a fit subject for admission to a hospital for the mentally disordered." On September 25, 1963, he was sent to a state mental institution for up to 180 days.

Subsequent to his release from prison in 1964, Bobby Glenn Pearce wandered up and down the East Coast. At one point, he married, separated after a few months, and had a daughter seven months after he left his wife. In December 1973, he was arrested in Miami Beach for "buying, receiving, or concealing stolen property"—in this case a TV set and three paintings that had been taken from a hotel. After posting bond of $2,000, Pearce jumped bail and fled and spent the next decade as a fugitive. It was during this period that he began passing himself off as Jim Pierce.

In 1984, his lawyer arranged a plea bargain and Bobby Glenn, a.k.a. Jim, pled *nolo contendere* to the stolen property charge. He paid a $1,000 fine to resolve the matter. By then he had married his second wife, Yannick Adjadj, and had another daughter, Mary, who would soon set out on the junior tennis tour. Sordid and distressing as this story is on a personal level, and much as tennis authorities might wish to dismiss it as an exceptional case, the saga of Jim Pierce does raise difficult questions that cut to the heart of the most serious problems on the women's circuit.

When Cindy Hahn attempted to talk to Pierce about his past, he "grew increasingly agitated," according to *The New York Times*. Then Pierce told her, "I'm not threatening you, and I don't ever want to hear that I threatened you, but I'll be fifty-six in January. I don't have nothing left. When I go, I want everybody to go with me. You have no idea how my mind works. Anything could happen."

When Gerry Smith, Executive Director of the WTA, learned of Pierce's remarks and the article *The New York Times* planned to run, Smith backed away from his repeatedly stated position that the Code of Conduct applied only to players. Within forty-eight hours, Smith and the Women's Tennis Council, the tour's administrative body, had passed a new regulation that prohibited abusive conduct on the part of a player's coach, representatives, or relatives. The new regulation, commonly known as the "Jim Pierce Rule," gave no explanation of what would be considered abusive nor did it indicate how entourages would be monitored.

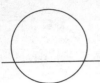

Afterword

Even those who are actively involved in the day-to-day operation of women's tennis—one is tempted to say, *especially* those who are actively involved—find it difficult to grasp the essence of the tour. As Gerry Smith, the WTA's Executive Director and CEO, told me, "It's hard to get your hands around the game. It's like a huge piece of Jell-O. How can you pick up a piece of Jell-O?"

With its hectic schedule, its constantly changing cast of characters, its recurrent controversies and ever-evolving idea of itself, women's tennis resists interpretation the way Wallace Stevens said a modern poem should—almost, but not quite, completely. As I mull over my time on the tour, I am mindful of a word that kept cropping up in my conversations with players—*balance*. That was the virtue so many of them said they aspired to—balance, as in an even distribution of weight as they set up for shots; balance, as in a rational assessment of their ambitions and abilities; balance, as in an emotional equilibrium that would allow them to evaluate the benefits and liabilities of life on the circuit.

Balance is the quality I hoped to achieve as I attempted to wrest some comprehensible shape from hundreds of personal interviews, press conferences, matches, chance encounters, and elliptical telephone conversations. The challenge came down to something comparable to describing a butterfly. Seen from the most flattering angle, women's tennis, like a butterfly, is a thing of beauty and grace, of bold colors and gauzy pastels. But beneath the delicate, variegated wings there beats the pulse of an ugly little bug. The two are inextricably connected. To focus on one side to the exclusion of the other is not simply to promote a consoling illusion. It's to deny reality and prevent people from understanding, much less solving, the problems of women's tennis. In the final analysis, a one-sided view is also unfair to the players, whose accomplishments cannot be fully appreciated without reference to the difficulties they have to confront.

No one could spend time on the WTA tour and not be impressed by the quality of the competition, the commitment of the players, coaches, and officials, and the irrefutable truth that excellence in any endeavor requires hard work. Years of training and hours of daily drills are the necessary foundation for a game that, at its ultimate, appears to be effortless. As Don Candy put it, "Show me a young lady who travels the tour and wins matches and I'll show you a tough lady. Regardless of the sadness and loneliness, they come through. Dad may watch from the sidelines and think she wins because she's a bloody good tennis player. But she wins because she's tough."

And yet, in contrast to the men, female competitors are expected to fall back into more demure roles as soon as they come off court. Tenacious and hard-nosed as they may be during matches, they have to be charming, good-humored, modest, soft spoken, and ingratiating afterward. The mark of a male champion can be a Sequoia-size chip on the shoulder. But women champions are judged not just on their results but on their ability to strike a series of traditional ladylike poses.

The miracle is that so many female players manage to swing with such apparent ease between the conflicting demands of their profession. Over and over I was struck by the poise and politeness of girls, some barely beyond adolescence, who spent hours digging out a close win or going down to a disappointing defeat, then sat patiently and answered my questions. In almost all cases, they were more gracious, good humored, and forgiving than anybody had a right to expect them to be.

Still, much as I found admirable about them, it would be less than honest of me to ignore everything that the players would prefer that the public not know. Yes, on balance—that word again—pro tennis can be a positive experience for some women. It offers them a chance to compete, to stretch and test their limits, to fulfill their potential and win a measure of financial independence. But the price they pay is often cruelly high.

Given the money and vested interests involved, it is utopian to propose the most logical solution to the tour's greatest problems. Yet there's no doubt that a single rule change could dramatically reduce the damage. At present, girls are allowed to turn pro during the month of their fourteenth birthday. It doesn't strike me as unreasonable to demand that the age limit be brought into line with other pro sports and raised to seventeen or eighteen. This way players could finish high school and reach a basic level of physical and emotional maturity before setting off on the circuit. Older players would be less vulnerable to sexual abuse, financial exploitation, and parental manipulation and battering.

Apologists for the status quo will argue that since youngsters are capable of becoming top-ten stars, they deserve to be allowed to compete. But nobody would buy this line of reasoning in other areas of life. A thirteen-year-old girl is also physically capable of having children. Yet what responsible person would encourage her to do so? What parent wouldn't protest that such a decision should be delayed until after a girl finished her education and gained sufficient experience to make an informed choice about her future?

It always amused me on the circuit to hear parents say, "How can I stop her? She just loves to play tennis. How can I tell her no?" Yet these same parents wouldn't let their underage kids drink and drive, no matter how much they "loved" to do it. My presumption—and it's one shared by substantial numbers of sports psychologists, players, and coaches—is that it's as risky to let an adolescent girl travel the tour as it is to let her drink and drive.

Since I'm certain the WTA won't change its minimum-age requirement, and that agents and parents would mount legal resistance to any such suggestion, I have another modest proposal. Why doesn't the WTA arrange to have teachers, counselors, and psychiatrists accompany the players on the circuit? In other professions, the Department of Labor looks after the interests of underage workers and insists that measures be taken to ensure their safety and well-being. Why shouldn't tennis be obliged to meet the same minimal standards? After all, it's a business now, not a game.

It is fascinating to note that during Wimbledon in 1991 a circus traveling through England was closed down by social workers who protested that no provisions had been made for the health and schooling of teenage performers. It didn't matter that the children themselves claimed that they enjoyed what they were doing. Meanwhile, Wimbledon went on as usual, despite ample evidence that its hoards of school dropouts worked long hours and were at high risk for physical and emotional injury.

In the absence of a rule change or a concerted effort by the WTA, the only hope, as Dr. James Loehr pointed out, lies with parents. If they choose to let their daughters travel the tour, they should know what awaits them. As it is now, most parents and players are in no better position than starry-eyed fans. Blinded by the vivid colors, the swirl of glamour, the lure of fame and money, they see only one side of the butterfly. While this book is, in part, a portrait of that side of women's tennis, it is also an attempt to redress the imbalance and show something of what lies beneath the game's seductive surface.

Little, Brown now offers an exciting range of quality titles by both established and new authors. All of the books in this series are available by faxing, or posting your order to:

Little, Brown Books,
Cash Sales Department,
P.O. Box 11,
Falmouth,
Cornwall,
TR1O 9EN
Fax: 0326-376423

Payments can be made as follows: Cheque, postal order (payable to Little, Brown Cash Sales) or by credit cards, Visa/Access/Mastercard. Do not send cash or currency. U.K. customers and B.F.P.O.: Allow £1.00 for postage and packing for the first book, plus 50p for the second book, plus 30p for each additional book up to a maximum charge of £3.00 (7 books plus). U.K. orders over £75 free postage and packing.

Overseas customers including Ireland, please allow £2.00 for postage and packing for the first book, plus £1.00 for the second book, plus 50p for each additional book.

NAME (Block Letters) ....

ADDRESS ....

....

....

☐ I enclose my remittance for ....

☐ I wish to pay by Visa/Access/Mastercard

Number ☐☐☐☐☐☐☐☐☐☐☐☐☐☐☐☐

Card Expiry Date ☐☐☐☐